Formal Specification of Interactive Graphics

Programming Languages

ACM Distinguished Dissertations

1982

Abstraction Mechanisms and Language Design,
by Paul N. Hilfinger

*Formal Specification of Interactive Graphics Programming
Languages,* by William R. Mallgren

Algorithmic Program Debugging,
by Ehud Y. Shapiro

Formal Specification of Interactive Graphics Programming Languages

William R. Mallgren

The MIT Press
Cambridge, Massachusetts
London, England

Publisher's note: This format is intended to reduce the cost of publishing certain works in book form and to shorten the gap between editorial preparation and final publication. Detailed editing and composition have been avoided by photographing the text of this book directly from the author's typescript or word-processor output.

Dissertation submitted in September 1981 to the Department of Computer Science, University of Washington in partial fulfillment of the requirements for the degree of Doctor of Philosophy (University of Washington Technical Report No. 81-09-01).

All formatting and typesetting was done using the Xerox 8010 Star Information System.

T
385
,M34
1983

Library of Congress Cataloging in Publication Data

Mallgren, William R.
    Formal specification of interactive graphics programming languages.

    (ACM distinguished dissertations)
    Originally presented as the author's thesis--University of Washington, 1981.
    Bibliography: p.
    Includes index.
    1. Programming languages (Electronic computers)--Computer graphics. I. Title. II. Series.
T385.M34   1983   001.64'43   83-938
ISBN 0-262-13191-9

Series Foreword

The Distinguished Doctoral Dissertation Series is a welcome outgrowth of ACM's annual contest, co-sponsored by The MIT Press, for the best doctoral dissertation in computer-related science and engineering.

During the judging process that is designed to select the annual winner, it has inevitably developed that some of the theses being considered in the final round are of such high quality that they also deserve publication. This book is one of those dissertations. In the judgment of the ACM selection committee and The MIT Press, it truly deserves special recognition as a Distinguished Doctoral Dissertation.

Dr. William Mallgren wrote his thesis on "Formal Specification of Interactive Graphics Programming Languages" at the University of Washington under the direction of a committee chaired by Professor Alan Shaw. It was submitted for the 1982 competition. The Doctoral Dissertation Award committee of ACM recommended its publication because it provides a comprehensive structure of graphics programming languages. As such, it serves well as a valuable monograph on the subject.

Walter M. Carlson
Chairman, ACM Awards Committee

Contents

Special Symbols

∘	function composition
≡	equivalence (by definition)
≈	object correspondence
∈	set membership
⊆	set containment
⊂	strict set containment
∩	set intersection
∪	set union
⇒	logical implication
⇔	logical equivalence
¬	logical not
&	logical and
|	(binary operation) logical or (in set descriptions) "such that" (bracketing characters) absolute magnitude
•	(flag character) basic generator operation
*	(binary operation) multiplication (flag character) hidden operation

Type Names

abbreviation	name (identifier)	specification
cg	core graphics	Appendix E.1
ci	core graphics interaction	Appendix E.2
co	color(color)	Appendix B.8
e	(used in examples)	
gf	geometric function (geomfcn)	Appendix B.5
gt	graphical transformation (grtrans)	Appendix B.4
im	implicit axioms	Appendix B.
ih	prototype language interaction	Appendix D.2
ip	prototype language interaction	Appendix C.2
ix	XPL/G interaction	Section 4.5
n	name (name)	Appendix B.8
p	continuous picture (picture)	Appendix B.1
ph	picture-hierarchy	Appendix D.3
pt	point(point)	Appendix B.7
rg	region (region)	Appendix B.6
s	ordered set of items (set(item))	Appendix B.9
sp	simple picture (spicture)	Appendix B.3
st	string (string)	Appendix B.10
tp	tree-structured picture(tpicture)	Appendix C.3
tr	picture-tree (tree)	Appendix B.2
ui	universal input primitives	Section 4.4

Figures

Acknowledgments

I am deeply grateful to Professor Alan Shaw for his expert guidance and unfailing support during the course of this work. I am also indebted to Professors Steven Tanimoto and Edward Lazowska for their careful reading and helpful criticism of the dissertation, and to Professor Walter Ruzzo for his advice on critical portions of Chapter Four. Special thanks to my wife, Teri, for her patience and encouragement throughout my graduate school career.

This research was supported in part by the National Science Foundation under grants MCS-7519480 and MCS-7826285.

To my father and mother

Formal Specification of Interactive Graphics Programming Languages

Chapter 1

Introduction

1.1 The Problem

The value of formal specification of software systems is widely recognized. Despite considerable recent effort on graphics standards, however, software for graphics applications (including standards) is invariably described by informal means. Referring to the 1976 IFIP Workshop on Methodology in Computer Graphics [GUER79], Newman and van Dam [NEWW78] note,

> One ... outcome of the Seillac workshop was an understanding of the value of formal specification techniques for graphics systems.

To date, little work has been done in this area. A useful starting point is the specification of languages in which graphics applications are written. There is no fundamental reason why the semantics of a graphics programming language cannot be described with the precision that is customary for language syntax and has become increasingly common for the semantics of general purpose languages. With the language specification available as a foundation, the properties of graphics software can be stated in a precise way also. The goal of this work is to develop means by which programming languages tailored for interactive computer graphics applications can be formally specified. We restrict our attention to picture generation; picture recognition and picture processing applications are not considered.

1.2 Applying Specification Methods to Graphics Languages

The purpose of a formal specification is to provide a precise characterization of a software system at some convenient level of abstraction. In this work we use specifications to describe the semantics of systems at a level that includes just their externally visible behavior. Efficiency constraints and implementation details are excluded. Such a specification is a useful tool during the design of a software system, as the defining document during its implementation, and for communicating its essential characteristics to those who will use it. Being unambiguous, a formal specification provides a sound basis for proofs of correctness of the software it describes. When a specification is given for a programming language, it also provides a basis for reasoning about programs written in that language. While a formal specification may not be directly suitable as user documentation, it can be a valuable aid in writing such documentation and should serve as the ultimate reference source when questions arise.

Formal semantic specifications have been written for some of the general purpose languages, such as Pascal [HOAC73] and Euclid [LONR78], but not for any of the graphics languages. The fact that formal specification techniques have seen so little application in computer graphics suggests that there are problems in applying existing specification techniques to this new domain. The main problems that we have identified are the following:

1) A variety of special constructs are used in graphics applications that are not found in general purpose languages.

2) Not all of these special constructs have been analyzed adequately in the literature to provide a sound basis for their specification.

3) Graphics applications frequently involve direct interaction with human users.

Specifications of general purpose languages have been successful largely because they are based on a small number of well understood, broadly applicable concepts, such as the data type, the assignment statement, and standard control constructs. If specifications of graphics languages are to be similarly useful, they must be based on equally well understood concepts appropriate to computer graphics.

Some of the special concepts used in graphics are the picture, region, graphical transformation, and hierarchic picture structure. The literature on graphics programming discusses many specific applications of concepts such as these, but their fundamental meanings often are not addressed. Our first problem, then, is to define the fundamental concepts of computer graphics in a way that is precise yet general enough to encompass the many forms in which they can appear.

Even with a good understanding of the underlying concepts, however, the sheer diversity of constructs poses a challenge to the specification of graphics languages. If many different methods must be used to specify a single language, little has been gained. One strategy is to devise a specification technique powerful enough to describe each of the constructs known to appear in graphics languages. This work has a different emphasis: Rather than trying to specify all existing graphics languages, we propose that graphics languages be designed in a way that reduces the diversity of constructs and facilitates specification with known techniques. The data type, already a part of many programming languages, captures a wide variety of concepts in convenient form and has received considerable study. By expressing the special concepts of a graphics programming language using data types, not only can we improve the language by unifying the representation of graphical constructs, but we also gain some applicable specification techniques. Among these techniques, we have chosen algebraic specifications as especially suitable.

Finally, we must deal with user interaction. While interaction is used in many areas of computing, it is especially important to computer graphics, where often the major objective is effective communication with the human user. Thus, a method for specifying graphics programming languages is incomplete unless it can describe language primitives for user interaction. User interaction involves not just input-output in the usual sense, but special synchronization constraints as well. To describe all of the forms user interaction can take, it is useful to think in terms of concurrent processes representing computing activity in the machine(s) and simultaneous actions on the part of the user(s). While various specification techniques exist for parallel computation, many have purposes different from ours and none blends smoothly with algebraic specifications. By extending the algebraic specification technique to handle data types shared among concurrent processes, we can specify interaction primitives in a way that is fully compatible with our data type specifications.

The usual axiomatic specification of declaration, assignment, and control statements completes the formal description of entire graphics languages.

1.3 Contributions

The main contribution of this work is a comprehensive method for formally specifying the semantics of interactive graphics programming languages. It employs the axiomatic specification technique of Hoare [HOAC69] for the language statements, the algebraic data type specification technique of Guttag, Zilles, and Goguen et al. [GUTJ75, ZILS74, GOGJ78] to describe graphical data types, and a new technique based on algebraic specifications to describe interaction primitives. Other contributions of the research are as follows:

1) precise definitions for some important graphical concepts, such as picture, graphical transformation, and hierarchic picture structure,

2) a unifying framework for graphics language design that allows many different graphical concepts to be expressed using a common construct, the graphical data type, and

3) a new specification technique applicable not just to user interaction but to other kinds of resource sharing in parallel systems.

The value of these results is demonstrated by using the design framework to create a prototype graphics language, by giving a complete specification of the prototype language, and by using the language and its specification in several verification examples. Two actual systems are specified: a portion of the GSPC Core Graphics system [GSPC79] and the input primitives of the language XPL/G [MALW76].

A formal specification for a complete graphics language has never been published. Eckert [ECKR77] has specified a portion of a non-interactive, Core-Graphics-related system using the state machine model of Parnas [PARD72]. However, the specification is unwieldy, and, not being completely formal, does not lend itself to precise reasoning, either about the system or programs that use it. Work closely related to ours is a specification of a graphics display interface by Guttag and Horning [GUTJ80]. Their approach is similar to ours in that the basic unit of specification is the data type, and the algebraic technique is used. Their major concern, however, is the use of specifications as a general system design tool. While their display interface provides a good example of the use of data types to construct graphics software, their treatment of the special requirements of graphics programming does not go beyond their example, and user interaction is not considered at all.

1.4 Organization

We begin in Chapter 2 by giving precise definitions for some important graphical concepts. These concepts are used in Chapter 3 as the basis for several graphical data types, which are formally specified using the algebraic technique. A specification technique for shared data types is developed in Chapter 4 and applied to programming language primitives for user interaction. Chapter 5 presents a framework for graphics language design and a prototype graphics language based on this framework. The techniques of Chapters 3 and 4 are used to specify both the prototype language and the Core Graphics system. Chapter 6 explores one of the ways in which formal specifications can be used: the verification of programs. Special problems associated with verifying graphics programs are addressed, and examples based on the prototype graphics language are presented. The appendices contain details of proofs alluded to in the text, as well as formal specifications of all the graphical data types introduced, the prototype graphics language, and a portion of the Core Graphics system.

Chapter 2

Basic Concepts

In this chapter we examine concepts that are basic to graphics programming and hence to graphics programing languages. Definitions are given for the concepts region, picture, graphical transformation, hierarchic picture structure, and user interaction, with examples of each. Properties of these concepts are considered with a view toward identifying constraints that must be imposed on corresponding language constructs and establishing an assertion language for reasoning about interactive graphics programs.

This material serves both to clarify some important ideas associated with graphics programming and to provide definitions we can draw upon in later chapters to illustrate the programming constructs, specification techniques, and proof methods we propose. Many of these definitions are discussed further in [MALW78].

2.1 Pictures as Partial Functions

Region

A *region* is defined as a set of points in some *universe* U. If pictures are taken to be continuous, then the universe is the plane or all of three-space, and regions correspond to areas or volumes. For raster graphics, pictures are made up of points on a discrete two-dimensional grid, and U consists of the grid points.

For simplicity, the discussion that follows uses the Cartesian coordinate system in two dimensions. The same ideas apply to higher dimensions and other coordinate systems, however.

<u>Example 2.1-1</u>.

The region consisting of the unit square at the origin can be written $R_1 = \{(x_1, x_2) \mid 0 \le x_1 \le 1, 0 \le x_2 \le 1\}$.

The important operations on regions are the usual set operations, intersection, union, and difference, and predicates for determining whether a region is empty or whether it contains a specified point or another region. Regions are useful for defining both pictures and graphical transformations.

Picture

Any two-dimensional picture can be modelled as a function that assigns a value to each point in the plane [ROSA69]. For convenience in dealing with pictures of finite extent in either two or three dimensions, we define a *picture* as a partial function P, where the *domain* D of the picture (the domain of the partial function) is a subset of the chosen universe. The range of P can be any set of values that it is reasonable to associate with the points of a picture. A particular interpretation for these values is not needed here; we will refer to them simply as *colors*.

<u>Example 2.1-2</u>

Some possible sets of colors are the following:

1) for binary pictures, two values representing black and white,

2) for gray-scale pictures, a subrange of the non-negative integers,

3) for colors of the spectrum, scalars correlated with frequency, or vectors containing red, green, and blue components,

4) more complex visual attributes such as transparency, reflectivity, and texture.

<u>Example 2.1-3</u>

Figure 2-1 shows two ways a picture consisting of a diagonal line segment from the origin to point (1,1) can be defined:

a)   In Figure 2-1a the line segment is defined by the domain D_1 of the picture P_1; only points on the line segment are part of the picture.

b)   In Figure 2-1b the domain D_2 includes the entire unit square, and the form of the picture function defines the line segment.

If the value 0 is interpreted to be "background", the two pictures look the same when displayed.

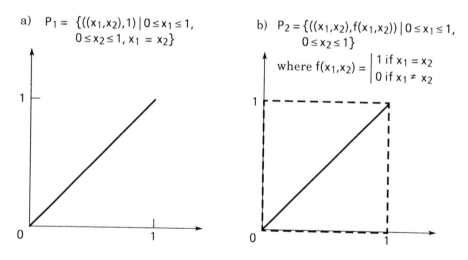

a) $P_1 = \{((x_1,x_2),1) \mid 0 \le x_1 \le 1,$
$\qquad 0 \le x_2 \le 1, x_1 = x_2\}$

b) $P_2 = \{((x_1,x_2),f(x_1,x_2)) \mid 0 \le x_1 \le 1,$
$\qquad 0 \le x_2 \le 1\}$

where $f(x_1,x_2) = \begin{vmatrix} 1 \text{ if } x_1 = x_2 \\ 0 \text{ if } x_1 \ne x_2 \end{vmatrix}$

Figure 2-1 Examples of a picture

Picture Sum

An important picture operation is *sum*, which can be thought of as the overlaying of pictures. The sum P_0 of two pictures P_1 and P_2 with domains D_1 and D_2 is defined as follows:

$$(P_1 + P_2)(q) = \begin{vmatrix} P_1(q) \text{ for all } q \in D_1 - D_2 \\ P_2(q) \text{ for all } q \in D_2 - D_1 \\ P_1(q) + P_2(q) \text{ for all } q \in D_1 \cap D_2 \end{vmatrix}$$

The sum $P_1 + P_2$ has domain $D_1 \cup D_2$ and is the same as as P_1 in the region where only P_1 is defined, P_2 where only P_2 is defined, and a combination of the two where they overlap. This combination is determined by the *color sum* $P_1(q) + P_2(q)$. Many different versions of the the summing function for colors are used in existing systems. See for example the "RasterOp" operations in [NEWW79]. A definition that is useful for gray-scale line drawings is $c_1 + c_2 = maximum(c_1, c_2)$, where c_1 and c_2 are non-negative integers [MALW78]. Other choices for the color sum are discussed in Section 2.4.

Picture Properties

Since the drawing of pictures is the distinguishing characteristic of graphics programs, properties of pictures are the most important vehicle for reasoning about graphics programs. Consideration of picture properties is also relevant to program optimization and error detection.

We denote the domain of picture P as $domain(P)$. Picture P is *visible* with respect to region R if

$$domain(P) \cap R \neq \emptyset,$$

that is, if any part of P lies within R. The visibility criterion is the basis of the *visibility test* (see Section 2.4) that can be used to speed up the display of structured pictures. P is *bounded* with respect to R if

$$domain(P) \subseteq R,$$

that is, if P lies wholly within R. The determination of whether all of a picture will be shown on a screen or fit on a reasonable amount of plotter paper is a boundedness test. Finally, we can say P is *resolvable* with respect to some threshold M if

$$|\text{domain}(P)| \geq M,$$

that is, if P is at least M in size by some measure appropriate to the application. Resolvability criteria can be used to eliminate unnecessary detail from a picture, as determined by either the nature of the application or the resolution of the output device.

Determination of the domain-related picture properties above is often made in practice using an *extent* of a picture, a region (presumably of a more convenient shape) that includes the picture domain.

Numerous binary relations can be defined on pictures. Some relations used in later chapters are the following:

Pictures P_1 and P_2 are *equal* if they are the same partial function, that is,

$$\text{domain}(P_1) = \text{domain}(P_2) \text{ and } P_1(x) = P_2(x)$$
$$\text{for all } x \in \text{domain}(P_1).$$

P_1 and P_2 are *coincident*, if they exactly coincide, i.e.,

$$\text{domain}(P_1) = \text{domain}(P_2).$$

P_1 *contains* P_2 if P_2 fits entirely within P_1, i.e.,

$$\text{domain}(P_2) \subseteq \text{domain}(P_1) \text{ and } P_1(x) = P_2(x)$$
$$\text{for all } x \in \text{domain}(P_2).$$

P_1 and P_2 are *disjoint* if they do not overlap, i.e.,

$$\text{domain}(P_1) \cap \text{domain}(P_2) = \varnothing.$$

2.2 Graphical Transformations

A *graphical transformation* is a function that maps pictures to pictures.

Example 2.2-1

The following are graphical transformations:
a) translation, scaling, rotation, and skewing,
b) changing all reds in a picture to blues,
c) a two-dimensional Fourier transform,
d) changing all squares in a picture to circles,
e) hidden line/surface removal.

The *composition* of two graphical transformations T_1 and T_2, denoted $T_1 \circ T_2$, is ordinary function composition, that is,

$$\text{for all } P, \; T_1 \circ T_2(P) \; = \; T_1(T_2(P)).$$

Our definition of graphical transformation is very broad. The graphical data types defined in Chapter 3 make use of two particular kinds of graphical transformations: geometric transformations and restriction transformations.

Geometric Transformation and Geometric Function

A *geometric transformation* is a graphical transformation that moves the points of a picture without changing their colors; thus any geometric transformation can be characterized by a mapping between points. Accordingly, we define a *geometric function* as a function G from points to points; that is, $G: U \rightarrow U$. For now, we require G to be one-to-one in order to simplify the mathematics (see [MALW78]). The effect of a geometric transformation $T^g\langle G \rangle$ on a picture P is defined

$$T^g\langle G \rangle(P) \; = \; P \circ G^{-1} \; = \; \{(G(x), P(x)) \mid x \in \text{domain}(P)\},$$

where **G** is the geometric function that *characterizes* T9. The notation T9⟨G⟩ is abbreviated to T9 when it is not necessary to show G explicitly.

<u>Example 2.2-2</u>

The graphical transformation T9 for scaling by amount s is characterized by the geometric function $S(x_1, x_2) = (s*x_1, s*x_2)$. The following illustrates the application of T9⟨S⟩ to the picture shown in Figure 2-1b:

T9⟨S⟩(P) = T9⟨S⟩($\{((x_1,x_2),P(x_1,x_2)) \mid 0 \le x_1 \le 1, 0 \le x_2 \le 1\}$)
   = $\{(S(x_1,x_2),P(x_1,x_2)) \mid 0 \le x_1 \le 1, 0 \le x_2 \le 1\}$
   = $\{((s*x_1,s*x_2),P(x_1,x_2)) \mid 0 \le x_1 \le 1, 0 \le x_2 \le 1\}$
   = $\{((y_1,y_2),P'(y_1,y_2)) \mid 0 \le y_1 \le s, 0 \le y_2 \le s\}$

where $P(x_1,x_2) = \begin{cases} 1 \text{ if } 0 \le x_1 \le 1, 0 \le x_2 \le 1, x_1 = x_2 \\ 0 \text{ if } 0 \le x_1 \le 1, 0 \le x_2 \le 1, x_1 \ne x_2 \end{cases}$

and $P'(y_1,y_2) = \begin{cases} 1 \text{ if } 0 \le y_1 \le s, 0 \le y_2 \le s, y_1 = y_2 \\ 0 \text{ if } 0 \le y_1 \le s, 0 \le y_2 \le s, y_1 \ne y_2. \end{cases}$

Some important operations on geometric functions are application to a point, application to a region, composition, and inversion. A geometric function **G** is *applied to a point* q by computing G(q). G is *applied to a region* R by applying G to each of the points in R individually:

$$G(R) = \{G(q) \mid q \in R\}.$$

The *composition* of two geometric functions G_1 and G_2, denoted $G_1 \circ G_2$, is just function composition:

$$\text{for all } q \in U, G_1{\circ}G_2(q) = G_1(G_2(q)).$$

The *inverse* G^{-1} of a geometric function G is defined by the relation

$$\text{for all } q \in U, G^{-1}(G(q)) = G(G^{-1}(q)) = q.$$

Restriction Transformation

A *restriction transformation* removes selected parts from a picture. A familiar example is the use of clipping to remove parts of a picture that will not fit on the screen. Any restriction transformation can be characterized by a region. When the transformation is applied to a picture, all points outside the characteristic region are removed.

The effect of a restriction transformation $T^r\langle R\rangle$ on a picture P is defined as follows:

$$T^r\langle R\rangle(P) = \{(p,P(p)) \mid p \in (R \cap \text{domain}(P))\}$$

where R is the region characterizing $T^r\langle R\rangle$. As before, the shorthand notation T^r is also used.

Example 2.2-3

The restriction transformation $T^r\langle Q\rangle$, which removes all points outside the unit square centered at the origin, is characterized by the region $Q = \{(x_1,x_2) \mid |x_1| \le 0.5, |x_2| \le 0.5\}$. $T^r\langle Q\rangle$ can be applied to the picture shown in Figure 2.1-1a as follows:

$$T^r\langle Q\rangle(P) = T^r\langle Q\rangle(\{((x_1,x_2), 1) \mid 0 \le x_1 \le 1, 0 \le x_2 \le 1, x_1 = x_2\})$$
$$= \{((x_1,x_2), 1) \mid 0 \le x_1 \le 1, 0 \le x_2 \le 1, x_1 = x_2, |x_1| \le 0.5, |x_2| \le 0.5\}$$
$$= \{((x_1,x_2), 1) \mid 0 \le x_1 \le 0.5, 0 \le x_2 \le 0.5, x_1 = x_2\}.$$

Combining Graphical Transformations

For composing graphical transformations where just geometric and restriction transformations are involved, several rules can be derived from the definitions:

composition rules
1) $T^g\langle G_1\rangle \circ T^g\langle G_2\rangle = T^g\langle G_1 \circ G_2\rangle$
2) $T^r\langle R_1\rangle \circ T^r\langle R_2\rangle = T^r\langle R_1 \cap R_2\rangle$

commutation rules
1) $T^g\langle G\rangle \circ T^r\langle R\rangle = T^r\langle G(R)\rangle \circ T^g\langle G\rangle$
2) $T^r\langle R\rangle \circ T^g\langle G\rangle = T^g\langle G\rangle \circ T^r\langle G^{-1}(R)\rangle$

Using these formulas and the fact that composition of graphical transformations is associative [MALW78], the composition of any sequence of geometric and restriction transformations can be reduced to the form $T^g \circ T^r$ for some T^g and T^r. Since this is an important canonical form, we introduce the notation $T^{gr}\langle G,R\rangle$ to stand for the expression $T^g\langle G\rangle \circ T^r\langle R\rangle$. (As before, the shorthand notation for $T^{gr}\langle G,R\rangle$ is T^{gr}.)

The class of graphical transformations that can be written in the form T^{gr} is exactly the class that can be expressed as the composition of a picture with a partial function on points, that is, by forming $T(P) = P \circ F$ for some partial function $F: U \rightarrow U$. If T is a restriction transformation $T^r\langle R\rangle$, then F is the partial identity function defined only on R. If T is a geometric transformation $T^g\langle G\rangle$, then F is exactly G^{-1}.

Color Transformation

One might ask the meaning of composing a function with P in the other order, namely $T(P) = C \circ P$ for some function C. If the result is to be a picture (which maps points to colors), C must be a function from colors to colors. Such *color transformations*, denoted $T^c\langle C\rangle$, describe, among other things, the effect of color mapping hardware in many raster display devices. The characteristic function C: colors $\rightarrow$ colors is a *color function*.

We define the application of a color transformation $T^c\langle C\rangle$ to a picture P as

$$T^c\langle C\rangle(P) = \{(x, C \circ P(x)) \mid x \in \text{domain}(P)\} = C \circ P.$$

Color transformations can describe any change to the colors of a picture, provided the new color at each point depends only on the previous color at that point. Local averaging, for instance, is not a color transformation, since the new color at a point depends on the colors of surrounding points.

By allowing C to be a partial function, it is possible to express "restriction" transformations that remove portions of a picture on the basis of color rather than location.

<u>Example 2.2-4</u>

The following are color transformations:

1) Color correction, used to make an image more faithfully represent an actual scene.
2) The negative of a picture: for gray-scale pictures with intensities between 0 and m, the transformation $T^c(N)$ where $N(c) = m-c$.
3) The transformations used in color-table animation [SHOR79].
4) Thresholding, in which those portions of a picture with a color value beyond a certain limit are not displayed.

The following additional combining rules can be derived for color transformations:

composition rule

3) $T^c(C_2) \circ T^c(C_1) = T^c(C_2 \circ C_1)$

commutation rules

3) $T^r(R) \circ T^c(C) = T^c(C) \circ T^r(R)$
4) $T^g(G) \circ T^c(C) = T^c(C) \circ T^g(G)$

2.3 Other Graphical Transformations

In this section we briefly examine some other kinds of graphical transformations that are included in the general definition of Section 2.2.

Many-to-One Geometric Transformations

So far we have required the geometric function G characterizing a geometric transformation $T^g(G)$ to be one-to-one. This restriction can be relaxed to include many-to-one functions, and many of the same results still hold. We use the notation T^h to represent a geometric transformation of this more general form. Let H be an arbitrary total function from U to U. The application of $T^h \langle H \rangle$ to a picture is defined

$$T^h \langle H \rangle (P) = \{(x, \text{SUM}_w\, P(w)) \mid x \in H(D),\ H(w) = x\},$$

where $\text{SUM}_w\, P(w)$ is the color summation over all points w in the inverse image of x under H, and H(D) is the image of set D under H. If H is one-to-one, the definition for $T^h \langle H \rangle (P)$ reduces to that for $T^g \langle H \rangle (P)$. This can be seen more easily by rewriting the earlier definition in the form

$$T^g \langle G \rangle (P) = \{(x, P(w)) \mid x \in G(D),\ G(w) = x\}.$$

Example 2.3-1

The following geometric transformations are many-to-one:
a) 3D to 2D projections, such as perspective projections and parallel projections,
b) the mapping from a continuous picture to a raster picture.

The following combining rules involving geometric transformations (see Section 2.2) still hold:

composition rule 1) $T^h \langle H_2 \rangle \circ T^h \langle H_1 \rangle = T^h \langle H_2 \circ H_1 \rangle$
commutation rule 1) $T^r \langle R \rangle \circ T^h \langle H \rangle = T^h \langle H \rangle \circ T^r \langle H^{-1}(R) \rangle$,

where $H^{-1}(R)$ is the inverse image of set R under H. (There is no inverse function for H.)

Commutation rules 2) and 4) do not hold for non-one-to-one geometric transformations.

Graphical Transformations of Other Forms

As we have seen, a wide variety of graphical transformations are of the form $T(P) = F_2 \circ P \circ F_1$ and can therefore be expressed as combinations of geometric, restriction, and color transformations.

In transformations of this form, the presence and color of each point in the resultant picture depends on a single point (and its color) in the original picture. However, our definition of a graphical transformation includes any function T: pictures → pictures, and some of the more complex graphical transformations, especially those used in picture processing, are not of this form.

Example 2.3-2

The following graphical transformations cannot be expressed using geometric, restriction, and color transformations:

   a) hidden line / hidden surface removal
   b) shading and texturing
   c) defocusing and weighted averaging
   d) Fourier transformations
   e) many image enhancement techniques.

2.4 Hierarchic Picture Structures

The most common way of structuring pictures in graphics programming systems is in a hierarchy, so that a picture is made up of subparts that are themselves pictures, and so on. Graphical transformations can be included within picture hierarchies to modify pictures according to their structure.

Some Hierarchic Structures

We define a *rooted hierarchy* H as a set of *nodes* and a decomposition of H into a *root node* n ϵ H and a collection of subsets $H_1, H_2, ..., H_k$, $k \geq 0$, such that each H_i is a rooted hierarchy, and the union of all the H_i is H–{n}. The H_i are called the *progeny* of n, and n is a *parent* of each H_i. A node with no progeny is called a *leaf*. A *hierarchy* is a rooted hierarchy except that its decomposition has no root node. (Its progeny are still rooted hierarchies.) By drawing a directed arc from each root node to the root node of each of its progeny, a hierarchy can be represented by an acyclic directed graph, and a rooted hierarchy as a singly rooted acyclic directed graph [KNUD73].

Our definition of a hierarchy agrees with that of Parnas [PARD74]. It is very general so as not to preclude any of the kinds of hierarchic picture structures used in existing systems. If the progeny H_i of each node n are disjoint sets, then a rooted hierarchy becomes a *tree*, and a hierarchy becomes a *forest*. If the ordering of the progeny is important, a hierarchy is *ordered*. The fundamental difference between a tree and a general hierarchic structure is that no node in a tree can have more than one parent. The simplest form of hierarchy is a single level "rake" structure, which is a tree in which all progeny of the root are leaves. Figure 2-2 includes illustrations of a) a general hierarchic structure, b) a tree structure, and c) a single-level tree structure.

a) General hierarchic   b) Tree Structure   c) Single-level tree
    structure   structure

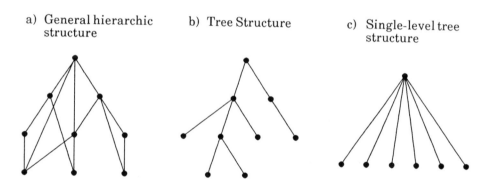

Figure 2-2 Examples of a hierarchic structure

Several relations can be defined between nodes of a hierarchy. Node n_1 is said to be *progeny-of* node n_2 if n_2 is the root of one of the progeny of n_1. The relation *descendent-of* is the transitive closure of progeny-of. N_1 is a *sibling-of* n_2 if both are progeny of the same root. Another definition of a hierarchy is that the descendent-of relation forms a partial order; thus error checking criteria for hierarchic structures can be expressed in terms of these relations.

Henceforth we use the terms hierarchy and hierarchic structure to refer to any of the kinds of hierarchies defined above.

Picture Structures

A data structure that is used to represent one or more pictures is a *picture structure*. If the structure is a hierarchy, we call it a *hierarchic picture structure*.

Example 2.4-1

The following are hierarchic picture structures:

a) A segmented display file is a one-level tree structure.

b) The layout of a VLSI chip is conveniently designed as a general hierarchic structure. Major functional blocks (such as memories, ALUs, busses) are built up from smaller functional units (registers, multiplexors, programmed logic arrays) and so on, everything ultimately being formed from a few primitive elements (wires, pads, contacts).

c) A document consisting of chapters, sections, subsections, paragraphs, and sentences is an example of an ordered tree structure [SHAA80b].

Pictorial information can be associated with a hierarchy in any number of ways to form a hierarchic picture structure. Pictures are generally stored either at the leaves only, or are allowed at any node. Graphical transformations are placed at all nodes, at non-leaf nodes only, or in the links between nodes.

Example 2.4-2

a) The picture structure associated with display procedures [NEWW72, MALW76] is a general hierarchy with pictures in any node and transformations in the links.

Three realizations of hierarchic picture structures are presented in later chapters:

b) Data type picture-tree (Section 3.3.1) provides ordered tree structures with pictures at the leaves and transformations at the non-leaf nodes.

c) Data type tree-structured picture (Section 5.3.1) provides ordered tree structures with pictures at any node and transformations in the links.

d) The picture hierarchy (Section 5.3.2) provides a general unordered hierarchy with pictures in the leaves and transformations in the non-leaf nodes.

In this work we consider a hierarchic picture structure to contain just pictures and graphical transformations, but, of course, other kinds of information can also be present in the structure, such as highlighting information, detectability with a pointing device, or non-graphical attributes of the object(s) being represented by the structure.

Our hierarchic picture structures are used for picture generation only. Hierarchic structures of a kind unrelated to ours are used in image analysis [TANS80].

The Representative Picture

The picture represented by a picture structure is the *representative picture* of that structure. We call the operation that produces the representative picture from a picture structure the *display* operation. Informally, we can define (recursively) the representative picture of a hierarchic picture structure as the picture at the root (if any) plus the sum of the representative pictures of the progeny.

Of course, the representative picture depends not only on the pictures within the structure, but also on the transformations. Once it is decided where pictures and transformations are to be located, a precise definition of the representative picture can be given.

Example 2.4-3

Given below are representative picture definitions for each of the hierarchic picture structures in Example 2.4-2. H denotes the picture structure in each case.

a) $P_H = P_0 + SUM^k_{i=1} T_i(P_i)$,

where P_0 is the picture at the root of H, T_i the transformation at the link to progeny H_i, and P_i the representative picture of H_i.

b) $P_H = \begin{vmatrix} \text{if H contains only a leaf, the picture at the leaf,} \\ \\ \text{otherwise } T_0(SUM_i\, P_i), \end{vmatrix}$

where T_0 is the transformation at the root of H and P_i is the representative picture of progeny H_i.

c) same as a).

d) $P_H = SUM_i\, P_i$,

where P_i is the representative picture for progeny H_i as defined in b). (Recall that there is no top level root.)

We are not concerned here with the interesting and difficult problem of designing algorithms for rendering realistic views of 3D scenes. This process can be viewed either as a transformation applied to the representative picture or as a computation performed on a picture structure before it is displayed. The representative picture concept is the same in either case.

Definitions b), c), and d) in the example are the basis of specifications of the display operations for corresponding structures in Chapters 3 and 5.

Hierarchic Composition

The definitions we have given for the representative picture of a hierarchic picture structure correspond with one's intuition about what the structures should mean. However, the order of computation they imply is not always the best choice for an algorithm that computes the representative picture for display. All of the definitions in Example 2.4-3 define the representative picture in a "bottom up" manner, starting at the leaves and successively applying transformations and additions to reach the root. A different method, which we will call *hierarchic composition*, is to traverse the structure in pre-order, composing transformations during descent, applying the appropriate composite transformations to the pictures at the nodes, and summing up the results. Hierarchic composition is often more efficient because the number of times pictures must be transformed is reduced, and in many cases entire substructures can be bypassed by means of a *visibility test* involving only the transformations [MALW78]: Whenever the restriction part of transformation T is the null region, T(P) is invisible for any picture P, and composition of further transformations with T cannot change this.

A hierarchic composition algorithm for the hierarchic picture structure of Example 2.4-2b) is presented in [MALW78].

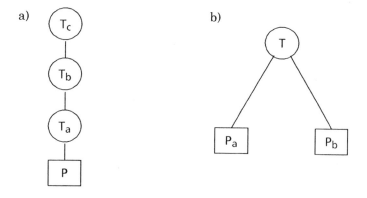

Figure 2-3 Two hierarchic picture structures

Figure 2-3a shows a simple hierarchic picture structure of the kind defined in Example 2.4-2b), with transformations at the non-leaves and a picture at the leaf. Using definition b) of Example 2.4-3 the representative picture is

$$T_c(T_b(T_a(P))) \;=\; (T_c \circ (T_b \circ T_a))(P)$$

whereas hierarchic composition computes the result

$$((T_c \circ T_b) \circ T_a)(P).$$

The two expressions are the same provided the composition of graphical transformations is associative. Fortunately, graphical transformations are just functions on pictures, and the composition of functions is associative [KELJ55], so this requirement is met for all graphical transformations.

A second requirement that must be met for hierarchic composition to be valid can be seen by examining the hierarchic picture structure in Figure 2-3b. Here the representative picture is defined as $T(P_a + P_b)$ whereas hierarchic composition results in the expression $T(P_a) + T(P_b)$. It is thus necessary that the graphical transformation operation distribute over picture sum. This requirement is always met for geometric transformations and restriction transformations. Proofs are outlined in Appendix A.

Color transformations only distribute over picture sum for certain color functions and color sum operations. To find sufficient conditions for the distributive law to hold for color transformations, we evaluate the two expressions $T^c\langle C\rangle(P_1) + T^c\langle C\rangle(P_2)$ and $T^c\langle C\rangle(P_1 + P_2)$ using the definition of a color transformation above.

$$T^c\langle C\rangle(P_1) + T^c\langle C\rangle(P_2) = P',$$

$$\text{where } P'(x) = \begin{cases} C \circ P_1(x) \text{ for all } x \in D_1 - D_2 \\ C \circ P_2(x) \text{ for all } x \in D_2 - D_1 \\ C \circ P_1(x) + C \circ P_2(x) \text{ for all } x \in D_1 \cap D_2. \end{cases}$$

$$T^c\langle C\rangle(P_1 + P_2) = P'',$$

$$\text{where } P''(x) = \begin{cases} C \circ P_1(x) \text{ for all } x \in D_1 - D_2 \\ C \circ P_2(x) \text{ for all } x \in D_2 - D_1 \\ C \circ (P_1(x) + P_2(x)) \text{ for all } x \in D_1 \cap D_2. \end{cases}$$

We see immediately that $\text{domain}(P') = \text{domain}(P'')$. P' and P'' are the same picture provided $P'(x) = P''(x)$ everywhere inside this domain. Examining the expressions above, we see that this condition is met if

$$C(c_1) + C(c_2) = C(c_1 + c_2), \quad \text{for all colors } c_1, c_2,$$

Thus, if color function C distributes over the color sum, then $T^{C}(C)$ distributes over the picture sum, as required for hierarchic composition.

Evaluating Alternatives for the Color Sum

Example 2.4-4

The following are possible choices for a summing function on "colors" consisting of scalars representing gray-scale values:

a) the maximum function $\quad max(c_1, c_2)$ [MALW78]
b) the sum $\qquad\qquad\qquad c_1 \oplus c_2$
c) the average $\qquad\qquad\quad (c_1 \oplus c_2)/2$
d) the bounded sum $\qquad\; min((c_1 \oplus c_2), M)$ [RIEJ75]
e) preemption $\qquad\qquad\quad c_2$

where $\oplus$ denotes scalar addition.

Several desirable properties for the color sum can be listed:

1) commutativity, $c_1 + c_2 = c_2 + c_1$,
2) associativity, $(c_1 + c_2) + c_3 = c_1 + (c_2 + c_3)$,
3) existence of an "inverse" (subtraction) satisfying for all $1 \le k \le n$,

$$(SUM_{i=1}^{n}\, c_i) - c_k = (SUM_{i=1}^{k-1}\, c_i) + (SUM_{i=k+1}^{n}\, c_i),$$

4) distributive property with color functions,

$$C(c_1 + c_2) = C(c_1) + C(c_2).$$

Properties 1) through 3) seem so reasonable in light of our experience with addition for integers and reals that it is tempting to make them absolute requirements. Property 4) need hold only if hierarchic composition is to be done.

Surprisingly, however, we have found that many color summing functions with an acceptable visual effect do not meet these criteria. Of the choices listed in Example 2.4-4, e) is not commutative, c) is not associative, only b) has a subtraction operation, and only e) is distributive with all color functions. Thus the particular color sum operation to be used in a given context must be evaluated against the relative importance of each criterion.

2.5 User Interaction

What is Interaction?

An important aspect of many computer graphics applications is interaction with human users. We list below some characteristics observed in systems generally agreed to be interactive:

1) User interaction is a form of input/output. Data is passed bidirectionally between program and user. Program output is generally in the form of pictures and text, shown on a display device. Input is often entered through several devices with different characteristics. (A categorization of the common input device types is given below).

2) Interaction involves parallel activity between a computer process and the human user who controls the input devices. This is not just logical parallelism but physical concurrency, with accompanying synchronization requirements. The program and user are independent of one another, except when the program needs information from the user, or the user needs a response from the program. Then, the two must synchronize to effect the information transfer.

3) The user side of the interactive interface is often poorly defined. While the program accesses the interactive interface in a uniform way using a set of operations provided for the purpose, the actions performed by the user in conveying his intentions to the program are many and varied. Each kind of interactive input device requires a different technique for its use: pushing a button, typing on a keyboard, turning a dial, pointing with a

stylus or a finger, and moving a joystick or mouse are common examples.

4) Time plays an important role in many interactive systems. Some kinds of interactive input are accomplished by sampling a changing value at regular time intervals, such as the entry of curved lines and character recognition. Dragging and rubberbanding techniques also fit into this category. For other kinds of input, an automatic timeout may be desired if there is no response from the user within a specified period.

5) In an interactive environment, input and output cannot always be cleanly separated. An example is pick (pointing) input, in which the user points to something already displayed on the screen. The input received by the program is a function of more than just the action taken by the user. The user selects a location on the screen, but the data passed to the program depends on what part of a picture or what menu item has been displayed at that location. Dynamic feedback effects such as dragging and rubberbanding also involve relationships between input and output.

In a broad sense, any input/output is a form of interaction; however the more interesting kinds of interaction are those in which a machine process and a user are "closely coupled". At the IFIP Workshop on Methodology of Interaction (Seillac II) [GUER80] the definition of interaction that emerged was "interaction is a style of control and interactive systems exhibit that style." Without attempting to decide the desirable properties of user interaction, we can at least characterize an "interactive style of control" that precludes systems that run in the familiar "batch" mode.

We will say that, *interaction* occurs whenever the actions of a user affect the execution of a program in real time, and user actions are potentially influenced by previous behavior of the program. Interaction can affect the flow of control through a program, the value of program variables, and the timing of program execution. Note, however, that "being interactive" is not a property of a program, but rather a property of an *execution* of a program. While programs that do no user input-output can never be executed interactively, any program can be run non-interactively, by buffering a record of enough user actions to allow the program to reach completion. Clearly, in this case, results of the program have no effect on user actions, and the program process never has to wait for a user action in order to proceed. We define a *non-interactive program* as a program that cannot be run interactively, because it does no user input.

Interaction Primitives

Confusion often arises concerning the languages and interfaces associated with interactive systems. A working group at the Seillac II workshop addressed this issue ([GUER80] p. 83):

> In the interactive world, we distinguish two interfaces to the computer. The first between the user or operator and the computer is called the User Interface. The second between the programmer of the system and the computer is called the Program Interface. Each interface needs a Specification Language. In addition, the User Interface provides a means to communicate with the computer by using the Dialogue Language. The Dialogue Language is handled by its counterpart on the programmer side: the Programming Language.

In this view, the user communicates through the user interface with a program that implements the dialogue language. The major concern in our work is the program side of the user interface, that is, the set of operations available in the programming language for accessing the user interface to implement a dialogue language. Thus, we define an *interaction primitive* as a programming language operation that handles input/output with the user.

Virtual Devices

In present-day systems, output to the user is generally accomplished through display screens. While display devices are certainly not all alike, they can generally be treated in a uniform manner by doing output in terms of a canonical coordinate system. User input, on the other hand, frequently involves several different devices with radically different characteristics. Numerous authors have given classifications of the input devices in common use (e.g. [TRAU75, WALV76]), and it is now common for graphics languages to provide *virtual devices* of a few standard kinds, relieving the programmer of concern for the peculiar characteristics of individual physical devices.

Example 2.5-1

The virtual devices suggested in [FOLJ74] are used in both the GPGS system [CARL77] and the Core Graphics system [GSPC79]:

pick   points to things displayed on the screen; the closest physical analogue is a light pen.

button   indicates a choice by entering a single bit of information (usually used in groups), e.g. a function key.

keyboard   enters a text string, e.g. a terminal keyboard.

locator   enters a position (point in screen space), e.g. a data tablet.

valuator   enters a scalar quantity, e.g. a potentiometer.

Input devices can be operated using either of two basic protocols: 1) the device is sampled by the program to determine its current value, or 2) the device causes events to notify the program that data is available.

Through the design of the interaction primitives, virtual devices such as those in the example can be used as the basis for still higher level devices [WALV76]. These high-level devices often involve both output and input in a specific relationship.

Example 2.5-2

The following are examples of devices that can be implemented in terms of lower level devices:

a) The keyboard device, although presented as a low-level virtual device in Example 2.5-1, can be implemented using a set of button devices. Enough button inputs, perhaps signalled by an "end-of-message" button, are collected to form a complete message. The echoing of partial messages on the screen and even simple editing functions can be built into the device definition. In fact, any of the low-level virtual devices can be implemented using other devices when a closely corresponding physical device is not available.

b) A dragging device for moving pictures around can be implemented by using the input from a locator device to control the transformation of a picture. A similar example is a rubberband device where one end of a line segment tracks the motions of a locator device.

c) A stroke device can be implemented by gathering locator inputs into a list until some end signal is given. Again, simple forms of editing can be included.

Other high-level devices are those that automatically queue outstanding user input, device associations in which an event from one device causes the value of another to be sampled [GSPC79], and local processors (e.g. "smart terminals") that carry on conversations of their own with the user. Van den Bos in [BOSJ80] has proposed language facilities that support entire hierarchies of programmer-defined devices. Device definitions implement dialogues of their own using lower level devices and can be stored in libraries for use in other programs.

Universal Low-Level Input Primitives

It is important that the interaction primitives in a programming language not impose arbitrary restrictions on the range of dialogue languages that can be implemented. This is especially true for primitives that provide the lowest level of access to the user interface.

<u>Example 2.5-3</u>

The initial version of the input primitives for the language XPL/G [MALW76, TURC75] included the operations getkey, getmsg, and getxy to wait for input from each of the three supported devices and corresponding operations to obtain their data, the objective being to make the input system as simple as possible. These input primitives impose two restrictions on the way user input can be handled. First, it must always be known in advance which device will be next, because once the program commits to wait for one of the devices, no other device can be serviced. Second, the program can do nothing, not even output to the user, while it is waiting for user input.

The operation keyorxy was later added, making it possible to wait for either a keystroke or input from the locator device. This, and other changes prompted by users unsatisified with the original design, resulted in a more complex system that still precluded certain kinds of dialogues. (A specification of the XPL/G input primitives is given in Section 4.5.)

The following *universal input primitives* provide simple, unrestrictive, low-level tools for controlling user input. There are three operations, each of which accepts one or more device names as parameters.

The operation

$$wait(device_1, ..., device_n : devicename) : devicename$$

$(n > 0)$ waits until one of the devices in its parameter list has input, then returns that device name as its value. Thus, a wait for device A *or* device B is performed by the statement

$$d \leftarrow wait(A, B),$$

and to wait for device A *and* device B either

$$wait(A); wait(B) \text{ or } wait(B); wait(A)$$

is used. A wait with timeout can be accomplished by making one of the devices in the parameter list a clock.

For polling an input device, we include the operation

$$\text{test(device : devicename) : boolean.}$$

Test returns the value true or false depending on the status of the named device. In either case the program retains control. This operation can be omitted in systems where it is necessary that programs relinquish the CPU while waiting for user input.

Data is obtained from a device using the operation

$$\text{read(device : devicename) : data.}$$

Read can be used after calling wait or test to guarantee fresh data is available, or it can be called at periodic intervals to track the activity of a device as a function of time. (In strongly typed languages, special provision must be made for reading data of different types from different devices.)

The universal input primitives are discussed further and specified formally in Section 4.4.

Chapter 3

Graphical Data Types and
Their Algebraic Specification

The definitions in Chapter 2 capture the meaning of
fundamental concepts underlying graphics programming.
Unfortunately, manifestations of these concepts found in
programming languages vary in form from one language to the
next and often do not lend themselves to formal description; or
they are not supported at all and must be provided within
individual application programs. In this chapter we examine a
programming language construct that is suitable for expressing
many of the concepts we have discussed, is a convenient
programming tool, and is amenable to precise specification: the
graphical data type. After some initial motivation, we present a
collection of types that exemplify concepts from Chapter 2. We
then examine data type specification techniques and, using the
definitions of Chapter 2 as a guide, give algebraic specifications of
the types presented.

3.1 Why Graphical Data Types?

Definitions

The data type concept is present in some form in the majority
of programming languages, and yet it has no universally accepted
definition. (See for instance [SIGP81] and [DEMA78].) We define a
data type as a set of objects together with specific operations that
provide access to those objects. For now, we will confine our
discussion to data types that are used by a single sequential
process. The value of data types in this work will be as a means of
providing *abstractions*. A general definition of abstraction is given
by Standish [STAT78]:

The act of abstraction consists of focusing on properties thought to be essential, or characteristic, and of ignoring properties thought to be irrelevant.

Any data type provides some degree of abstraction, since the operations can be used in place of the code that implements them. The term *abstract data type* or *data abstraction* refers to a data type that provide a particular well-defined level of abstraction: The semantics of the operations are considered characteristic, and the objects are taken as atomic; the implementation of the operations and the representation of the objects are considered irrelevant. We will use the definition given by Liskov and Zilles [LISB74]:

> An *abstract data type* defines a class of abstract objects which is completely characterized by the operations available on those objects. ... When a programmer makes use of an abstract data object, he is concerned only with the behavior which that object exhibits, but not with any details of how that behavior is achieved by means of an implementation.

This definition can be applied in two different contexts. In the context of specifying an abstract data type, it means that the specification is representation independent, that is, no implementation is precluded whose operations give the specified results. We will discuss this issue further in Section 3.5. In the context of implementing an abstract data type, the definition requires *encapsulation*: it must be guaranteed (by compile time or run time checks) that the only access to objects is through operations defined for their type.

Neither the data types of Fortran nor the classes of Simula 67 are abstract data types, because access to object representations is not controlled. The languages Clu, Alphard, and Ada (as well as later versions of Simula) do contain this notion of encapsulation. All of the data types in this work are abstract data types and the terms will be used interchangeably in what follows.

Finally, a *graphical data type* is a data type that provides an abstraction especially useful in graphics applications.

The Need for Graphical Data Types

An important premise of this dissertation is that data types are a useful way to organize the special purpose concepts needed in a graphics programming language. General purpose languages have included data types from the beginning. Examples are types integer, real, character, boolean, string, and record, each of which normally has a well-defined set of operations for manipulating its objects. It is rare that a high level language allows the programmer to get at the individual bits in the machine representation of a real number. Such representation details are abstracted out -- the programmer is not concerned with them and in fact is not given access to them. Generally, the only access to real numbers is through arithmetic operations and relational tests.

By contrast, graphical objects, such as pictures and graphical transformations, have traditionally been handled by building structures from general-purpose data types. This approach requires the programmer to be aware of representation detail that is not relevant to the task of manipulating and displaying pictures. Not only does this make graphics programs hard to write, but the integrity of structures maintained at such a low level cannot be guaranteed. For example, it may be possible to accidentally build a "hierarchic" picture structure containing cycles, causing the display routine to enter an infinite loop. Even the information directly relevant to picture generation can become unmanageable if it must all be kept in mind at once. These problems can be addressed by making commonly needed graphical abstractions available in the language.

Consider hierarchic picture structures as an example. They give necessary organization to pictures at a level much higher (more abstract) than mappings from points to colors. The basic operations for manipulating a hierarchic picture structure remain the same regardless of the interpretation given to the pictures in the leaves. Another example is the picture primitive, such as a line segment, filled polygon, or text string. A picture primitive is known to have certain properties, such as being bounded by a given region, having certain end points or shape, or spelling out a particular English phrase, but, for many purposes, its lower level details can be ignored. Graphical transformations are still another example. A well chosen abstraction can make knowledge of matrix manipulation unnecessary. Each of these abstractions can be readily expressed as a data type. The direct provision of abstractions like these in a graphics programming language can only aid in program development and improve the clarity of the end result.

The use of graphical data types also contributes to the modularity and extendability of a graphics language. By their very nature, data types are logically independent of one another and of other features in a language. New data types can be added to a language without impacting what is there already, and a given collection of types can be embedded in several different languages.

A final argument for the use of graphical data types is that they allow the incorporation of graphics features into a language in a way that can be precisely specified using well-known techniques. The ability to formally specify such features aids in the design, implementation, and documentation of graphics programming systems.

Related Work

Programming facilities similar to our graphical data types have appeared in [KJET72], which describes a Simula-based language with built-in class definitions for points, lines, circles, and hierarchically structured pictures; in [SCHG76, SCHG80] which describe a data type for line drawings that has been implemented as an extension to Fortran; and in [THAD79] where a Pascal extension containing a similar data type for line drawings is presented. Although [SCHG76] discusses some of the problems involved in specifying pictorial data types, none of these works gives a formal specification.

The work most closely related to ours is that by Guttag and Horning discussed in Section 1.3 [GUTJ80]. They have designed a hierarchy of types to serve as the basis for a display device interface, and specified them algebraically. While their data types are specific to a particular interface design, they do provide examples of graphical data types different from ours.

3.2 The Basic Graphical Data Type: Continuous Picture

The first graphical data type that we will define captures the picture concept at the lowest level of abstraction -- as a partial function from a universe of points to colors, corresponding to the definition of a picture in Section 2.1. Type *continuous picture* provides a model for any picture with a finite number of colors, while abstracting out details of how pictures are represented, either in the memory of a machine or on a display medium. It is not, however, an example of a data type that would be used in a program. Instead it provides a restatement of our picture definition that will be helpful in defining the semantics of other graphical data types.

We will describe the type by giving its operations and informal descriptions of their semantics. A formal specification is given in Appendix B.1. The operations can be divided into three groups, for creating, examining, and transforming continuous pictures.

Picture Generating Operations

The first problem we must consider is how pictures are to be generated. We wish to define pictures on a continuous (non-discrete) space, in which most useful regions contain an uncountable number of points. It is also useful to allow pictures to be infinite in extent. However, in order to be of practical use, the type must allow any picture object of interest to be created in a finite number of operations. We solve this problem by considering pictures as partial functions from regions to colors rather than from points to colors. Of course, finitely generated pictures are still limited to containing a finite number of colors, but this is not a serious limitation in the context of picture generation. Intuitively, we may still think of a picture as a set of ordered pairs, but the first element of each pair is a region instead of a point. We will call such a colored region a *patch*.

Any continuous picture can be built up using just a constant for the empty picture and an operation to add patches to it. (For convenience we will treat constants as operations with no parameters.) The names and functionalities of these operations are as follows:

$$nullpict \qquad\qquad\qquad\qquad\qquad\qquad \rightarrow picture$$
$$inspatch \qquad picture \times region \times color \rightarrow picture.$$

The operation nullpict takes no parameters and returns an object of type (continuous) picture. Inspatch(P,R,c) takes existing continuous picture P, and region R and color c (describing a patch), and produces a new picture incorporating the patch (R,c). Even if a color was already assigned to all or part of R, the new color c prevails within R.

Existing pictures are added together using the operation

$$sum \qquad\qquad\qquad\qquad picture \times picture \rightarrow picture.$$

Sum(P$_1$,P$_2$) is defined in accordance with the picture sum of Section 2.1.

The "background" of a continuous picture can be filled in with the operation

$$fill \qquad\qquad\qquad\qquad picture \times color \rightarrow picture.$$

The continuous picture fill(P,c) is the same as P except that it contains all of the universe and has color c everywhere outside the domain of P.

The picture generating operations we have given make use of the types region and color. The continuous picture abstraction is of greatest use if no unnecessary assumptions are made about these types. For now, we merely assume their existence. In order to formally specify type continuous picture, we will require that types region and color have certain operations, but the semantics of the operations will not be important. Specific examples of these types are given in Section 3.3.

Inquiry Operations

An object is of no use unless we can obtain information about it. A continuous picture cannot even be displayed unless it is possible to find out what points it contains and how those points are colored. In general, the only way to get information about an object is to map it onto an object of another type. Otherwise it is impossible to distinguish one object of a type from any other [GUTJ78a]. Even a predicate is a mapping onto objects of type boolean.

Following [GUTJ75], we refer to the type currently being defined as the *type of interest* and all other types as *outside types*. An operation that returns an object of outside type is an *inquiry operation* (after [LISB75]). For type continuous picture, the following inquiry operations are useful:

domain	picture → region
colors	picture × region → set(color)
getpatch	picture × color → region
getcolor	picture × point → color.

Domain(P) is the domain of P as defined in Section 2.1. Colors(P,R) is the set containing all the colors of P that are used inside region R. Getpatch(P,c) returns the region consisting of all parts of P that have color c. (Patches of the same color are combined.) Getcolor(P,p) is the color of P at point p.

Graphical Transformations

An important concept that we have not yet included in the continuous picture abstraction is the graphical transformation. Section 2.2 defines restriction transformations, geometric transformations, and color transformations. Corresponding to these we define the following three operations:

restriction	picture × region → picture
geomtrans	picture × geomfcn → picture
colortrans	picture × colorfcn → picture

Once again we have introduced some new types: geomfcn for geometric functions (from points to points) and colorfcn for color functions (from colors to colors). These types will be discussed further in Section 3.3.

Extensions

The following operations will be considered extensions to type continuous picture because they have a narrower purpose, and they can be expressed in terms of operations already given.

While the picture building operations already given are sufficient to create any continuous picture object, it is convenient to have picture primitives directly available that are appropriate to the application at hand. The following are some possible operations for producing picture primitives:

dot	point × color → picture
lineseg	point × point × color → picture
box	point × point × color → picture
text	string × point × color → picture.

Dot(p,c) is the continuous picture containing the single point p with color c. Lineseg(p_1,p_2,c) contains all the points on the straight line segment connecting p_1 and p_2 with color c. Box(p_1,p_2,c) consists of the area inside and on the rectangle with diagonal vertices p_1 and p_2. Text(x,p,c) is a continuous picture consisting of font for string s, starting at location p, with color c. (We leave choice of font and base line direction unspecified.)

In Section 2.1 some properties of pictures were discussed. Each of these properties can be expressed using the inquiry operations already defined, but having some especially useful predicates predefined will make it easier to write program assertions involving pictures (see Section 6.1):

equal	picture × picture → boolean
coincident	picture × picture → boolean
contains	picture × picture → boolean
disjoint	picture × picture → boolean
visible	picture × region → boolean
bounded	picture × region → boolean.

The meanings of these predicate operations correspond to the definitions in Section 2.1.

3.3 Data Type Examples

In this section we present a collection of graphical data types to illustrate how the concepts of Chapter 2 can be packaged as abstractions directly useful in writing graphics programs. Only a brief discussion of each type is given here. Many are described further in the context of the prototype language in Section 5.3. Formal specifications for all of the data types introduced in the dissertation are given in Appendices B, C, and D.

Operations are denoted using a functional syntax. However, we do not intend to preclude other notations, such as the infix $p_1 + p_2$ in place of $sum(p_1, p_2)$, or $p_1 = p_2$ for $equals(p_1, p_2)$. Thus, included in the specifications in the appendices (under **synonyms**) are alternate forms for some of the operations. The synonyms listed are used in later sections as well as in the specifications themselves.

We do, however, restrict operations to be pure functions, that is, each operation returns a value that depends only on the parameters of the call, and there are no side effects, either on the parameters or any other part of the system state. While operations more general than this can be specified without undue difficulty [GUTJ80, LEVM80], these restrictions simplify the specifications, allowing us to concentrate more on concepts and less on the mechanics of specification.

Included in the heading for each data type are a formal name for the type and a one- or two-character abbreviation. The formal names are used in describing the functionality of the operations and for referring to types within programs. The abbreviations are used in specifications for naming axioms and occasionally to prefix operation names (with a dot as separator) for readability. To the right of each data type heading, the appendix containing the corresponding specification is given.

3.3.1 Pictorial Data Types

Type continuous picture captures satisfactorily the concept of a picture as a partial function, but higher level picture abstractions are of greater use as programming tools. We present below two graphical data types as examples of picture abstractions suitable for inclusion in a programming language. Type simple picture allows pictures to be built up from a set of standard primitives. Type picture-tree organizes simple pictures into tree structures.

Type Simple Picture (spicture, sp)   Appendix B.3

$$
\begin{array}{lrcl}
\text{nullpict} & \text{color} & \to & \text{spicture} \\
\text{setcolor} & \text{spicture} \times \text{color} & \to & \text{spicture} \\
\text{moveto} & \text{spicture} \times \text{point} & \to & \text{spicture} \\
\text{lineto} & \text{spicture} \times \text{point} & \to & \text{spicture} \\
\text{text} & \text{spicture} \times \text{string} & \to & \text{spicture} \\
\text{append} & \text{spicture} \times \text{spicture} & \to & \text{spicture} \\
\text{curpos} & \text{spicture} & \to & \text{point} \\
\text{curcolor} & \text{spicture} & \to & \text{color}
\end{array}
$$

An empty simple picture with an initial current color is created by nullpict. Setcolor and moveto change the current color and current position without affecting the picture's appearance. Picture primitives for line segments and text strings are added using lineto and text. The color and location of the added primitives is determined by the current color and current position of the original picture. Simple pictures are combined using the append operation; the current color and position of the result are those of the second argument to append. The inquiry operations curpos and curcolor allow the current position and color of a simple picture to be obtained.

Type Picture-Tree (tree, tr)   Appendix B.2

leaf	spicture x name → tree
node	grtrans x name → tree
insprogeny	tree x tree → tree
instrans	tree x grtrans → tree
delprogeny	tree x name → tree
getname	tree → name
getpict	tree → spicture
gettrans	tree → grtrans
getprogeny	tree x name → tree
isleaf	tree → boolean

Objects of type picture-tree are created by assembling simple pictures into a tree structure. All picture-trees have names so that they can be accessed within larger structures. A picture tree is either a leaf containing a simple picture or a (non-leaf) node containing a graphical transformation. Nodes can have progeny, which are inserted by the insprogeny operation and deleted by delprogeny. The transformation at a node is replaced using instrans. The inquiry operations provide for obtaining the name of a picture tree, the simple picture at a leaf, the graphical transformation at a node, a progeny of a node, and the function of a picture-tree (leaf or node).

Type picture-tree exemplifies a hierarchic picture structure with pictures at the leaves and transformations at the non-leaf nodes, as discussed in Section 2.4. This contrasts with type tree-structured picture, presented as part of the prototype language in Section 5.3.1, which has transformations in the links and pictures in any node.

The Representative Picture

The above data types provide two different kinds of picture structures. A property common to all picture structures is that they represent displayable pictures. We define any program object that can be graphically displayed as a *pictorial object*. A graphical data type with pictorial objects is a *pictorial data type*; it includes an operation for displaying its objects.

In order to precisely describe the picture a hierarchic picture structure represents, we introduced in Section 2.4 the concept of a representative picture. One function of a graphics system is to make visible the pictures represented by pictorial objects by creating an image on a display device. A displayed image can only approximate the picture it is intended to convey, however. Display devices, be they cathode ray tubes, pen and ink plotters, or line printers, have limited size, accuracy, resolution, color selection, and dimensionality, so they must employ various "cheats" to display most pictures. For instance, a straight line segment might appear as a wiggly row of dots on a printer or raster display, as a series of connected steps on a plotter, or as a smooth linear streak on a vector CRT, but, in any case, the viewer thinks "line segment", even though a true line segment is perfectly straight and has no thickness. Similarly, many display devices approximate smooth curves as series of straight line segments. The rendering of 3D scenes on raster display devices is an especially difficult picture approximation task.

Our concern in this work is the picture conveyed from a program through a display device, not the physical pattern of dots or strokes that actually appears. It is here that type continuous picture can help us. It provides a set of objects that correspond to idealizations of displayed images. Instead of trying to say exactly what is to appear on a display device, we specify a mapping from pictorial objects to continuous picture objects. Thus, we define the *representative picture of a pictorial object* to be a unique object of type continuous picture. The display system is assumed to provide a recognizable approximation of this representative picture.

To describe mappings from pictorial objects to their representative pictures, we introduce a special operation, called display, for each pictorial data type. For the two types above the operations are

        * display   spicture → picture

for type simple picture and

        * display   tree → picture

for type picture-tree. The display operation allows representative pictures to be defined within the same framework as ordinary operations associated with a data type. The apparent naming ambiguity is not a problem. The display operation is a *generic operation* that has meaning for all pictorial data types. The intended meaning can always be determined from the type of the argument.

The symbol "*" denotes that the display operation is a *hidden operation*. Hidden operations cannot be used within programs and need not be implemented; they are defined only to aid in the specification of a data type. The display operation aids in specifying the mechanism for displaying pictorial objects. In fact the entire type continuous picture is hidden in the same way; it is not intended for use in programs, but it will play a central role in the specification of graphics languages (Chapter 5) and the verification of graphics programs (Chapter 6).

3.3.2 Other Graphical Data Types

Several graphics-related concepts other than pictures are discussed in Chapter 2 for which the data type model is also appropriate. We discuss below data types that capture each of the concepts color, point, region, geometric function, color function, and graphical transformation. The data type descriptions given here serve a dual purpose: to indicate how the concepts developed in Chapter 2 are translated into the data type model, and to provide specific data type examples for later reference. Thus, for each type we discuss both the general properties it must have in order to fit the concept, and specific choices we have made in order to provide convenient examples. These example types are described in more detail as part of the prototype language in Section 5.3.

Type Color (color, co)   Appendix B.8

The color data type has a very simple basic structure. The essential operations are a collection of constants, an equality test and the summing function to be used in adding pictures:

$$
\begin{array}{ll}
color_1 & \rightarrow \ color \\
\dots & \dots \\
color_n & \rightarrow \ color \\
equal & color \times color \rightarrow boolean \\
sum & color \times color \rightarrow color.
\end{array}
$$

Beyond this, the complexity of the type depends on the nature of the attributes used to describe the appearance of each point in a picture.

For our purposes, the interpretation of the color values and the definition of the color sum are left open. Some possible definitions for the color sum were discussed in Section 2.4. We use familiar color names as constants.

Type Point (point, pt)   Appendix B.7

Each object of type point corresponds to a point in the universe. All that is required is a set of constants and a means of determining their spatial relationship to one another. The usual way of satisfying these requirements is by choosing a coordinate system, whichs maps points onto tuples of some scalar data type.

For our illustrative needs, we choose the universe to be the plane, the scalar type to be the real numbers, and the coordinate system to be either Cartesion or polar, with provision for converting between the two:

point	real × real → point
polarpt	real × real → point
origin	→ point
abscissa	point → real
ordinate	point → real
radius	point → real
angle	point → real.

It is also convenient to have available operations for simple vector arithmetic and for comparing points:

sum	point × point → point
difference	point × point → point
equal	point × point → boolean.

Type Region (region, rg)

Just as the coordinate system to be used in building pictures is determined by type point, the kinds of shapes that can appear within pictures is determined by type region. Since regions are most naturally thought of as sets of points, we include the familiar set operations:

complement	region → region
intersec	region × region → region
union	region × region → region
difference	region × region → region
empty	region → boolean
contains	region × region → boolean
equal	region × region → boolean.

Missing from this list are operations for the initial creation of regions. The most general way to build regions is by combining points, but most useful regions cannot be finitely generated this way. In fact, by basing type continuous picture on regions instead of points, we have only deferred the finite generation problem for pictures (see Section 3.2) to the region data type. A solution is to provide specific operations for generating the shapes needed in a particular range of applications. The following generator operations provide the empty region, the universe, a single point, straight line segments, solid rectangular boxes (of predetermined orientation), and regions containing the points on a text string (of predetermined font):

nullregion	→ region
universe	→ region
point	point → region
lineseg	point × point → region
box	point × point → region
text	string × point → region.

Type Geometric Function (geomfcn, gf)   Appendix B.5

Referring to Section 2.2, we can identify some operations that apply to any geometric function:

compose	geomfcn × geomfcn → geomfcn
invertible	geomfcn → boolean
inverse	geomfcn → geomfcn.

Since we are using objects to represent functions an additional operation is needed to apply a geometric function to a point:

transform	geomfcn × point → point.

Intuitively, transform(G,p) = G(p).

Just as for type region it is convenient to choose generators according to application, rather than attempt complete generality. For illustrative purposes we include translation and uniform scaling in two dimensional cartesian coordinates. (This the only type other than type point in which a particular coordinate system is referenced.)

identity	→ geomfcn
scale	real → geomfcn
translate	real × real → geomfcn

Type Graphical Transformation (grtrans, gt)   Appendix B.4

In its most general form, a graphical transformation is any function from pictures to pictures (see Section 2.2), so we define the operations

compose	grtrans × grtrans → grtrans
* transform	grtrans × picture → picture

corresponding to functional composition and the transformation of pictures. We have chosen (arbitrarily) to make graphical transformations act only on objects of type continuous picture. Since type continuous picture is a hidden data type (see Section 3.2), this definition does not allow transformations to be applied directly to pictorial objects in a program. They can, however, be imbedded in a pictorial object to change the representative picture.

To provide a particular data type for later use, we restrict graphical transformations to be of the form T^{gr}, that is, consisting of geometric and restriction parts only (see Section 2.2). The following operations then complete the data type:

grtrans	geomfcn × region → grtrans
identity	→ grtrans
gpartof	grtrans → geomfcn
rpartof	grtrans → region.

The data type defined by these operations is still very general. Since there are no limitations imposed on types geometric function and region, any transformation that moves or deletes all or part of a picture is included. The versions of these two constituent types given above determine the properties of the graphical transformation type we will use in later examples.

3.3.3 General Purpose Types

A number of data types commonly found in general purpose languages are useful in graphics applications, including the types boolean, integer, real, character, string, and set. We will employ the standard logical operators for type boolean and the arithmetic operators for types integer and real without further definition. Commonly used definitions for the types string and set vary considerably, so we define our own versions of these below. In addition we define a name data type to provide a supply of names.

Type Name (name, n) Appendix B.8

In its simplest form, type name contains just a collection of constants and an equality test:

$$
\begin{array}{lcl}
name_1 & \rightarrow & name \\
\cdots & & \cdots \\
name_n & \rightarrow & name \\
equals & name \times name \rightarrow & boolean.
\end{array}
$$

For some uses a total ordering on names is required:

$$
\begin{array}{lcl}
lessthan & name \times name \rightarrow & boolean.
\end{array}
$$

Type String (string, st) Appendix B.10

A string is a sequence of characters. We will only need operations for generating and concatenating strings:

$$
\begin{array}{lcl}
nullstr & \rightarrow & string \\
inschar & string \times char \rightarrow & string \\
concat & string \times string \rightarrow & string.
\end{array}
$$

Other operations such as substring, length, and search would probably be included for most applications.

Type Ordered Set of Item (set(item), s) Appendix B.9

We will need a set abstraction for several purposes, so we give a single type definition that encompasses all of our needs. To obtain the necessary generality we define the set abstraction in terms of a *parameterized type* [THAJ78] or *type generator* [WULW76, ZILS80], which yields a unique type for each value of its parameter(s). In this case the parameter (item) is itself a data type, which determines the type for objects contained in sets. The reason for the name "ordered set" is that we require objects of type item to be totally ordered. Type item must have the operations equals and lessthan.

Type ordered set includes the usual set operations,

nullset	$\rightarrow$ set
insert	set $\times$ item $\rightarrow$ set
remove	set $\times$ item $\rightarrow$ set
union	set $\times$ set $\rightarrow$ set
intersect	set $\times$ set $\rightarrow$ set
difference	set $\times$ set $\rightarrow$ set
contains	set $\times$ item $\rightarrow$ boolean
equal	set $\times$ set $\rightarrow$ boolean
empty	set $\rightarrow$ boolean
size	set $\rightarrow$ integer,

and the additional ones,

first	set $\rightarrow$ item
rest	set $\rightarrow$ set
select	set $\rightarrow$ item.

First(s) is the least element contained in set s according to the total ordering defined on type item. Rest(s) is all of s except the least element. Select(s) returns an arbitrary element from s.

3.4 Specification Techniques

Now that we have presented some graphical data types, we need to describe their meaning more precisely. The concepts underlying these types were defined in Chapter 2 in terms of mathematical objects such as sets, partial functions, and directed graphs. Our aim in the rest of this chapter is to re-express our earlier definitions as graphical data type specifications. Many techniques have been proposed for specifying data abstractions. Desirable properties of specification techniques have been listed by several authors (for example [MARM76] and [LISB77]). In our view, the primary role of a data type specification is to make explicit the boundary between an abstraction and its implementation. An encapsulation "defends" this boundary by ensuring that programs cannot access the data type representation. A specification should provide all the information necessary for a programmer to use the data type and perhaps prove facts about his program, as well as make it unnecessary for an implementer of the type to know its intended use. A specification is also a valuable design tool. To be successful in these roles, a specification must be both mathematically sound and easily understood.

The major problem posed by graphical data types is the diverse nature of the concepts they represent. Techniques well suited to describing some types are awkward to apply to others. The specification technique we have chosen to use is the algebraic specification technique. Its primary attractions are its fundamental simplicity and its applicability to a wide variety of data organizations. We will use the algebraic technique to specify all but one of the data types in this dissertation, and then extend the technique to handle primitives for user interaction.

In what follows we give a brief overview of some specification techniques for data abstractions, then describe the algebraic technique in greater detail. An excellent survey of data type specification techniques can be found in [LISB77].

3.4.1 Overview of Techniques

One of our overriding concerns is that a specification capture only the externally observable behavior of a data type, that it describe only the abstraction and not place unnecessary constraints on (or provide unnecessary information about) an implementation. Data type specification techniques can be divided into two categories, *operational* and *definitional* [GUTJ77]. Operational specification techniques specify a data type by representing the objects and expressing the operations in terms of more primitive abstractions whose properties are already known. Such a defining implementation is referred to in [BERV79] as an *abstract model*. An implementation is correct with respect to an operational specification if its externally observable behavior agrees with that of the abstract model. A definitional specification, on the other hand, states only what the operations must do, without giving algorithms for doing it.

It has been shown by Berzins [BERV79] that the externally observable behavior of a data type can be precisely characterized as a heterogeneous (or many sorted) algebra, which we will refer to as the *defining algebra* of the type. An operational specification determines this algebra by example; a definitional specification gives its properties directly. In either case, an implementation of a data type is correct if the algebra A_i of the implementation is compatible with the defining algebra A_0, that is, if there is a homomorphism from A_i onto A_0. The correctness of data type implementations is treated in more detail in [HOAC72a], [GUTJ78c], and [BERV79].

An operational specification is generally written in terms of convenient abstractions from the realm of mathematics, such as graphs, sets, and sequences. Because the defining algebra is determined implicitly, proofs of programs containing the type are handled most easily by first proving a collection of generally useful theorems about the abstract model and using these as the basis of program proofs [LISB79]. The main advantages of operational specifications are that they are written in a style that is familiar to programmers and that consistency is not a problem. However, operational specifications can still be incomplete (if not all cases are considered), and there is a danger that the particular algorithm used in the abstract model will mistakenly be taken as part of the specification. The operational approach works best when abstractions can be used that are closely related to the concept being specified.

Example 3.4-1

As an example of an operational specification, we give a modified version of a specification from [BERV79] (p. 67) for type stack. The abstraction on which it is based is the mathematical sequence. Operations from the sequence abstraction are prefixed with "seq$".

type stack
with
create		→ stack
push	element x stack	→ stack
pop	stack	→ stack
top	stack	→ element
isempty	stack	→ boolean

representation sequence[element]
operations create() = seq$create()
   push(e,s) = seq$addlast(s,e)
   pop(s) = **if** seq$length(s) = 0 **then** ⟨stack underflow⟩
      else seq$subrange(s,1,seq$length(s)-1)
   top(s) = seq$last(s)
   isempty(s) = **if** seq$length(s) = 0 **then** true **else** false

Definitional specification techniques include various axiomatic methods [HOAC72a, WULW76, SPIJ75] and more recent work based on denotational semantics [DEMA78]. Axiomatic methods give the properties of the defining algebra directly by means of axioms. The proof of correctness of an implementation reduces to showing that it satisfies the axioms. The same axioms in turn form a convenient basis for proofs about programs containing the type. Unfortunately, not only can a list of axioms be incomplete, but it can be inconsistent as well, since it is possible for axioms to contradict each other. The attraction of a definitional specification is its "purity": only the essential part of a data abstraction, the external behavior (or defining algebra), is mentioned.

<u>Example 3.4-2</u>

As an example of an axiomatic specification that does not use the algebraic technique, we give an axiomatic specification for type stack adapted from [SPIJ75] (p. 129). The data type defined here differs from the one in Example 3.4-1 in that the operation pop accepts an integer argument, the operation used replaces isempty, and the operations push and pop return results through an argument.

create		$\rightarrow$ stack
push	element $\times$ stack	$\rightarrow$ stack
pop	integer $\times$ stack	$\rightarrow$ stack
top	stack	$\rightarrow$ element
used	stack	$\rightarrow$ integer

(S1) WS(create(),0).

(S2) (u<MaxNum & WS(s,u,i,e)) {push(e',s)}
     (WS(s,u + 1,i + 1,e) & WS(s,u + 1,0,e')).

(S3) (j≤u & j≤i & WS(s,u,i,e)) {pop(j,s)} WS(s,u-j,i-j,e).

(S4) WS(s,u,i,e) {invoke top(s)} WS(s,u,i,e).

(S5) WS(s,u,i,e) {invoke used(s)} WS(s,u,i,e).

where s ∈ stack, u,i ∈ integer, e ∈ element,
       WS(s,u,i,e) ≡ (0≤i<u | i = u = 0) & used(s) = u
                     & (u >0 {pop(i,s)} top(s) = e),
       WS(s,0) ≡ WS(s,0,0,e), and
       MaxNum is the maximum size of a stack.
(WS is the predicate "well-formed stack".)

3.4.2 The Algebraic Specification Technique

The algebraic specification technique, developed by Guttag [GUTJ75, GUTJ78], Zilles [ZILS74, ZILS80], and Goguen et al [GOGJ78], is an axiomatic technique that employs some assumptions and restrictions to make the presentation of a data type specification especially simple. The axioms are restricted to consist of a finite number of equations containing the operations, free variables (universally quantified), and conditional tests. It is assumed that the only objects of the type are those created by finite application of the listed operations.

Example 3.4-3

Given below is an algebraic specification for the stack abstraction of Example 3.4-1.

st1 pop(create) = undefined
st2 pop(push(e,s)) = s
st3 top(create) = undefined
st4 top(push(e,s)) = e
st5 isempty(create) = true
st6 isempty(push(e,s)) = false

The equations (axioms) of an algebraic specification determine the defining algebra by grouping the expressions that can be formed from the operations into *equivalence classes*. Each equivalence class of expressions corresponds to an object in the algebra. This notion of object is meaningful only if the equivalence classes are preserved by the operations (informally $a = b \Rightarrow f(a) = f(b)$, for all operations f), An equivalence relation that meets this criterion is a *congruence relation*, and the equivalence classes are then *congruence classes*.

Equations between expressions of the type of interest determine the equivalence classes (and therefore the objects) of that type. For example, axiom st2 above states that pop(push(e,s)) represents the same stack object as s itself, for all possible substitutions for s and e. Axiom st1 states that pop(create) does not represent a proper stack object. (Exception conditions are discussed further in the next section.) The set of objects for each type is totally determined by the specification for that type, so equations between expressions of outside type assign the results of inquiry operations to existing objects without defining any new ones. According to axiom st5 above, isempty(create) is another expression for the boolean object true.

If the results of applying all inquiry operations to all objects of the type of interest are determined by the axioms, the specification is *complete*. If these values are uniquely determined, the specification is *consistent*. It follows that a specification is not consistent unless the congruence classes are preserved under the operations. (Otherwise an inquiry operation applied to two expressions for the same object could yield different results.) Guttag [GUTJ78a] has shown that it is possible to algebraically specify any type of practical interest (any type that is computable and finitely generated) provided, in some cases, that certain operations included in the specification are not considered part of the type. That such *auxiliary operations* are necessary to define certain types has been shown by Thatcher et al [THAJ78]. Further study of the power of various forms of equational specifications appears in [BERJ79] and [KAMS79].

Unfortunately, the completeness of an arbitrary algebraic specification is undecidable. However, heuristics applicable to primitive recursive operations are given in [GUTJ78a] that aid in writing recognizably complete axiomatizations, and operations more general than this seldom occur in programming applications. We give our own method for writing algebraic axioms based on these heuristics in the next section.

Likewise, the question of consistency is undecidable for the general case. However, if a provably correct implementation can be constructed for a particular specification, or the axioms can be shown to have the Church-Rosser property (i.e. the order of application of the axioms does not matter), then consistency is assured. We have found that in practice a good intuitive understanding of the type being defined together with the heuristics given in the next section are generally sufficient to avoid inconsistent axiomatizations.

We have chosen to use the algebraic specification technique for a number of reasons: a few simple concepts are sufficient to specify a wide variety of data types, it is a definitional technique so that the defining algebra is determined directly, heuristics can aid in making a specification consistent and complete, and the technique is widely known and studied. Disadvantages are that the form of the axioms can be somewhat unnatural to the uninitiated, auxiliary operations must be introduced to specify some types, and for a few types an algebraic specification is cumbersome. We have found the algebraic specification technique to be well suited for specifying nearly all of the graphical data types we have looked at (see Section 3.7) and the resulting specifications to be useful for reasoning about graphics programs.

3.5 A Methodology for Algebraic Specification

We will illustrate our method for constructing algebraic specifications with examples from the types continuous picture (Section 3.2) and simple picture (Section 3.3.1). Complete specifications are in Appendices B.1 and B.3 respectively.

3.5.1 The Form of a Specification

The heading contains the name of the type, the type identifier, and its one- or two-character abbreviation (see Section 3.3), for example,

Data Type Continuous Picture (picture, p).

Next the operations and their functionalities are listed. The following operations are part of the continuous picture data type:

operations
- nullpict   → picture
- inspatch   picture × region × color → picture
      lineseg   point × point × color → picture
      sum   picture × picture → picture
      domain   picture → region
      getcolor   picture × point → color

Alternate ways of denoting the operations are listed as synonyms:

synonyms
$$sum(P_1, P_2) \equiv P_1 + P_2$$

Under the heading **axioms** is a list of equations that completely and consistently define the type. Each equation (axiom) is preceded by a "number" consisting of the type name abbreviation and a sequence number. Axioms used as examples in this section are labelled with type abbreviation "e" (example), with the corresponding number from the appendices, if any, indicated also. Finally, under **theorems** are listed useful facts that can be proven from the axioms.

3.5.2 Constructing the Axioms

A complete and consistent set of axioms can be constructed in a straightforward manner if the operations are partitioned into the three groups: inquiry operations, generator operations, and basic generator operations. Other authors have used similar partitionings under various names [LISB77, GUTJ78b, ZILS80, LISB79]. The methodology given here is most closely related to that of [GUTJ78b].

The *generator operations* return objects of the type of interest. For type continuous picture nullpict, inspatch, lineseg, and sum are generator operations. The remaining operations (domain and getcolor in the list above) return objects of outside types and are called *inquiry operations*. (The third category, basic generator operations, is defined below.)

In line with our earlier definition (Section 3.4.2), an axiomatization is complete if the result of applying every inquiry operation to every expression formed from the generators is determined. The use of variables makes this feasible with a finite number of axioms: one for each inquiry operation applied to each generator. The domain operation, for instance, can be completely defined by giving meaning to each of the expressions domain(nullpict), domain(inspatch(P,R,c)), domain(lineseg(p_1,p_2)), and domain(sum(P_1,P_2)), and similarly for the getcolor operation, which results in the following list of axioms:

e1/p1	domain(nullpict) = nullregion
e2/p2	domain(inspatch(P,R,c)) = R ∪ domain(P)
e3	domain(lineseg(p_1,p_2,c)) = rg.lineseg(p_1,p_2)
e4	domain(sum(P_1,P_2)) = domain(P_1) ∪ domain(P_2).

$e5/p7$ getcolor(nullpict,p) = undefined

$e6/p8$ getcolor(inspatch(P,R,c),p) =
       if p ϵ R then c else getcolor(P,p)

$e7$ getcolor(lineseg(p_1,p_2,c),p_3) =
       if p_3 ϵ rg.lineseg(p_1,p_2) then c else undefined

$e8$ getcolor(sum(P_1,P_2),p) =
       if p ϵ domain(P_1) & p ϵ domain(P_2)
       then getcolor(P_1,p) + getcolor(P_2,p)
       else if p ϵ domain(P_1) then getcolor(P_1,c)
       else if p ϵ domain(P_2) then getcolor(P_2,c)
       else undefined

This method does indeed produce a complete specification provided expressions can be found for the right hand sides of the equations. However, for the entire continuous picture data type in Appendix B.1, there are 12 generator operations and 10 inquiry operations so that 120 axioms would be required! The number of axioms grows roughly as the square of the number of operations with this method (assuming the ratio of generator operations to inquiry operations is roughly constant).

Fortunately, it is usually possible to reduce the number of axioms by further partitioning the generator operations, selecting as *basic generators* only those operations necessary to generate every object of the type of interest. For type continuous picture, the operations nullpict and inspatch are sufficient. Accordingly, they are flagged with the symbol "•" in the list of operations. Now we need two kinds of axioms: axioms that define the results of the inquiry operations applied to the basic generators, for example axioms *e1*, *e2*, *e5*, and *e6* above, and axioms that express the remaining generators in terms of the basic generators, for example,

$e9/p25$ lineseg(p_1,p_2,c) = inspatch(nullpict,rg.lineseg(p_1,p_2),c)

$e10$ sum(P_1,P_2) = ...,

Axioms for the inquiry operations applied to non-basic generators (axioms *e3*, *e4*, *e7*, and *e8* above) are not needed.

The result is a complete axiomatization, because, in any expression of outside type, the non-basic generators can be reduced to basic generators, and the basic generators and inquiry operations can then be removed entirely. For example,

$$
\begin{aligned}
&\text{domain(lineseg(p_1,p_2,c))} \\
&= \text{domain(inspatch(nullpict,rg.lineseg(p_1,p_2),c))} \quad \text{by axiom } e9, \\
&= \text{rg.lineseg(p_1,p_2)} \cup \text{domain(nullpict)} \qquad\qquad\;\; \text{by axiom } e2, \\
&= \text{rg.lineseg(p_1,p_2)} \qquad\qquad\qquad\qquad\qquad\quad\; \text{by axiom } e1,
\end{aligned}
$$

which agrees with axiom *e3* that we wrote earlier. Using this strategy, the maximum number of axioms required is the product of the number of basic generators (2) and the number of other operations (20), or 40 in all for the continuous picture data type. Note that as long as the basic generators do not change, the number of axioms grows linearly with the number of operations.

3.5.3 Auxiliary Operations

Of course, no method for determining the left hand sides of the axioms is of any value unless we can complete the right hand sides. Axiom *e10* above is an example where, within the allowable form for algebraic axioms, no right hand side can be written. The only way the sum operation can be defined in terms of the basic generators is to introduce an *auxiliary operation*, an operation that is necessary to the specification but is not part of (the defining algebra for) the type. Since auxiliary operations are never made available to the users of a type (or required to be implemented) they are always hidden operations (see Section 3.3.1) and are flagged as such by the symbol "*". It is possible to write axioms for sum in terms of the operation

  * addpatch   picture × region × color → picture,

which adds a single patch to a picture, combining colors where they overlap. Addpatch in turn can be defined in terms of inspatch: (Recall that inspatch inserts a new patch by preempting any overlapped colors.)

$e11/p9$ $\text{sum}(P, \text{nullpict}) = P$

$e12/p10$ $\text{sum}(P_1, \text{inspatch}(P_2, R, c)) =$
$$\text{sum}(\text{addpatch}(P_1, R, c), \text{restriction}(P_2, \sim R))$$

$e13/p11$ $\text{addpatch}(\text{nullpict}, R, c) = \text{inspatch}(\text{nullpict}, R, c)$

$e14/p12$ $\text{addpatch}(\text{inspatch}(P, R_1, c_1), R_2, c_2) =$
$$\text{inspatch}(\text{inspatch}(\text{addpatch}(P, R_2 - R_1, c_2), R_1 - R_2, c_1),$$
$$R_1 \cap R_2, c_1 + c_2).$$

(Restriction is not an auxiliary operation; it is included in the complete definition of type continuous picture in the appendix.)

Thus, we have presented two complete axiomatizations for the six operations listed at the beginning of this section, the first consisting of axioms $e1$ through $e8$, and the second of axioms $e1$, $e2$, $e5$, $e6$, $e9$, and $e11$ through $e14$ (plus the axioms for restriction). The second method, which makes use of basic generators, requires far fewer axioms (31 in all) when applied to the entire continuous picture data type, and is the method used for all of the specifications in this work.

3.5.4 Additional Axioms

Sometimes it is desirable to include axioms that refine the congruence classes among expressions, and therefore the object definitions, beyond what is required for completeness. For example, the two expressions,

$$\text{lineseg}(p_1, p_2, c) + \text{lineseg}(p_3, p_4, c) \text{ and}$$
$$\text{lineseg}(p_3, p_4, c) + \text{lineseg}(p_1, p_2, c),$$

give the same result for all inquiry operations and seem intuitively to represent the same picture, but they cannot be shown to be equivalent. Reduction to basic generators yields the expressions

$$\text{inspatch}(\text{inspatch}(\text{nullpict}, \text{rg.lineseg}(p_1, p_2), c), \text{rg.lineseg}(p_3, p_4), c)$$

and

$$\text{inspatch}(\text{inspatch}(\text{nullpict}, \text{rg.lineseg}(p_3, p_4), c), \text{rg.lineseg}(p_1, p_2), c).$$

While axioms constructed as above do completely define the external behavior of a data type, they may not allow all indistinguishable objects to be directly proven equivalent. The most convenient solution is to combine some of the congruence classes, by adding new axioms between expressions containing just basic generators (we call these *basic generator expressions*), bringing the congruence classes defined by the axioms into one-to-one correspondence with objects that can be distinguished with the inquiry operations:

e15/p21 inspatch(P,nullregion,c) = P
e16/p22 inspatch(inspatch(P,R_1,c),R_2,c) = inspatch($P,R_1 \cup R_2,c$)
e17/p23 inspatch(inspatch(P,R_1,c_1),R_2,c_2) =
        inspatch(inspatch(P,R_2,c_2),$R_1 - R_2,c_1$).

Axiom *e17* establishes equivalence between the two expressions above.

    Up to now the consistency of a specification has been implicit in our method of constructing the axioms. By definition the basic generator expressions comprise all objects of the type of interest. The methodology we have described does not give equivalences between these expressions, so each is effectively a separate object. Since each basic generator expression is represented only once in the left hand side of the axioms for an inquiry operation, the value of an inquiry operation applied to a basic generator expression is always uniquely determined. All other generator expressions (those containing non-basic generators) are uniquely reducible to basic generator expressions using the remaining axioms.

    Axioms such as *e15*, *e16*, and *e17* that equate basic generator expressions introduce a new problem, however. There is no guarantee that the larger equivalence classes established by the new axioms are preserved as conguence classes by all operations. For the present work, we rely on our intuitive understanding of the type to get these axioms right, recognizing that a precise treatment would require formal consistency proofs.

    Guttag [GUTJ78a] avoids the problem in principle by taking all expressions to be equivalent that cannot be proven different, that is, the equivalence classes are as large as possible without contradicting the axioms. With this view, axioms such as *e15*, *e16*, and *e17* are never written. The problem of proving equivalence of expressions like the above remains, however.

3.5.5 Exception Conditions

Several methods have been proposed for handling exception conditions (errors) in an algebraic context [GUTJ75, GOGJ77, GUTJ77, MAJM79, BERV79, GUTJ80]. Since none of the proposed methods has clearly established itself over the others, we have elected to avoid the issue, and treat error conditions only at a superficial level. The method we use is from early work by Guttag [GUTJ75].

The unique object undefined is implicitly a member of every type. Any application of an operation that cannot be given a well defined meaning, such as asking the color at a point in the null picture (axiom *e5* above), is assigned the value undefined. To avoid having to write extra axioms for every type to deal with this special object, the following *implicit axiom* is considered to be a part of every data type specification:

> *im0* The result of applying any operation to the value undefined (in any argument) is the value undefined.

We do not intend the object undefined to mean that "any result is correct", but rather that some indication is given that the attempted operation has no meaningful result.

Unfortunately, this method of treating errors introduces a technical problem: inconsistencies arise between *im0* and the other axioms defining a type [GUTJ77]. Since the axioms are generally treated as reduction rules, we can avoid these inconsistencies in practice by requiring that, in reducing an expression, axiom *im0* always has priority over any other axiom that can be applied.

3.5.6 The Implicit Axioms

Because of the organization we impose on the axioms, certain axioms can be omitted from a specification without ambiguity. It might seem that omitting axioms can only contribute to confusion; however, when axioms of certain common forms occur frequently enough, the readability of a specification is improved by leaving them out. For example, the following axioms appear in the specification of type simple picture in Appendix B.3:

$sp7$ curcolor(nullpict(c)) = c
$sp8$ curcolor(setcolor(P,c)) = c
$sp9$ curcolor(moveto(P,x)) = curcolor(P)
$sp10$ curcolor(lineto(P,x)) = curcolor(P)
$sp11$ curcolor(box(P,x_1,x_2)) = curcolor(P)
$sp12$ curcolor(text(P,s)) = curcolor(P)

Axioms $sp9$ through $sp12$ are all of the same form. The intuitive significance is that the current color of a simple picture is not affected by the operations moveto, lineto, and text, but only by nullpict and setcolor. With the proper assumptions, this information is conveyed just as well by axioms $sp7$ and $sp8$ alone.

Our method for constructing axioms requires that the axioms for each inquiry or non-basic generator operation F have left hand sides of the form F(B(...),...), where B must range over all of the basic generators. The only exception is when an operation can be defined completely in terms of another operation (for example axiom $e9$ above). This makes it easy to recognize when an axiom is missing.

Let I,G, and B represent an inquiry operation, a generator operation, and a basic generator operation respectively. Let variable t be of the type of interest, each o_i of an outside type, and each a_i and b_i of any type. The following implicit axioms define the default to be used when a required axiom with corresponding left hand side is missing. (The ordering of parameters is arbitrary.)

for an inquiry operation:

$im1$ $I(B(o_1,...,o_{n(B)}),a_1,...,a_{n(I)})$ = undefined

$im2$ $I(B(t,b_1,...,b_{n(B)}),a_1,...,a_{n(I)})$ = $I(t,a_1,...,a_{n(I)})$

for a generator operation:

$im3$ $G(B(o_1,...,o_{n(B)}),a_1,...,a_{n(G)})$ = $B(o_1,...,o_{n(B)})$

$im4$ $G(B(t,b_1,...,b_{n(B)}),a_1,...,a_{n(G)})$ =
$B(G(t,b_1,...,b_{n(G)}),b_1,...,b_{n(B)})$.

These axioms, plus axiom $im0$ above, are considered part of every specification.

Axioms $sp9$, $sp10$, $sp11$, and $sp12$ are all instances of implicit axiom $im2$. Since none of the data types already introduced contain good examples of the other implicit axioms, we will create a fictitious operation for type simple picture,

revstrings   spicture → spicture,

which textually reverses all of the strings displayed in a picture. The axiomatization might be as follows:

$e18$ revstrings(nullpict(c)) = nullpict(c)

$e19$ revstrings(setcolor(P,c)) = setcolor(revstrings(P),c)

$e20$ revstrings(moveto(P,x)) = moveto(revstrings(P),x)

$e21$ revstrings(lineto(P,x)) = lineto(revstrings(P),x)

$e22$ revstrings(text(P,s)) = text(revstrings(P),st.reverse(s)).

The revstrings operation leaves a simple picture unchanged except for the text strings. Accordingly, axiom $e18$ can be supplied by implicit axiom $im3$, and axioms $e19$, $e20$, and $e21$ by $im4$, so that only axiom $e22$ need be shown explicitly in a specification.

Our conventions of marking the basic generator operations with the symbol "•" and grouping the axioms for each operation ensure that it can always be determined when an axiom required for completeness is missing. In each case, the appropriate implicit axiom is considered part of the specification and can be used in proofs.

While all of the axioms are shown in the specification for type simple picture in the appendix, the specification for type tree-structured picture in Appendix C.3 (discussed in Section 5.3.1) uses the implicit axioms to great advantage: the specification would be almost twice as long if all of the axioms were shown explicitly. The implicit axioms are especially valuable to the event algebra specification technique presented in Chapter 4.

3.6 The "Generates" Relation

We have discussed graphical data types as embodying abstractions and have referred to different levels of abstraction, with the implication that a collection of related types forms some kind of hierarchy. We have not said how such a hierarchy can be determined or even shown a hierarchy for the data types we have defined.

Many different relationships among modules of software systems appear in the literature, from the ring mechanism of the Multics system [ORGE72] to the "uses" hierarchy of Parnas

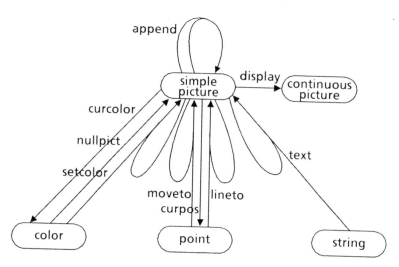

Figure 3-1 The signature for type simple picture

[PARD76]. Guttag and Horning present an informal hierarchy among data types that are similar to ours in [GUTJ80]. A way of depicting the relationship among the data types in a language would provide a global view of the language, valuable both in the design process and, later on, to those who use it. However, unlike the modules of an operating system constructed as nested layers representing successively more abstract virtual machines, it is not clear what the fundamental relationships among the data types in a language are. For instance, what does it mean for one data type to be more abstract than another? Our aim in this section is to discover an easily determined relationship among the data types of a language that contributes to global understanding.

Both [GOGJ78] and [ZILS80] employ a diagram such as Figure 3-1 to show the *signature* of a data type. Each operation is represented as a complex arc with a tail at each argument type and a head at the result type. Such a diagram can be extended to include all of the types in a language, but the result is too detailed to show relationships among the types clearly.

An ordinary directed graph can be derived by disregarding individual operations and drawing a single directed arc from type A to type B if an operation exists with functionality

$$a_1 \times \ldots \times A \times \ldots \times a_n \rightarrow B.$$

The graph for the operations from type simple picture is shown in Figure 3-2. Still the diagram is too complex to be manageable for a large number of types, and the numerous two-way arcs do little to tell us *how* the data types they connect are related. Ideally, an arc from A to B would mean "type A is less abstract (at a lower level) than type B". It is worthwhile to ask what relationship each arc represents, retaining only those that have the desired meaning.

The arcs in the graph represent both inquiry operations and generator operations. While inquiry operations play the important role of giving meaning to a data type (see Section 3.2), the relation defined by the generator operations is closer to what we want here. The inquiry operations included in a type are somewhat arbitrary, in that it is possible, and often convenient, to define mappings

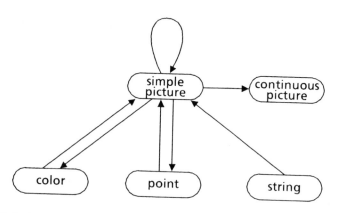

Figure 3-2 A graph derived from the signature for type simple picture

(operations) from the type of interest onto any number of outside types. The types used to generate objects of the type of interest, on the other hand, are relatively fixed for a given abstraction. Furthermore, the fact that objects of type B are generated from objects of type A is a sound basis for saying that B represents a higher level abstraction than A. By eliminating from the graph arcs due only to inquiry operations and arcs from a type to itself, we get a *generation graph*. Figure 3-3 shows the generation graph

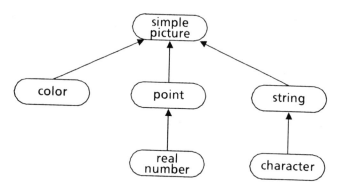

Figure 3-3 A generation graph for type simple picture

corresponding to the previous two figures, except that we have extended the graph to include additional types. The result is a tree structure expressing the fact that simple pictures are made up of colors, points, and strings, that points are made up of real numbers, and that strings are made up of characters. If there is an arc from A to B in the generation graph, we say that A is a *constituent* of B.

While Figure 3-3 expresses the kind of relationship among types that we have been seeking, there are still some problems. First, the "generates" relation as we have defined it is somewhat arbitrary, since the assignment of operations to data types is not unique. Some operations can be equally well defined as generator operations for one type or inquiry operations for another. For example, the operation

$$\text{transform} \qquad \text{geomfcn} \times \text{point} \rightarrow \text{point}$$

is an inquiry operation for type geometric function, but it could also be defined as belonging to type point, making it a generator operation. Second, the generation graph sometimes shows unwanted constituents.

Figure 3-4 shows the generation graph for type continuous picture. Having claimed that a continuous picture is made up of a set of patches (region-color pairs), it is hard to justify types geometric function, color function, string, and point as constituents. Type geometric function is shown because of the operation

$$\text{geomtrans} \qquad \text{picture} \times \text{geomfcn} \rightarrow \text{picture}.$$

However, the role of G in the expression geomtrans(P,G) is to perform a transformation on picture P; the result certainly does not *contain* G in any sense. Now, consider the operation

$$\text{instrans} \qquad \text{tree} \times \text{grtrans} \rightarrow \text{tree}$$

of type picture-tree (Section 3.3.1 and Appendix B.2). We think of picture-tree instrans(P,T) as actually containing graphical

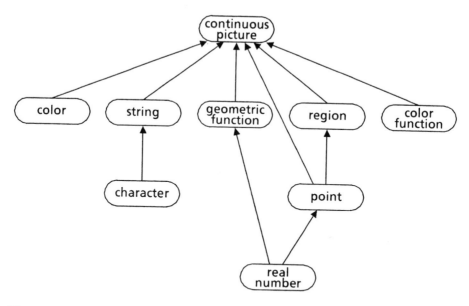

Figure 3-4 A generation graph for type continuous picture

transformation T. What criterion can be used to distinguish these two cases?

Finally, some operations that are generator operations in syntax are like inquiry operations in function. The operation

getprogeny   tree x name → tree

returns part of a picture-tree that happens to also be of type picture-tree, but it actually generates nothing at all.

To make the graph better reflect the way objects are generated and hence the notion of nested abstractions, it is necessary to take into account the semantics of the operations. A simple method that gives intuitively reasonable results is to make use of the basic generators identified as part of an algebraic specification. Since the basic generators represent a minimal set of operations that generate all objects of a type, they define a minimal set of constituent types as well.

We therefore define the *"generates" relation* as follows: Type A *generates* type B, provided A and B are different types, and there is a basic generator operation defined for type B with functionality

$$a_1 \times \ldots \times A \times \ldots \times a_n \rightarrow B.$$

The generation graph corresponding to the "generates" relation for type continuous picture is shown in Figure 3-5.

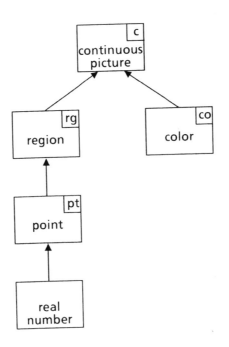

Figure 3-5 The "generates" relation for type continuous picture

When a generation graph is acyclic we can refer to it as a *generation hierarchy*. All of the generation graphs in this work are hierarchical, but cyclical "generates" relations are also possible. To the extent that the "generates" relation forms a partial ordering on a set of types, it defines a nesting of abstract levels; types included in a cycle are at the same level.

Figure 3-6 shows the generation hierarchy for the types presented in this chapter. It is a hierarchy with two roots: type picture-tree and type continuous picture. The special role of type continuous picture in defining representative pictures (see Section 3.3.1) is shown by means of the dashed arrows. These are not part of the "generates" relation but reflect the generic inquiry operation display that is defined for all pictorial types. Being a hidden type, continuous picture would not appear in a generation hierarchy of types available in a language.

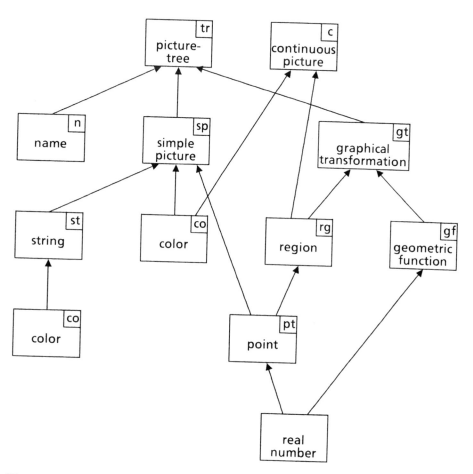

Figure 3-6 The "generates" relation for the graphical data types of Chapter 3

3.7 Observations

Having presented some graphical data types and a specification technique, we conclude this chapter with some observations concerning the specifications of these types in Appendix B.

A Special Case: The Region Data Type

All of the data types we have presented can be specified with the algebraic technique. It was this wide applicability, together with fundamental simplicity, that led us to choose the algebraic specification technique over the many other techniques for specifying data abstractions that have appeared in the literature. Unfortunately, and in contrast with our other data types, type region has an algebraic specification that is cumbersome and seemingly more complex than the underlying concept.

We believe the awkwardness for this one type is due to the fact that the simplest and most natural basic generator operations cannot be used, because of the necessity for finite generation (see Sections 3.2 and 3.3.2). In fact, a simpler data type for regions of finitely many points is easy to specify algebraically using an operation that inserts one point at a time as a basic generator. To handle continuous spaces with uncountably many points, however, it is necessary to employ generators of a higher level of complexity, and the specification becomes more difficult. Rather than give an algebraic specification that would be hard to understand or use in proofs, we specify type region operationally (see Section 3.5.1) using sets of points as the underlying model. Since objects of the defining algebra can be placed in one-to-one correspondence with sets of points, the operational specification in Appendix B.6 is straightforward.

Modularity of Specifications

In Section 3.1 we advocated the use of graphical data types primarily on the basis of their role in programs. It is apparent from

Appendix B that the decomposition of a graphics system into data types has a positive effect on its specification as well. The inherent modularity of data types translates directly into a specification composed of manageable sized pieces (compare with the Core Graphics System specification in Appendix E). The data types provide abstractions that build on one another, so that specifications of high-level concepts can defer more detailed aspects to a lower level. Important design decisions can be localized, so that the likelihood of inconsistencies in the overall specification is reduced, and changes can be made more easily.

For example, the specification of type graphical transformation determines that all transformations shall be of the form $T^{gr}(G,R)$ for some geometric function G and region R, but the choice of the kinds of geometric and restriction transformations to allow is deferred to types geometric function and region. Similarly, type picture-tree provides a tree structure within which individual pictures can be organized, but does not impose restrictions on the form of the pictures at the leaves. The choice of picture primitives, is determined at a lower level by type simple picture, and simple picture objects can have an elaborate structure of their own with no effect on the picture-tree specification. As another example, neither type continuous picture nor any of the pictorial types we have defined makes any mention of what the universe is or what (if any) coordinate system is used within it. These choices are localized in the lower level types, point and geometric function. In fact, simple picture is the only type that assumes the universe is two-dimensional, and even that assumption is easily changed by replacing the picture primitive operations.

Restrictions Among Data Types

In spite of the modularity provided by data types, each data type specification assumes properties of the outside types. For a specification to be meaningful, these assumptions must be correct. Two kinds of restrictions can result: restrictions on the form of a specification and restrictions that affect the semantics (defining algebra) of a type.

Each reference to an outside operation (an operation from an outside type) carries with it the assumption that the operation is defined somewhere. For example, the specification for type continuous picture references the binary operation sum for colors, but only its existence is assumed, its definition can be arbitrary. The semantics of type color are not restricted, because the color sum could be kept out of the defining algebra by making it a hidden operation.

Sometimes outside operations must be required to have certain semantic properties. For example, type ordered set requires type item to have the operation lessthan, which is further restricted to define a total ordering. While lessthan must have the right semantic properties in order to correctly define what goes on inside type ordered set, once again the defining algebra of the outside type (item) is not restricted, because a total ordering can be defined on any finitely generated type. An example of a restriction that does affect the defining algebra of an outside type is provided by type geometric function. Type graphical transformation requires type geometric function to have an inverse operation, which is expected to behave in the normal way, so that all geometric functions must be one-to-one. (A different definition of type graphical transformation might not impose this restriction; see Section 2.3).

We have not tried to deal with restrictions among types in a formal way. The generation hierarchy can be helpful, however, by indicating places where restrictions are likely to occur.

Nondeterministic Operations

One last point needs to be made regarding the completeness of specifications. Requiring that the specification of an operation be complete in the sense we have defined implies that the operation has a uniquely determined value over its entire domain. This completeness criterion does not apply to nondeterministic operations, where more than one result may be considered correct, and successive invocations with the same arguments may give different (correct) results. The select operation for type ordered set (discussed further in Section 6.4) is the only example of a nondeterministic operation in this chapter. The specification of nondeterministic operations is treated in greater detail in [SUBP79].

Chapter 4

Algebraic Specification of User Interaction

In Chapter 3 we showed that many important graphical concepts can be captured as graphical data types, a form in which they can be conveniently used in programs and precisely specified. However, one increasingly common aspect of computing, which is especially important to computer graphics, cannot be encapsulated using ordinary data abstractions: interaction with a human user. In many of the applications for which pictures are useful, direct user interaction is also desirable.

Just as for graphical data types, our objective in studying user interaction is to develop formal ways of describing the pertinent language features. Our attention is therefore directed at interaction primitives (operations) suitable for inclusion in a high level language, rather than the design of particular user interfaces. Interaction primitives whose semantics are precisely specified make it possible to write and prove assertions about user interfaces and interactive programs.

Previous work on specifying interaction has been concerned with user interfaces and dialogue languages rather than programming language primitives. For example, Lamport, in [LAML79], specifies the required behavior of an interactive text formatter. Shaw, in [SHAA80a], uses flow expressions to describe the interleaving of machine processes and user actions for several interactive applications.

Probably the earliest formal method for describing interactive dialogues was by means of state machines. This method is exemplified by "reaction handler" systems for responding to user input, such as that provided by the language Dial [NEWW70]. While finite state machines are too restrictive for our purposes, the specification method we will use for describing interaction primitives is also based on state transitions.

4.1 The Data Type Model and Interaction

For each of the graphical language concepts specified so far, we have first expressed the concept as a collection of objects accessed through a well defined set of operations, then written a specification for the data type that results. Unfortunately, the semantics of interaction primitives cannot be fully captured by ordinary data abstractions. What it means for a program to be interactive was discussed in Section 2.5. In this section we will look at the specific characteristics of user interaction that make the ordinary data type model inappropriate.

It is possible to specify a simple user interface with techniques used for data types by viewing interaction primitives as operations acting on a user interface object. Some of the operations are called by the program for reading data entered by the user; the rest are invoked in some way by the user to provide that data. By treating states of an interface as the objects of a data type, we can write algebraic axioms in the usual way, provided the operations are restricted to the kinds we know how to axiomatize. The user interface becomes a single variable to which objects of type "interface" are assigned. When an operation is invoked that changes the state of the interface, a new interface object replaces the old one.

Example 4.1-1

The following "data type" specification defines a user interface with two input devices, a menu selection device, such as a set of function keys, and a positioning device, such as a data tablet with stylus.

program operations
- init $\qquad\qquad\qquad\qquad\qquad$ → interface
  tstmenu $\qquad\qquad$ interface → flag
  readmenu $\qquad\qquad$ interface → menuitem
- clrmenu $\qquad\qquad$ interface → interface
  tstpen $\qquad\qquad\quad$ interface → flag
  readpen $\qquad\qquad$ interface → point
- clrpen $\qquad\qquad\quad$ interface → interface

user actions
- menuentry $\qquad$ interface x menuitem → interface
- penentry $\qquad\qquad$ interface x point → interface

axioms

tstmenu(init) = empty
tstmenu(clrmenu(S)) = empty
tstmenu(menuentry(S,m)) =
$\qquad$ **if** tstmenu(S) = empty **then** full **else** overrun

readmenu(init) = undefined
readmenu(menuentry(S,m)) =
$\qquad$ **if** tstmenu(S) = empty **then** m **else** readmenu(S)

tstpen(init) = empty
tstpen(clrpen(S)) = empty
tstpen(penentryf(S,x)) =
$\qquad$ **if** tstpen(S) = empty **then** full **else** overrun

readpen(init) = origin
readpen(penentryf(S,x)) =
$\qquad$ **if** tstpen(S) = empty **then** x **else** readpen(S)

As in Chapter 3 the symbol "•" is used to indicate the basic generator operations, and the implicit axioms described in Section 3.5 supply the axioms needed for completeness. The operations tstmenu and tstpen test for the presence of data (or data overrun) on the menu selection or positioning device respectively. Data is read in with the operations readmenu and readpen. The same data may by read repeatedly until clrmenu or clrpen is used to clear the device status and make it ready for

User input is provided by the special operations menuentry and penentry, which are not used in programs.

The following (nonterminating) program adds lines and solid rectangles to a picture using the interactive input operations defined above. Availability of the data types menuitem, point, and spicture is assumed.

```
program solids;
    var S: interface, cmd: menuitem, p1,p2: point, pic: spicture;
begin
    S ← init;  pic ← nullpict;
    while true do begin
        while tstmenu(S) = empty do {empty statement};
        cmd ← readmenu(S);  S ← clrmenu(S);
        while tstpen(S) = empty do;
        p1 ← readpen(S);  S ← clrpen(S);
        while tstpen(S) = empty do;
        p2 ← readpen(S);  S ← clrpen(S);
        case cmd of
            line: pic ← lineto(moveto(pic,p1),p2);
            box: pic ← box(pic,p1,p2)
        end
    end
end.
```

The interactive interface specified in the example illustrates some limitations of the traditional data type model for defining interaction primitives. Because side effects cannot be handled cleanly within the data type paradigm, a separate clear operation is required to indicate that data can be discarded after each read. A more convenient read operation would combine these two functions, returning the next item of data while updating the state of the interface as a side effect. A second limitation is illustrated by the sample program. All synchronization necessary to maintain an orderly protocol with the user must be handled by the program. The **while** loops before each read are needed to wait until data is available. Worse yet, the additional synchronization requirements available. Worse yet, the additional synchronization requirements brought on by concurrent access to state variable S (by program and user) cannot be handled at all by ordinary sequential language constructs.

The synchronization requirements for user interaction are complex enough that it is preferable to build the synchronization into the interaction primitives themselves. The interface that results is not only simpler to use but leads to more readable programs. In many computing environments busy waiting, such as that performed by **while** loops is undesirable. Leaving the synchronization to the system can allow computing resources to be managed more efficiently. However, the semantics of such an interface cannot be described within the ordinary data type model.

Example 4.1-2

The sample program in Example 4.1-1 can be simplified by defining interactive primitives that combine the functions of separate test, read, and clear operations for each device. This operation waits until data is available, then returns that data as its value and clears the device. The following four operations are now sufficient to define the interface:

program operations
    getmenu   → menuitem
    getpen   → point

user actions
    menuevent   menuitem →
    penevent   point →

Using these operations, the program in Example 4.1-1 becomes much simpler:

```
program solids2;
    var cmd: menuitem, p1,p2: point, pic: spicture;
begin
  pic ← nullpict;
  while true do begin
    cmd ← getmenu; p1 ← getpen; p2 ← getpen;
    case cmd of
      line: pic ← lineto(moveto(pic,p1),p2);
      box: pic ← box(pic,p1,p2)
    end
  end
end.
```

In the next section we introduce shared data types and a method for specifying them algebraically. Using this more powerful data type model, it is possible to specify a variety of interaction primitives in a way that fits in well with our graphical data type specifications.

4.2 Event Algebras: A Technique for Specifying Shared Data Types

4.2.1 Shared Data Types

Up to this point the terms "data type" and "data abstraction" have referred to collections of immutable (unchangeable) objects that are accessed from a sequential process via a well-defined set of operations. Immutable objects can be manipulated in just two ways: by creating new objects (via the operations) and by assigning them to variables; once created they cannot be changed. In this section we will refer to this kind of data type as a *sequential data type*.

In order to specify operations for user interaction, we find it necessary to use objects that are available to several processes concurrently and have a mutable (changeable) internal state; thus we introduce the notion of a *shared data abstraction* [OWIS76b] or *shared data type.* As before, each data type has associated with it a set of operations that provide the only means of access to objects of the type. Unlike sequential data types, however, shared objects have an internal state, and restrictions can be imposed on this state. One way to express the set of allowable states for objects of a given type is by means of a *type invariant*, a predicate that is always true for any object of the type. The maintenance of the invariant imposes *synchronization constraints* on the order in which operations on a single object may execute. An operation that would cause a violation of the invariant cannot proceed; its calling process is held up until another process changes the object state so that it can continue.

<u>Example 4.2-1</u>

A simple shared data type is the semaphore type with operations P and V. The state of a semaphore may be thought of (or implemented) as an integer value, initially zero. The invariant is that this value be non-negative. A V operation has the effect of incrementing the value of the semaphore by one, so a V operation can always proceed. A P operation, however, decrements the value by one, so it may have to wait (if the result would be negative).

In this section only, the Simula "dot notation" is used to express operation calls. Thus, calls to the operations of a semaphore s are denoted s.P and s.V. Elsewhere the dot notation is used as described in Section 3.3.

Since algebraic specifications have been used to define the data types introduced thus far, it would be desirable to use them here as well. However, shared data types cannot be defined using algebraic axioms in the usual way. In the strictest sense, an operation cannot be defined algebraically unless it can be modelled as a pure function. The function model is appropriate for operations that return a single value, have no side effects, and execute indivisibly, and when the time interval needed to execute an operation is not of concern. The operations we wish to specify are more general:

1) An operation can wait for its associated object to reach a particular state (because of synchronization constraints) before returning to the calling program. This means that operations do not execute indivisibly and the time of return is important.

2) Operations can have side effects on the state of the object they are associated with.

One way to describe the synchronization behavior of shared operations is by giving a data type invariant as in the previous example. Another way is to describe the synchronization constraints for each operation directly. Using the latter approach, a complete specification for a shared data type can be constructed by including the following information for each operation:

1) the conditions under which the operation can proceed,

2) the value returned by the operation, and

3) the effect of the operation on the state of the object.

Example 4.2-2

Consider a one-slot buffer with operations

put   item →
get   → item.

Let buf1 refer to a one-slot buffer object. The effect of the call buf1.put(x) is to put item x into the buffer (increasing the number of items it contains by one). The operation buf1.get returns the item currently in buf1 (decreasing the number of items by one). A put cannot proceed if the buffer contains an item; a get cannot proceed if it is empty. (The invariant is that the buffer contain either zero or one items.)

Using notation similar to that of Owicki [OWIS76b], we can construct a workable specification for a one-slot buffer using explicit synchronization constraints:

initially count(buffer) = 0, contents(buffer) = undefined
operation put(x : item)
    wait until count(buffer) = 0
    return value undefined
    state change count(buffer) ← 1
        contents(buffer) ← x
operation get **returns** item
    wait until count(buffer) = 1
    return value contents(buffer)
    state change count(buffer) ← 0

The functions count and contents are introduced to denote the
state of a buffer object.

From our point of view, there are two disadvantages to the
specification in the example. First, it is written in a language
totally different from the algebraic axioms we have used so far.
Secondly, the specification consists of an implementation using a
particular abstract machine. Not only does this cause unnecessary
detail to appear in the specification, but it is unlikely that a single
underlying machine will be suitable for defining all the data types
needed in a graphics language. Algebraic specifications have
already shown themselves to be practical for a wide range of data
type definitions. We can use them here as well.

4.2.2 Events and Abstract States

As a first step in this direction, a "universal" representation
for the state of an object is needed. The most general approach is to
think of each possible history for an object as a unique state. We
define an *event* as the entry or exit of an operation call together
with the arguments to that call. An object enters a new state each
time an event for that object occurs. There are as many different
states as there are different sequences of events.

More formally, we associate with each operation

$$Op_i \qquad\qquad t_1 \times \ldots \times t_m \to v$$

the two *event functions*

$$Op_i\$call \qquad state \times t_1 \times \ldots \times t_m \to state$$
$$Op_i\$return \qquad state \times t_1 \times \ldots \times t_m \to state$$

The initial state of an object is defined by the special event function

$$\$init \qquad\qquad\qquad \to state$$

An *abstract state* is an element in an algebra with the functions $\$init$, $Op_1\$call$, $Op_1\$return$, ..., $Op_n\$call$, $Op_n\$return$. Initially the abstract state of any object is simply $\$init$. When operation Op_i is called with arguments a_1, ..., a_m, the abstract state becomes $Op_i\$call(S,a_1,\ldots,a_m)$, where S is the previous abstract state of the object. When Op_i returns, the abstract state becomes $Op_i\$return(S,a_1,\ldots,a_m)$, where S is the state just before the return.

The notion of abstract states is meaningful for any shared object regardless of implementation. The abstract state of an object at any time is uniquely determined by the sequence of events in its history up to that time.

Example 4.2-3

For an object of type one-slot buffer the event functions are

$$\$init \qquad\qquad\qquad \to state$$
$$put\$call \qquad state \times item \to state$$
$$put\$return \qquad state \times item \to state$$
$$get\$call \qquad\qquad state \to state$$
$$get\$return \qquad\qquad state \to state.$$

After execution of the statements (using Simula-like notation)

$$buf1 \leftarrow \textbf{new } buffer; \; buf1.put(x)$$

the abstract state of buffer **buf1** is

$$\text{put\$return(put\$call(\$init,x),x).}$$

In general, an implementation needs to keep track of only a small number of states explicitly, rather than the tremendous number that exist in the abstract sense. Thus, the states explicitly provided for in an implementation, called *concrete states*, correspond to sets or equivalence classes of abstract states.

<u>Example 4.2-4</u>

The event functions for type semaphore are **$init** (with functionality "→ state") and **P$call, P$return, V$call,** and **V$return** (all with functionality "state → state"). Assume an implementation data structure that consists of an integer variable, as described in Example 4.2-1. We can show the correspondence between abstract and concrete (integer) states for such an implementation by means of a mapping

$$\Phi \qquad \text{abstract states} \;\to\; \text{concrete states}$$

defined as follows:

$$\Phi(\$init) = 0$$
$$\Phi(P\$call(S)) = \Phi(S)$$
$$\Phi(P\$return(S)) = \Phi(S) - 1$$
$$\Phi(V\$call(S)) = \Phi(S)$$
$$\Phi(V\$return(S)) = \Phi(S) + 1$$

where free variable S denotes an arbitrary abstract state.

The concrete state of semaphore **sem** after the statements

$$\text{sem} \leftarrow \textbf{new}\ \text{semaphore;}\quad \text{sem.V}$$

is the integer

$$\Phi(V\$return(V\$call(\$init)))$$
$$= \Phi(V\$call(\$init)) + 1$$

$$= \Phi(\$init) + 1$$
$$= 1$$

Since not all of the possible states for a shared data object are actually permissible due to synchronization constraints, a correct implementation must not only guarantee that the operations return the proper values, but also that they are synchronized so that only valid states occur. In order to formally specify both of these aspects of an object's behavior, we associate with each operation

$$Op \qquad\qquad t_1 \times \ldots \times t_n \to v$$

the two *characteristic functions*

$$Op:wait \qquad state \times t_1 \times \ldots \times t_n \to boolean$$
$$Op:value \qquad state \times t_1 \times \ldots \times t_n \to v$$

$Op:value(S,a_1,\ldots,a_n)$ is the value returned by the operation call $X.Op(a_1,\ldots,a_n)$, where S is the state of object X at the time of return. $Op:wait$ captures the synchronization constraints for Op. Op can return to its caller only when $Op:wait(S,a_1,\ldots,a_n)$ is false. Each operation for a shared data type is completely specified by giving its wait and value characteristic functions.

4.2.3 Specifying Shared Data Types Algebraically

There are many disciplines suitable for describing the characteristic functions, since they are nothing more than functions in the ordinary mathematical sense. The definitions up to this point, however, were chosen to facilitate the algebraic specification technique. By using algebraic axioms to describe the characteristic functions of a shared type, we achieve our goal of using a uniform language for all of our data type specifications and, as shown in the next section, for user interaction as well.

We specify a shared data type in terms of a heterogeneous algebra in much the same way as for sequential data types (see Section 3.4). We call the defining algebra for a shared data type an *event algebra*. The abstract states (both valid and invalid) are the objects of the "type of interest". If the shared data type has operations op_1, ..., op_n, its event algebra contains the corresponding event functions $op_1\$call$, $op_i\$return$ and characteristic functions op_1:wait, op_1:value ($i = 1, ..., n$) in its list of operations. As usual, there may be auxiliary operations also.

<u>Example 4.2-5</u>

The characteristic functions for the one-slot buffer are

put:wait	state x item → boolean
put:value	state x item → null
get:wait	state → boolean
get:value	state → item,

and the event functions are (from Example 4.2-3)

\$init	→ state
put\$call	state x item → state
put\$return	state x item → state
get\$call	state → state
get\$return	state → state.

Using the event functions as the basic generators (or *basic state generators*), we can completely specify the event algebra for type one-slot buffer with the following axioms:

put
    b1 :wait($init,x) = false
    b2 :wait(put$return(S,$x_1$),$x_2$) = true
    b3 :wait(get$return(S),x) = false
get
    b4 :wait($init) = true
    b5 :wait(put$return(S,x)) = false
    b6 :wait(get$return(S)) = true
    b7 :value($init) = undefined
    b8 :value(put$return(S,x)) = x.

It is not difficult to see the intuitive meaning of each of the axioms. Initially, a put operation can proceed because a newly created buffer is empty (axiom *b1*). If a previous put operation has just completed, a put must wait (*b2*) until a get operation completes (*b3*). These are the only events that affect put operations. The value of a get operation is undefined for a new buffer (*b7*), but then a get cannot return in this case anyway (*b4-b6*). Otherwise, the value of a get operation is the most recent item placed in the buffer by a put (*b8*).

As before, the axioms explicitly shown in the example are not sufficient to form a complete axiomatization. Just as for sequential data types, axioms of certain standard forms are omitted for readability. The implicit axioms listed in Section 3.5 still apply. The axiom

$$\text{put:wait(put\$call}(S,x_1),x_2) = \text{put:wait}(S,x_2),$$

for example, is an instance of implicit axiom *im2* and is considered part of the specification. We use other notational shortcuts that apply only to shared data type specifications:

1) The names and functionality of event functions and characteristic functions are not listed since they are completely determined by the operations for the type.

2) For operations that do not return a value (i.e. procedures), the corresponding value characteristic functions are omitted from the specification. The following functionality and axiomatic definition are assumed:

$$\text{Op:value} \quad \text{state} \times t_1 \times \dots \times t_n \rightarrow \text{null}$$
$$\textit{im5} \quad \text{Op:value}(S, a_1, \dots, a_n) = \text{undefined}$$

where null is a special type that has the single object undefined and no operations.

3) For operations that always return immediately (i.e. operations with no synchronization constraints) the corresponding wait characteristic functions are omitted with the following axiom assumed for each:

$$im6 \quad Op{:}wait(S, a_1, ..., a_n) = false.$$

4) When the basic state generators are separate from the event functions, axioms must be written for the event functions. In this case, an event function can be defined to have no effect on the abstract state, resulting in an especially simple axiom that we will omit from specifications. One of the following implicit axioms then applies:

$$im7 \quad Op\$call(S,a_1,...,a_n) = S$$
$$im8 \quad Op\$return(S,a_1,...,a_n) = S.$$

4.2.4 Correctness of Implementations

In order to define what it means for an implementation to be correct, we need to say more precisely what we mean by a valid object state. The abstract state of an object of type T is *valid* if it is one of the following:

1) $\$init$,
2) $Op_i\$call(S,a_1,...,a_n)$, provided S is a valid state, or
3) $Op_j\$return(S,a_1,...,a_n)$, provided S a valid state and $Op_j{:}wait(S,a_1,...,a_n)$ is false,

where Op_i and Op_j are operations defined for type T. According to requirement 2) an operation call can occur at any time, as determined by the processes in the system. Synchronization constraints are imposed by delaying the return of operation calls so that requirement 3) is met; no operation can return until its wait characteristic function is false for the current state of the object. Of course, a return cannot occur until the corresponding call has been made.

For an implementation of a shared data type to appear correct to a user just two things are necessary: only valid sequences of events are allowed to occur, and operations always return the correct value. We define correctness in exactly this way. An implementation for a shared data type is *correct* with respect to its specification if, for all objects X of the type and all calls $X.Op(a_1,...,a_n)$ to operations defined for the type,

1) X takes on only valid abstract states, and
2) the value of $X.Op(a_1,...,a_n)$ is $Op:value(exitstate(X),a_1,...,a_n)$.

Exitstate(X) denotes the abstract state of object X determined by the sequence of events for X up to the time of return from Op. (The abstract state of X immediately after the return is $Op\$return(exitstate(X),a_1,...,a_n)$.)

Our definition of correctness is as unrestrictive as possible in order to allow any implementation of a shared data type that has the right external behavior. In particular, event functions, characteristic functions, and abstract states need not be implemented. We do assume, however, that access to objects is allowed only through their operations.

Some means of controlling synchronization is needed in any shared data type implementation, both to enforce synchronization constraints for the type and to protect the integrity of state information. Especially convenient for both purposes is the **with/when** critical section statement due to Hoare [H0AC72b], which we will use in all of our examples. The meaning of the statement "**with** R **when** B **do** S" is as follows: The process is suspended for at least as long as either another process has exclusive access to resource R or boolean expression B is false. Then, statement S is executed as a critical section with exclusive access to R and with B guaranteed to be true. For our purposes R is always the resource containing the object state. No assumptions are made regarding the order of execution of multiple processes awaiting the same resource and condition simultaneously.

Example 4.2-6

The following is a specification for the semaphore data type:

operations

P   →

V   →

basic state generators

(The event functions are the basic state generators.)

auxiliary functions

semcount   state → integer

axioms

P:wait(S) = (semcount(S) = 0)

semcount($init) = 0

semcount(P$return(S)) = semcount(S) – 1

semcount(V$return(S)) = semcount(S) + 1

No axioms are shown for the V operation because it returns no value and is never required to wait. (See implicit axioms *im5* and *im6* above.)

The following implementation of type semaphore corresponds to the informal description in Example 4.2-1 and the state mapping function in Example 4.2-4:

```
var semval : integer;
initially semval ← 0;

procedure P;
begin
  with semval when semval > 0 do
      semval ← semval −1
end;
procedure V;
begin
  with semval when true do
      semval ← semval + 1
end;
```

The *auxiliary function* semcount in the specification above returns the current "value" of the semaphore. Auxiliary functions serve the same role in shared data type specifications as auxiliary operations for sequential data types. (See Section 3.5.) They may be introduced for readability, and they are sometimes necessary to make an algebraic specification possible.

4.2.5 The Canonical Model

We now present a general implementation of a shared data type in terms of the characteristic functions of its operations. This *canonical model* will be useful later for proving facts about programs that use shared data types, in particular programs with user interaction. Let operation Op have functionality $t_1 \times \ldots \times t_n \to v$. Then the event functions and characteristic functions for Op are

$$
\begin{array}{ll}
\text{Op\$call} & \text{state} \times t_1 \times \ldots \times t_n \to \text{state} \\
\text{Op\$return} & \text{state} \times t_1 \times \ldots \times t_n \to \text{state} \\
\text{Op:wait} & \text{state} \times t_1 \times \ldots \times t_n \to \text{boolean} \\
\text{Op:value} & \text{state} \times t_1 \times \ldots \times t_n \to v,
\end{array}
$$

and the following code defines the behavior of Op:

```
var S : state;                          {global declarations for}
initially S ← $init                     {all operations of the type}
   . . .
function Op(a1 : t1, a2 : t2, ... , an : tn) : v;
begin
   with S when true do
      S ← Op$call(S,a1,...,an);
   with S when ¬Op:wait(S,a1,...,an) do
      begin
         Op ← Op:value(S,a1,...,an);
         S ← Op$return(S,a1,...,an)
      end
   end.
```

Combining analogous implementations for each of the operations completely implements the type. We can show that this is a correct implementation by demonstrating that only valid abstract states occur and that an operation always returns the correct value. First, we note that the concrete states in the implementation correspond exactly to abstract states, so that the two may be treated interchangeably in assertions. Encapsulation guarantees that the state S of an object is accessed only by the operations, while, within an operation, S is accessed only inside two critical sections.

Initially, S is the valid state $init. We must show that both of the critical sections preserve valid states. The first critical section is

```
with S when true do
   S ← Op$call(S,a1,...,an).
```

Assume that at entry to the critical section S is the valid state S'. Then, at exit from the critical section, S is Op$call(S',a1,...,an), which is valid by definition. The second critical section is

```
with S when ¬Op:wait(S,a₁,...,aₙ) do
    begin
        Op ← Op:value(S,a₁,...,aₙ);
        S ← Op$return(S,a₁,...,aₙ)
    end.
```

Assume that, at entry, S is the valid state S''. At exit, S is $Op\$return(S'',a_1,...,a_n)$, but, by the condition on the **with/when** statement, $Op:wait(S'',a_1,...,a_n)$ must be false, so, by definition, S is a valid state at exit. Finally, we observe that the value returned by Op is $Op:value(S'',a_1,...,a_n)$, with S'' the state of the object just before return, as required. Thus, we have shown that the canonical model of a shared data type is a correct implementation.

<u>Example 4.2-7</u>

We conclude with a more complex specification example, a bounded buffer with a time-out capability. The read operation has parameters for process identity and a time-out interval in case there is no data in the buffer. A time-out interval is also specified in calls to the write operation in case the buffer is full. The write operation returns the value true to indicate success, and false when time-out occurs. When time-out occurs for the read operation the special value undefined is returned. Any number of processes can do reads and writes to a buffer. Elapsed time is computed with the aid of a clock process that is assumed to run all the time and to "tick" at a constant rate. The maximum size of a buffer is N.

Bounded Buffer with Time-out

operations

read	name x integer $\rightarrow$ item
write	name x integer x item $\rightarrow$ boolean
clocktick	$\rightarrow$

basic state generators

(The event functions are the basic state generators.)

auxiliary functions

bufsize	state $\rightarrow$ integer
fetchitem	state x integer $\rightarrow$ item
time	state x name $\rightarrow$ integer

axioms

read

:wait(S,id,t) = (bufsize(S) = 0) & (time(S,id) < t)

:value(S,id,t) = **if** bufsize(S) > 0
   then fetchitem(S,bufsize(S)) **else** undefined

write

:wait(S,id,t,x) = (bufsize(S) = N) & (time(S,id) < t)

:value(S,id,t,x) = (bufsize(S) < N) bufsize($init) = 0

bufsize(read$return(S,id,t)) = max(bufsize(S)–1, 0)

bufsize(write$return(S,id,t,x)) = min(bufsize(S) + 1, N)

fetchitem(write$return(S,id,t,x),n) =
      if bufsize(S) = N **then** fetchitem(S,n)
      else if n = 1 **then** x
      else fetchitem(S,n-1)

time($init,n) = undefined

time(read$call(S,$id_1$,t),$id_2$) = **if** id_1 = id_2 **then** 0 **else** time(S,id_2)

time(write$call(S,$id_1$,t,x),$id_2$) =
      if id_1 = id_2 **then** 0 **else** time(S,id_2)

time(clocktick$return(S),id) = time(S,id) + 1

4.2.6 Other Specification Techniques for Concurrency

Many techniques have been devised for specifying aspects of parallel computing. Our primary concern in choosing a specification technique was the ability to describe all of the properties of interaction primitives that are relevant to correctness. Correctness criteria for parallel systems can be separated into constraints on synchronization and requirements for the behavior of individual operations, such as their return values and side effects. The latter we will refer to as *data flow* requirements.

The majority of research in parallel computation has concentrated on synchronization problems, and published specification techniques reflect this bias. A number of techniques are based on regular expressions (a survey appears in [SHAA79]). Among these are path expressions [CAMR74] and flow expressions [SHAA78]. While path expressions are used in modules like our shared data types, they describe only the order of execution of operations; the operations themselves are defined by other means. Flow expressions have even been applied to problems in interaction [SHAA80a], but again only to describe allowable sequences of activity. Two specification languages based on orderings of events are those of Grief [GREI77] and Laventhal [LAVM79]. Laventhal's method is part of a system that automatically generates synchronization code for shared data types, but once again, some other method is needed to describe the operations themselves. While our essential objectives could probably be met by using algebraic axioms for the data part and one of the above methods for the synchronization part of a specification, we thought it worthwhile to see if the juxtaposition of such totally different styles of specification can be avoided.

A method for specifying both the data flow and synchronization aspects of shared data types is described by Owicki in [OWIS76b]. The notation is similar to that of Example 4.2-2 with special provisions to facilitate proofs of correctness. A specification method developed by Dahl [DAHO80] is based on time sequences in much the same way as our event algebras, and is capable of describing both the synchronization and data flow elements of parallel systems. The method consists largely of a "tool box" of operations for dealing with sequences. While the notation and computational techniques are quite different from ours, many of the ideas should be applicable to interaction.

4.3 Specification of User Interaction

User Actions

Event algebras are sufficiently powerful to describe the transfer of data through an interactive interface, the synchronization between program and user, and the side effects that take place. We need one more thing, however, before we can specify interaction primitives: a model for the user view of the interface. While the program is accessing the interface by means of the interaction primitives, the user is accessing the same interface from the other side by means of actions such as keystrokes, light pen hits, motions of a track ball, or drawing strokes on a data tablet.

As suggested by the examples in Section 4.1, a convenient way to model the behavior of a user is by defining a set of operations called *user actions*. Each user action corresponds to a specific user activity and captures just those aspects of the activity that affect the interface. A user action is considered to be invoked at the time the activity becomes known to the system. The input of data is modelled by user actions with parameters. In some cases a user action results in immediate feedback by the system without intervention by the application program. Feedback of this sort can be modelled by user actions that return values. An indicator light, for example, can be described by a boolean value.

Example 4.3-1

a) To enter a position with a "mouse", the user first positions the cursor to the desired location and then presses the enter button. The pertinent aspects of this activity are the identity of the input device, the location selected, and the time at which the enter key was pressed. The path that the cursor took in arriving at its final location does not matter in this case. We define a user action with a parameter of type point:

mouseposn   point →

The operation is considered to be invoked at the time the enter key on the mouse is pressed.

b) A keyboard with a type-ahead buffer can be modelled by a user action that has a parameter of type character and returns a boolean value:

keystroke   char → boolean.

The parameter gives the character value of the key that is struck. The boolean quantity returned is an indication to the user of whether the type-ahead buffer is full. The indicator might actually consist of a light or audible alarm.

c) Very complex input devices are possible (see Section 2.5), such as front end processors that carry on user conversations of their own before sending data to the host processor. In this case, the "user" seen by the host includes the front end processor, and the user actions can be formulated to abstract out the low level interactions invisible to the application program. (The interface between the front end and the user might warrant a specification of its own.)

The User Interface as a Shared Data Type

With user activities defined in terms of operations, an interactive interface can be thought of as a general communications interface among concurrent processes. One way to view such an interface is as an information depository, accessible to the several processes. Each process can enter or read information from the interface by using operations provided for the purpose. Since our intent is to specify the external behavior of an interface, not its implementation, we take an abstract view of the information contained in the interface. We will think of the interface as storing the complete history of operation calls (and their parameters) since initialization. Thus, information is added to the interface whenever any of its operations is invoked. The interface provides information in two ways: by returning a value to an operation call and by controlling the time at which the operation returns. Of course, an actual implementation of an interface only needs to keep enough information around to answer the queries provided for by its operations.

Most of our examples will have just two processes: program and user. Alternatively, each input device can be thought of as belonging to a separate process, but this interpretation is not necessary in any of our examples. We will need a third process, a real time clock, in examples where time is important. One can imagine systems in which a user interacts with several programs at once, perhaps via a network. We will not discuss such systems in this work, however.

In Section 4.1 we explored use of the data type model to describe the operation of an interactive interface. The results were unsatisfactory largely because sequential data types are not appropriate for dealing with the concurrency present in interactive systems. Section 4.2 introduced the shared data type, an extension of the sequential data type model for dealing with objects that are shared among concurrent processes. Shared data types are ideally suited to modelling an interface of the kind we have outlined. The interface itself is treated as a shared object. The operations for the type provide the means for communicating through the interface. The only thing unusual about a shared data type used in this way is that just one object of the type exists.

By treating the interactive interface this way, we can specify its semantics using an event algebra. Event algebras provide the kind of implementation independent specification we want. The notion of abstract state for shared data types corresponds exactly to the past history of an interface.

Example 4.3-2

The following is a specification for the interaction primitives in Example 4.1-2:

program operations
 getmenu   → menuitem
 getpen   → point

user actions
 menuevent   menuitem → penevent
 point   →

axioms
getmenu
 :wait($init) = true
 :wait(getmenu$return(S)) = true
 :wait(menuevent$return(S,m)) = false
 :value($init) = undefined
 :value(menuevent$return(S,m)) =
  if getmenu:wait(S) **then** m **else** :value(S)
getpen
 :wait($init) = true
 :wait(getpen$return(S)) = true
 :wait(penevent$return(S,x)) = false
 :value($init) = undefined
 :value(penevent$return(S,x)) =
  if getpen:wait(S) **then** x **else** :value(S)

The previous example and those in the next two sections deal only with user input, but there is nothing special about the direction of data flow. Output to the user can be described in the same way. User actions associated with output are quite different from those for input, however, since now the active side of the interface is the program, with the user in a more passive role

They include such "actions" as waiting for prompts from the program and making use of what is on the screen to determine later actions.

<u>Example 4.3-3</u>

In this example we specify a set of operations for handling prompt messages. The program issues a prompt message using the program operation **prompt**. User action **waitprompt** represents the user waiting for a prompt message; **readprompt** represents the user making use of the message.

program operations
　　prompt　　　　　　　　　　　　　　　msg →

user actions
　　waitprompt　　　　　　　　　　　　　　　→
　　readprompt　　　　　　　　　　　　　　→ msg

axioms
waitprompt
　　:wait($init) = true
　　:wait(prompt$return(S,m)) = false
　　:wait(waitprompt$return(S)) = true
readprompt
　　:value($init) = undefined
　　:value(prompt$return(S,m)) = m

In order to examine how an interactive program behaves under various conditions, we must be able to model sequences of user actions. Since user actions can depend on what the program does as much as vice versa, it is convenient to write special programs called *user descriptions* to model user behavior. We use the same syntax for user descriptions as for ordinary programs, except that they begin with the keyword *user*. Of course, only user actions can be invoked inside a user description, not program operations. The next example gives a simple *program-user pair*, that is, a program and a user description that run in parallel.

Example 4.3-4

```
program simple-interaction        user simple-interaction
   const N;                          var B : array of point;
   var A : array of point;              i : integer;
      i : integer;                 begin
begin                                i ← 0;
   for i ← 0 to N do begin         while true do begin
      prompt("enter point");          waitprompt;
      A[i] ← getpen;                  penevent(B[i]);
   end                                i ← i + 1;
end.                               end
                                end.
```

This user description represents a user who enters a new position with a pen device each time a prompt appears. The program reads in N positions by first prompting the user for the next position and then reading the pen device. When the program terminates (with the user waiting for yet another prompt), the first N locations in array A contain the N locations entered by the user (modelled by array B). In Chapter 6 we look at how to prove theorems about program-user pairs.

4.4 Universal Input Primitives

In Section 2.5 a set of low-level primitive operations for controlling user input was described. In this section we give a formal specification of these primitives using an event algebra.

The universal input primitives are

```
wait(device1,device2,...),
test(device), and
read(device).
```

The wait operation waits until any one of the devices named in its parameter list has data, then returns that device name as its value. The test operation returns the value true if the named device has data, false otherwise. The read operation returns the data waiting to be read at the named device, if any.

We start by providing a precise functionality for the operations. In order to focus attention on the semantics of the operations rather than syntax issues, we have streamlined the operations somewhat and given them new names.

program operations

waitdev	set(device) → device
testdev	device → boolean
readdev	device → data

The parameter list for wait has been replaced by a single parameter of type set-of-devices. Also, data coming from all devices is assumed to be of the same type.

It remains to define the user side of the interface. The simplest possible multiple-device interface can be represented by one user operation that records an input event on any device:

user actions

usrevent	device x data →

To write down a formal specification it is necessary to know (or decide) exactly what the operations do. The informal description given above and in Chapter 2 says surprisingly little. Some of the questions that must be answered are the following:

1) The testdev operation indicates when data is available, but it is unclear when that data should become *un*available. That is, how soon should testdev start returning the value false -- as soon as the program is first informed of data (with testdev or waitdev), or not until the data is actually read by the program (with readdev)?

2) The waitdev operation has the ambiguity in 1) and an additional one: If more than one device is ready, which one is reported back to the program? Here there are as many different options as there are possible scheduling strategies.

3) Even the behavior of **readdev** is not completely determined by its description. If the user enters a second item of data before the first has been read, which of the two should be reported back by **readdev**? Should extra data be queued indefinitely (as practical), up to a stated buffer size, or discarded?

A formal specification is obviously of value even to define a set of operations as simple as these. In the specification that follows we have made these choices (among others):

1) **Testdev** returns false only after data has been read.

2) Conflicts in **waitdev** are resolved according to a predetermined priority among devices (see below).

3) Input is not queued; newly arriving data is discarded until the previous data is read.

program operations

waitdev	set(device) → device
testdev	device → boolean
readdev	device → data

user actions

usrevent	device x data →

auxiliary functions

getdata	state x device → data

axioms

waitdev:

ui1   wait(S,D) = **if** empty(D) **then** false
         else if testdev:value(S,first(D)) **then** false
         else if empty(rest(D)) **then** true
         else wait(S,rest(D))

ui2   value(S,D) = **if** empty(D) **then** error
         else if testdev:value(S,first(D)) **then** first(D)
         else value(S,rest(D))

testdev:

   ui3   value(\$init,d) = false

   ui4   value(getdata\$return(S,d_1),d_2) =
         if $d_1 = d_2$ **then** false **else** value(S,d_2)

   ui5   value(usrevent\$return(S,d_1,x),d_2) =
         if $d_1 = d_2$ **then** true **else** value(S,d_2)

readdev:

   ui6   value(S,d) =
         if ¬testdev:value(S,d) **then** undefined **else** getdata(S,d)

ui7   getdata(\$init,d) = undefined

ui8   getdata(usrevent\$return(S,d_1,x),d_2) =
         if $d_1 = d_2$ & ¬testdev:value(S,d_2) **then** x **else** getdata(S,d_2)

The specification for **waitdev** requires some elaboration. The resolution of the multiple-ready-device conflict is specified using the first and rest operations for type set (see Section 3.3.3). First chooses an element from a set according to an ordering defined on the type of the objects in the set. Rest forms a set made up of everything else from the original set. We assume that, for devices, the ordering reflects device priority.

It might be desirable to specify **waitdev** so that the scheduling strategy is left open. It happens that the axiom given above for the **waitdev:wait** characteristic function does not constrain the scheduling strategy at all. However, any deterministic function for **waitdev:value** will impose scheduling constraints. (Of course, a mathematical function is always deterministic, but we will use the term to include nondeterministic mappings also, that is mathematical relations.) A nondeterministic version of **waitdev:value** that does what we want may be specified by substituting the following axioms for axiom *ui2* above:

   ui2a contains(D,waitdev:value(S,D)) = ¬empty(D)
   ui2b testdev:value(S,waitdev:value(S,D)) = ¬empty(D)

(The implicit axioms in Section 3.5 do not apply to nondeterministic functions. These two axioms comprise the entire specification for **waitdev:value**.) The resulting specification is not complete in the sense of Section 3.5, but it does completely specify the semantics of waitdev up to the intended nondeterminism.

4.5 XPL/G Interactive Input Primitives

Thus far we have given specifications only for interaction primitives constructed for the purpose. We wish also to apply our specification technique to existing systems, both to determine its range of applicability and in the hope of gaining insight into existing systems. We conclude this chapter with a specification of the interaction primitives provided in the language XPL/G [MALW76, TURC75], a graphics language that implements William Newman's display procedures [NEWW72]. In Section 5.5 a portion of the GSPC Core Graphics System including interactive input is also specified.

The interaction primitives of XPL/G were designed to provide a uniform interface to the input capabilities of several different graphics display devices. The objective was to make it easy to write programs that could be run from any of several terminals without change. The specification of the XPL/G input primitives given below is surprisingly straightforward. A greater surprise were the omissions discovered in the original documentation for the system. It was enlightening also to observe the effect of a seemingly small language feature, added after the fact, on the complexity of the specification.

Three kinds of input are recognized by XPL/G: individual keystrokes, messages made up of several keystrokes, and positions ((x,y) coordinates). A program can ask for a particular kind of input using the operations getkey, getmsg, and getxy. The result is then available in the special variable keyboard (for getkey and getmsg) or penx and peny (for getxy). Added flexibility is provided by the operation keyorxy, which waits for either a keystroke or a position, deposits it in keyboard or penx and peny as appropriate, and returns the value 1 for keystroke or 2 for position. To make possible highly interactive effects like dragging and rubberbanding, a polling mode, controlled by the special variable xypolling, is available for the positioning device. With xypolling set to true, getxy obtains the current coordinates of the positioning device immediately without waiting for action from the user. Xypolling is automatically reset to false when the user enters a keystroke. A more complete description of the XPL/G input system can be found in [MALW76].

In the specification that follows, the special variables of XPL/G are treated as parameterless operations. Penx and peny are combined into a single operation that returns a point object. Xypolling, which can be modified as well as read, is split into two operations to perform these two functions. The user side of the interface is modelled with two user operations: keystroke, which corresponds to depressing a key on the keyboard, and position, which represents the reporting of a location by the positioning device (but no specific action by the actual user).

program operations

getkey		→
getmsg		→
getxy		→
keyorxy		→ integer
keyboard		→ string
pen		→ point
setxypolling	boolean →	
xypolling		→ boolean

user actions

keystroke	char →	
position	point →	

auxiliary functions

* lastkey	state → string	
* lastmsg	state → string	
* lastx	state → point	

axioms
getkey
 ix1 :wait(getkey$call(S)) = true
 ix2 :wait(keystroke$return(S,c)) = false
getmsg
 ix3 :wait(getmsg$call(S)) = true
 ix4 :wait(keystroke$return(S,c)) = (c = end-of-msg-character)
getxy
 ix5 :wait(getxy$call(S)) = ¬xypolling:value(S)
 ix6 :wait(keystroke$return(S,c)) = false
keyorxy
 ix7 :wait(keyorxy$call(S)) = ¬xypolling:value(S)
 ix8 :wait(keystroke$return(S,c)) = false
 ix9 :value(keyorxy$call(S)) = 2
 ix10 :value(keystroke$return(S,c)) = **if** c = space **then** 2 **else** 1
keyboard
 ix11 :value($init) = nullstring
 ix12 :value(getkey$return(S)) = lastkey(S)
 ix13 :value(getmsg$return(S)) = lastmsg(S)
 ix14 :value(keyorxy$return(S)) =
        if keyorxy:value(S) = 1 **then** lastkey(S) **else** value(S)
pen
 ix15 :value($init) = pt.origin
 ix16 :value(getxy$return(S)) = lastxy(S)
 ix17 :value(keyorxy$return(S)) =
        if keyorxy:value(S) = 2 **then** lastxy(S) **else** value(S)
xypolling
 ix18 :value($init) = false
 ix19 :value(setxypolling$return(S,b)) = b
 ix20 :value(keystroke$return(S,c)) = false

ix21 lastkey(keystroke$return(S,c)) = c
ix22 lastmsg(getmsg$call(S)) = nullstring
ix23 lastmsg(keystroke$return(S,c)) = lastmsg(S) ‖ c
ix24 lastxy(position$return(S,p)) = p

The process of writing the specification for XPL/G interactive input was at the same time both easier and more difficult than expected. The axioms were constructed in a straightforward manner by asking which events influence the outcome of each operation; few auxiliary operations were needed. The resulting specification corresponds very closely to what the actual implemented system does, closely enough, in fact, that an XPL/G programmer could get better information about the language from the specification above than he could from the original documentation.

This latter fact is what caused difficulties in writing the specification. The process of looking at each operation in turn to determine the influence of call and return events led to questions that were not addressed by the documentation; it was even necessary to refer to the code for the system in some cases to get the answers.

For instance, the documentation does not explicitly say what is contained in the variable keyboard. Probably most readers correctly guess that it contains a single character after getkey or keyorxy (returning the value 1), and a character string after getmsg. The documentation says only that it "always contains the most recent input from the keyboard", which turns out to be false. The keyboard variable contains the most recent keyboard input only after a call to getkey, getmsg, or keyorxy (returning the value 1); it is not changed at any other time.

The author's imperfect memory of the system caused an error in the specification that was discovered only inadvertently while looking through the XPL/G runtime support. It was assumed that keystroke input entered by the user between calls to getkey would be picked up by the next getkey call, and similarly for the other kinds of input. This is not the case. The next read to the keyboard is not issued until getkey, getmsg, getxy, or keyorxy is called. A keystroke entered by the user while the program is busy, that is before a call to one of these four operations, will be missed. The language documentation says nothing at all on the subject.

The ambiguities raised here seem minor, but any one of them is sufficient to cause a program to fail if the wrong assumptions are made. What is significant is that none of these errors and omissions were discovered, even during a revision of the documentation intended to clear up such problems. Certainly, if this specification had been available, documentation of the XPL/G interactive input system would have been easier to write, with the result more accurate and complete.

The above specification represents the XPL/G input system as originally designed and implemented. A feature was added later to reduce the number of keystrokes necessary for certain interaction protocols. The **getkey** operation was changed to make it possible to obtain the character entered by the user to signal the previous positioning input. It is instructive to look at the changes that are necessary to make the specification reflect this new feature. Two new auxiliary functions must be introduced:

* keypending   state → boolean
* getpendingkey   state → string.

Axioms *ix1* and *ix12* must be modified:

ix1'   wait(getkey\$call(S)) = ¬keypending(S)
ix12' keyboard:value(getkey\$return(S)) =
                if keypending(S) **then** getpendingkey(S) **else** lastkey(S).

Several new axioms must be included:

ix25   keypending(\$init) = false
ix26   keypending(getkey\$return(S)) = false
ix27   keypending(getmsg\$return(S)) = false
ix28   keypending(getxy\$return(S)) = ¬xypolling:value(S)
ix29   keypending(keyorxy\$return(S)) = false
ix30   getpendingkey(getxy\$return(S)) = lastkey(S).

Two observations can be made about the new specification: First, the increase in the size of the specification is considerable. Two new auxiliary functions are necessary when there were only three to begin with, and the number of axioms increases by 25 percent. Why should such a small change to the system require such a large change to its specification? The reason seems to be the nature of the change itself. It was not easy either to implement or to explain clearly in the documentation. We would like to think that there is a useful correlation between the ease with which an abstraction can be specified using our technique and a cleanness of design that aids in implementing and understanding it.

Our second observation is that, in spite of the size of the change, it was straightforward to accomplish. Only two of the original axioms had to be modified; the rest of the change was additions to what was there already. One of the nice properties of algebraic specifications is that new capabilities can be added to a type easily. Fortunately, this property carries over to event algebras as well.

Chapter 5

Design and Specification
of Graphics Programming Languages

Making meaningful and precise statements about picture-related concepts in programming languages is a problem that is central to our work. In Chapter 2 we used the language of mathematical functions and sets to describe pictures, graphical transformations, and hierarchic picture structures. In Chapter 3 we were able to express many of the same concepts using graphical data types. In Chapter 4 we introduced a way of precisely describing primitives for user interaction. We now bring these results together to formally specify the semantics of some complete graphics programming languages.

In the next section we examine some features of graphics programming languages that distinguish them from general purpose programming languages and pose problems of specification. In Section 5.2 we show that powerful and convenient graphics programming languages can be created by adding graphical data types and interaction primitives to a general purpose base language with suitable control and data structuring facilities. The semantics of such a language can be described formally using the techniques of Chapters 3 and 4 to augment a specification of the base language. We illustrate this design strategy by presenting a prototype interactive graphics language and a specification of its semantics. Finally, in Section 5.4, we show that our specification methods can be applied to graphics languages that are not data type based, by specifying a portion of the GSPC Core Graphics System.

5.1 Charactistic Properties of Graphics Programming Languages

By *graphics programming language* we mean any high level programming language with special facilities for generating and displaying pictures. Graphics languages include languages with special syntactic elements for dealing with pictures, such as Dial [NEWW70], SPDL [RIEJ75], Euler-G [NEWW72], Metavisu [BOUP72], and XPL/G [MALW76]. They also include graphics subroutine packages that can be used with a general purpose programming language, such as GPGS [CARL77], GINO-F [WOOP71], the GSPC Core Graphics system [GSPC79], and a multitude of support packages for specific graphics devices. *Interactive graphics programing languages* provide special facilities for user interaction as well. Although the many graphics languages in use seem outwardly quite different, especially those with special syntax, they generally provide the same basic tools for generating and displaying pictures. We will review some of these tools here and discuss problems that relate to the design and specification of graphics languages.

Picture Structures

To deal with pictures by computer, some form of picture structure is unavoidable, be it an array of pixels, a set of points, lines, and solids, or a heirarchic structure of successively smaller picture subparts. Although these structures are well understood in a general sense, the special requirements of displaying and performing computations on pictures impose constraints on the way the underlying structures are organized and used. One way to provide appropriate data structuring facilities for pictures is by defining special data types. Section 3.3.1 presents examples of such pictorial data types, with formal specifications of their semantics.

Pictorial Output

A property common to all graphics programs is the production of pictures. Describing the pictures that result is therefore an important specification task. There are two aspects to the problem. The first is the need to abstract away from the characteristics of particular display devices and capture the "ideal picture" being portrayed through the medium of a physical display. Secondly, for many graphics programs, particularly interactive ones, there is no one picture that can be called the result; there may be many pictures produced during the lifetime of the program process. The pictorial output of a program must therefore be treated as a mapping on program states. We defined the representative picture of a pictorial object in Section 3.3.1. In Section 5.4 we extend the representative picture notion to programs and introduce mappings that define pictorial program output.

User Interaction

Many of the graphics languages mentioned at the beginning of this section contain facilities to support user interaction. Thus, a specification technique without provision for describing these facilities is incomplete. A definition of interaction is given in Section 2.5. Chapter 4 develops a specification technique for interaction primitives. In Section 5.4 we show how specifications of interaction primitives can be integrated with those of the data types in a graphics language.

Input-Output Relationship

The task of specifying an interactive graphics language is often complicated by a close relationship between input and output. Some degree of interdependence is unavoidable: the user determines his actions in part by what is on the screen. Beyond this, though, the very meaning of input received from the user can depend on the screen contents. For instance, depending on the menu being displayed at the time, a delete command might mean "delete all", "delete picture part", or "delete menu display". For pointing input, the value passed to a program (the name of a picture part) is dependent on the picture most recently sent to the screen. Effects such as dragging and rubberbanding require that the displayed picture closely track the input from a positioning device. By using a conceptual state object to record the history of all user input and output, relationships such as these can be specified in the same way as other aspects of user interaction.

Timing Requirements

In one form or another the concept of time appears often in interactive graphics. Examples are the sampling of input devices at regular intervals and the provision of timeouts. Of course, animation is highly dependent on time, but we will not deal with the special problems of animation in this work. Time is provided for in our specifications by postulating a clock process, as in Example 4.2-7.

Modularity

A characteristic that graphics languages share with many other software systems is their customary lack of modularity. A typical graphics subroutine package, for instance, contains routines for manipulating a global picture structure and a collection of changeable modes that control various aspects of these routines. A monolithic structure such as this is undesirable for a number of reasons, but, to a degree, it is unavoidable. Systems with many dependencies between functional parts are undesirable because they are hard to understand, implement, maintain, or modify. However, as we have pointed out, there is often an inherent relationship between input and output functions of a graphics language. By employing data types as the basis for graphics language design, and specifying interaction in terms of a conceptual state object, we hope to achieve the dual goal of maximum modularity of design with clear identification of global relationships.

5.2 A Framework for Graphics Language Design

Three kinds of abstractions commonly appear in programming languages: control abstractions (such as **if-then-else**, **while-do**, and **case-of**), data abstractions (data types), and procedure abstractions (functions and subroutines). Most present-day graphics languages are based on procedure abstractions. In fact, the best known graphics languages are nothing but subroutine packages, called from a general purpose language (see Section 5.1). Even the special statements in languages tailored syntactically for graphics are often a disguise for sequences of subroutine calls, for example, the **draw** statement of the display procedure languages [NEWW72, BOUP72, MALW76]. In this section we outline an alternate approach to the design of graphics programming languages: the use of special graphics-oriented data types, such as those presented in Chapter 3.

The Base Language

For all but the most specialized applications, a graphics language needs all the capabilities of a general purpose language. No matter how important the role of pictures in a program, it is usually necessary to perform basic tasks such as building general data structures and doing file input-output.

This general computational power can be obtained without departing from facilities available in existing general purpose languages. The kinds of control flow needed in graphics programs are fundamentally the same as for any other application area. Even user interaction can be controlled conveniently by using ordinary control statements in conjunction with interaction primitives. The standard mechanisms for allocating variables, computing and assigning values, and defining and calling procedures are all useful in graphics programs, as are the common types Boolean, integer, real, string, array, and record. The sheer multitude of languages now in use provides a strong motivation to make use of existing language features where possible. The best way to do this is to use an existing general-purpose language as the base for any new graphics language.

But, which of the many existing general-purpose languages is best? The answer, of course, varies with application area, available hardware and software support, and programmer preference. An advantage data abstractions share with subroutines is that their functional properties need not depend on the language from which they will be used. Thus, for the prototype language presented in this chapter we did not feel compelled to choose a base language that would yield the best compromise over all possible applications. Instead we looked at our own application: the illustration of a general strategy for graphics language design and specification. The criteria we used were the following:

1) The language should have flexible control statements reflecting current thinking in programming methodology.

2) An assortment of useful data types should be available in the language, including at least the ones listed above.

3) The language should be widely known and accepted.

4) A formal specification of the language's semantics should be available.

The base language we have chosen is Pascal [JENK76].

Graphical Data Types

The specific facilities that must be added to a base language to make a useful graphics language depend on the kinds of pictures to be created. In flight simulation, for example, we want facilities appropriate for producing realistic, but mostly flat (that is, distant), scenes. For many computer aided design applications, line drawings are sufficient. The ideal language for architectural design would provide for both line drawings and 3D scenes with accurate shading and hidden surfaces removed. Document production applications require facilities tailored to formatted text and illustrations. Regardless of application area, however, tools are needed to support the following tasks:

1) creating primitive (atomic) pictures
2) combining pictures
3) modifying pictures
4) transforming pictures.

Picture primitives are generally organized into a few classes of related primitives, such as line segments with arbitrary endpoints, characters of different fonts, or n-sided polygons of different shapes.

Pictures are combined for two reasons: to create more complex pictures and to create pictures with a useful structure. Adding pictures together produces more complex pictures without additional structure; appending pictures to one another or building hierarchies of pictures creates pictures with structure that can be used in modifying them later.

By picture modifications we mean picture changes that are not naturally described as graphical transformations. Examples include deleting or replicating pictures or their parts and changing the structure of pictures. Graphical transformations are discussed in Chapter 2; examples include scaling, rotating, and Fourier transformations.

For the design framework we envision, these tools are provided not by separate procedures, but by a collection of graphical data types. The data types in Chapter 3 illustrate how this can be accomplished. The prototype language in the next section draws largely from the Chapter 3 examples.

We are not concerned with how new data types are added to the base language, although it is preferable that they be accessed in the same way as the indigenous types. It is conceivable that they be built into the compiler. A more flexible arrangement is to make tham available in a library. Greatest (but perhaps unnecessary) flexibility is obtained by making data types programmer definable. Numerous languages exist that support libraries of data types or programmer defined types, such as Clu, Alphard, Euclid, Modula, and Ada.

Interaction Primitives

To complete the design of a language for interative graphics, we must augment our list of tools to include

> 5) obtaining user input
> 6) controlling the display.

The complexity and power of primitives for handling user input varies greatly. The universal input primitives of Section 2.5 represent the low-level end of the scale. A useful addition is input buffering, such as the "type-ahead" feature provided by timesharing systems. Beyond this it is possible to build various protocols into the interaction primitives, such as associations between event devices and sampled devices, or to construct high level devices from lower level ones (see Section 2.5). We have chosen rather simple input primitives for the prototype language. A more complex input system is provided by the GSPC Core Graphics system discussed in Section 5.5.

The other part of user interaction is the output of pictures, prompt messages, menus, and so on to the screen. We refer to operations in this category as display control primitives, but we must bear in mind that input and output cannot always be cleanly separated in interactive systems; some primitives involve elements of both.

The simplest mechanism for controlling the display allows one picture to be displayed at a time. A segmented display structure allows a program to display several pictorial objects together and erase or replace individual objects from the image. Still fancier display control primitives allow transformation of pictures, for positioning or windowing, at the time of display. Greatest flexibility is provided by a structured display file [NEWW79] containing pictures and transformations in a general hierarchic structure. For the prototype language, we have chosen display control primitives that provide a segmented display.

5.3 A Prototype Graphics Language

The prototype language is the general purpose language Pascal, to which data types for dealing with pictures have been added. We present two versions of the language, both based on the design framework outlined in Section 5.2. The difference between the two languages is the way in which pictures are structured: as ordered trees in one case, and as a general hierarchy in the other. The particular data types chosen for the language are instances of the general concepts described in Chapter 2. We have deliberately kept them simple in order to make the language manageable as an illustrative medium and to emphasize the way in which the types fit together to form a complete language.

In addition to a picture data type, other data types have been incorporated to facilitate the building and transformation of pictures. Also, a set of operations is included for handling user interaction via a display device and various input devices. Since a description of the Pascal base language is available in [JENK76], only the new data types are included here. In the heading for each data type, both a type identifier and a one or two letter abbreviation is given. The type identifier is the formal name of the type in the language. The abbreviation is used outside the language to refer to operations, axioms, or theorems associated with a particular type. For example, "gt.identity" refers to the identity operation for the type graphical transformation (grtrans), and *gt2* is the name of the second axiom for grtrans.

The binary operation equals is implicitly defined for all data types. Two expressions (of the same type) are equal if and only if they represent the same object. This concept of equality is not especially useful for the complex types such as tree-structured picture, but is used often for the types name and color, which have no other structure.

5.3.1 The Prototype Language with Tree-Structured Pictures

The generation hierarchy (see Section 3.6) for the prototype language with tree-structured pictures is shown in Figure 5-1.

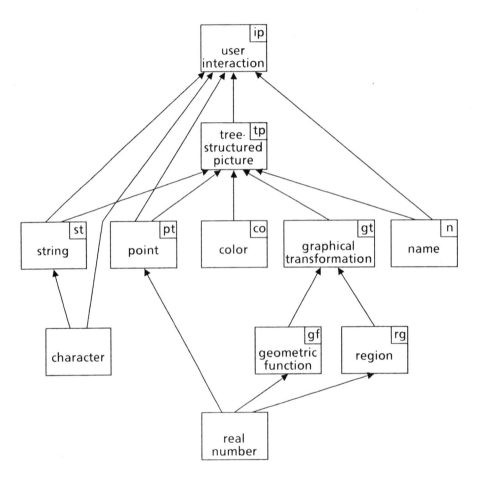

Figure 5-1 Generation hierarchy for prototype graphics language with tree-structured picture

There is a single pictorial data type called tree-structured picture (tpicture). Tpictures are ordered tree structures that contain two-dimensional line drawings and graphical transformations. They are constructed with the help of types point, color, and string. Types geometric function and graphical transformation facilitate transforming pictures. Interaction primitives are included to handle a keyboard, a positioning device, and a "pick" device for pointing to things on the screen. The new data types and interaction primitives for this version of the prototype language are formally specified in Appendices B and C. Section C.1 of Appendix C contains a summary of the operations. A sample program is included at the end of this section.

Tree-Structured Picture (tpicture, tp)

All pictures are of type tpicture. The simplest tpicture contains lines and text of arbitrary colors. More complex tpictures may be structured as ordered trees (see Section 2.4). Structuring is provided for by allowing a tpicture to contain other tpictures, called progeny, as well as lines and text. Each progeny has associated with it a graphical transformation and a name. The specification for type tpicture is in Appendix C.3.

function nullpict: tpicture

Empty tpictures are created by the nullpict operation. The current color is some default value; the current position is the origin.

function setcolor(P: tpicture, c: color): tpicture

The resultant tpicture is P with the current color set to c. Newly inserted lines and text will have the color c. (Progeny inserted into a tpicture P are not affected by the current color of P).

function moveto(P: tpicture, p: point): tpicture

The current position becomes p.

function lineto(P: tpicture, p: point): tpicture

Lineto inserts a line segment from the current position to point p. The current position becomes p.

function box(P: tpicture, p_1,p_2: point): tpicture

Box inserts a filled rectangle with diagonal vertices p_1 and p_2, edges aligned with the cartesian coordinate axes. The current position is unchanged.

function text(P: tpicture, s: string): tpicture
Text inserts the pictorial representation of string s starting at the current position, which remains unchanged.

function insprogeny(P_1,P_2: tpicture, T: grtrans, n: name): tpicture
The resultant tpicture is P_1 with P_2 inserted as one of the progeny. The new progeny is given the name n and has graphical transformation T associated with it. Later references to the progeny of a tpicture are made by name.

function curcolor(P: tpicture): color
Curcolor returns the current color of P.

function curpos(P: tpicture): point
Curpos returns the current position of P.

function getprogeny(P: tpicture, n: name): tpicture
Getprogeny returns the progeny of P with name n. If there is more then one progeny with name n, the most recently inserted one is returned. The result is undefined if there is no progeny named n.

function gettrans(P: tpicture, n: name): grtrans
Gettrans returns the graphical transformation associated with progeny n of P (the progeny with name n). If there is more than one progeny with name n, the most recently inserted one is used. The result is undefined if there is no progeny named n.

function delprogeny(P: tpicture, n: name): tpicture
The resultant tpicture is P with all progeny named n deleted. If there are no progeny named n, the value of P is returned unchanged.

function instrans(P: tpicture, n: name, T: grtrans): tpicture
The resultant tpicture is P with the graphical transformation for all progeny named n replaced by T. If P has no progeny with name n, the result is the same as P.

function append(P_1,P_2: tpicture): tpicture
Append forms a new tpicture containing all the elements (lines,

text, and progeny) of P_1 followed by all those of P_2. The current color and current position are those of P_2. Append(P_1,P_2) may also be written $P_1 + P_2$.

Graphical Transformation (grtrans, gt)

Tpictures are transformed by means of objects of type grtrans that are associated with them as progeny in a tree structure. A graphical transformation is made up of a geometric function part and a region part, both of which also have corresponding data types; see below. The region part restricts the screen representation of the associated progeny to only that portion which lies within the region. The geometric function part changes the size and location of the portion that remains. The specification for type grtrans is in Appendix B.4.

function grtrans(G: geomfcn, R: region): grtrans
The function grtrans is the basic generator of objects of type grtrans. A pure geometric transformation can be formed by setting R to the universe, a pure restriction transformation by setting G to the identity geometric function. Grtrans(G,R) can also be written T^{gr}(G,R).

function identity: grtrans
The identity graphical transformation has no effect on the screen representation of a tpicture. It is equivalent to grtrans(gf.identity,rg.universe).

function gpartof(T: grtrans): geomfcn
Gpartof returns the geometric function part of T.

function rpartof(T: grtrans): region
Rpartof returns the region part of T.

function compose(T_1,T_2: grtrans): grtrans
The result of composing two graphical transformations T_1 and T_2 is a new transformation whose effect on a tpicture is the same as that of applying T_2 then T_1. Compose(T_1,T_2) can also be written $T_1 \circ T_2$.

Geometric Function (geomfcn, gf)

An object of type geometric function defines a total one-to-one mathematical function between points. Geometric functions are used in graphical transformations to change the screen representations of tpictures without adding or deleting anything. In the prototype language, geometric functions can be defined for translation and scaling. The specification for type geomfcn is in Appendix B.5.

function scale(x: real): geomfcn
Scale specifies a uniform scale factor centered about the origin.

function translate(x_1,x_2: real): geomfcn
Translate specifies a translation by x_1 and x_2 in the horizontal and vertical directions respectively.

function compose(G_1,G_2: geomfcn): geomfcn
The composition of G_1 and G_2 is a new geometric function that has the effect of applying first G_2, then G_1 to any point. Compose(G_1,G_2) may also be written $G_1 \circ G_2$.

function identity: geomfcn
The identity geometric function leaves all points in the universe unchanged. Identity is equivalent to translate(0,0) or scale(1).

function inverse(G: geomfcn): geomfcn
The inverse of G is the geometric function that has the reverse effect of G on all points in the universe. Thus, G $\circ$ inverse(G) = inverse(G) $\circ$ G = identity. Inverse(G) can also be written G^{-1}.

function transform(G: geomfcn, p: point): point
Transform applies G to point p to produce a new point according to the above. For example, transform(identity,p) = p.

Region (region, rg)

A region can be thought of as a (possibly uncountable) set of points in some universe. Regions are used in graphical transformations to obtain selective parts of pictures. (See

Graphical Transformation above.) For the prototype language, the universe is the plane, and only regions made up of rectangles can be specified within it. The specification for type region is in Appendix B.6.

function universe: region
    The universe is all of two-space. Universe can also be written U.

function rectangle(x_1,x_2,x_3,x_4: real): region
    The most basic region object is the rectangle. X_1 and x_2 are the left and right boundaries, x_3 and x_4 the bottom and top boundaries, respectively, in the Cartesian coordinate system. If $x_1 > x_2$ or $x_3 > x_4$, the region is empty. It is also possible to generate regions consisting of a single point, a horizontal line segment, or a vertical line segment by suitable choice of arguments.

function intersect(R_1,R_2: region): region
    The intersection of two regions consists of the points common to both. Intersect(R_1,R_2) can also be written $R_1 \cap R_2$.

function union(R_1,R_2: region): region
    The union of two regions includes all points contained in either one. Union(R_1,R_2) may also by written $R_1 \cup R_2$.

function difference(R_1,R_2: region): region
    The difference of R_1 and R_2 is the region containing all points in R_1 but not in R_2. Difference(R_1,R_2) can also be written $R_1 - R_2$.

function empty(R: region): boolean
    A region is empty if and only if it contains no points.

Point (point, pt)

An object of type point corresponds to a point in the plane (the universe). Operations are provided to allow the use of either Cartesion or polar coordinates. The specification for type point is in Appendix B.7.

function point(x_1,x_2: real): point
    The point function generates a point from Cartesian coordinates.

function polarpt(x_1,x_2: real): point
    The polarpt function generates a point from polar coordinates. The value x_1 is the radius, and x_2 is the angle.

function origin: point
    Origin is equivalent to point(0,0) or polarpt(0,x).

function abscissa(p: point): real

function ordinate(p: point): real

function radius(p: point): real

function angle(p: point): real
    These four functions return Cartesian and polar coordinates.

function sum(p_1,p_2: point): point
    The result is the vector sum of p_1 and p_2. Sum(p_1,p_2) can also be written $p_1 + p_2$.

String (string, st)

    A string is a sequence of characters. The data type string defined here replaces the concept of a string as a packed array of characters, used in standard Pascal. The specification for type string is in Appendix B.10.

function nullstr: string
    Nullstr is the string containing no characters. Nullstr may also be written "".

function inschar(s: string, a: char): string
    The resultant string is s with character a inserted at the right. The expression inschar(...(inschar(nullstr,a_1),...),a_n) may also be written "$a_1...a_n$".

function concat(s_1,s_2: string): string
    The concatenation of two strings s_1 and s_2 is the string

consisting of those characters in s_1 in order followed by those in s_2 in order. Concat(s_1,s_2) can also be written $s_1 \parallel s_2$.

Color (color, co) and Name (name, n)

The only operations for these two data types are equals and some constants. Any data type on which the operation equals is defined can be used for either. Generally, type string or integer is most convenient. The Pascal type declaration mechanism makes it easy to assign actual types to the type identifiers color and name. The specifications for types color and name are in Appendix B.8.

User Interaction (ip)

The operations discussed in this section are not associated with any data type. Included are operations for prompting the interactive user, for getting data from one of the user input devices, and for maintaining the display seen by the user. Unlike the operations descussed so far, some are procedures which do not return a value, and some wait for a condition to be satified before they return.

A prompt message consists of a string which is displayed on the screen in some fashion. The user input devices are a keyboard for entering characters, a positioning device for entering points, and a pick device for pointing to parts of pictures on the screen. Changes are made to the display screen by posting (displaying) and unposting (removing) tpictures by name. The interactive primitives are specified in Appendix C.2.

procedure prompt(s: string)
The prompt operation outputs string s to the user, generally to indicate that input is expected.

function getkey
Getkey does not return until a new character (since the last call to getkey) is available from the keyboard. Its value is the character corresponding to the most recent keystroke.

function getposn

Getposn does not return until a new point (since the last call to getposn) is available from the positioning device. Its value is the point most recently entered with the positioning device.

function getpick

Getpick does not return until a new name (since the last call to getpick) is available from the pick device. Pick device inputs that do not actually "point to something" are ignored, and the user is notified when this happens. The value of getpick is the name of the tpicture most recently pointed to with the pick device. The name is that of the lowest-level tpicture that drew the item pointed to with a lineto, box, or text operation. The name of a top level tpicture is provided by the call to post that causes it to be displayed; the name of a progeny tpicture is provided by the call to insprogeny that creates it.

procedure post(P: tpicture, n: name)

A call to post causes the current version of P to be displayed on the screen and assigned the name n. Any previous tpicture posted with the same name is deleted from the screen. Future changes made to P are not reflected on the screen unless P is posted again.

procedure unpost(n: name)

Unpost removes the tpicture that was posted with name n (if any) from the screen.

User Actions

In order to specify the language operations for user interaction, the actions a user can take are formally defined as operations also. The user operations included correspond to waiting for a prompt and to entering input with each of the three input devices. Pascal syntax is used for convenience, even though these operations would never be used in a program. The user operations are specified in Appendix C.2.

function getprompt

Getprompt does not return until a new prompt (since the last getprompt) appears on the screen. Its value is the string argument of the most recent prompt by the program.

procedure keystroke

The keystroke procedure represents striking a key on the keyboard.

procedure position(p: point)

The position procedure represents entering a location (point) with the positioning device, (for instance a tablet or mouse).

function pick(p: point): boolean

The pick procedure represents pointing to something on the screen with the pick device (for instance a lightpen or any positioning device). If the pick action doesn't "point to anything", it is ignored, and an error indicator goes on to notify the user. The error indication is formalized by defining the pick operation as a boolean valued function: true means error (the pick action was ignored) and false means no error.

Sample Program

Figure 5-2 shows a simple interactive program written in the prototype language (translated from a sample XPL/G program in [MALW76]). A logic circuit diagram is drawn on the screen for the user to examine by moving around and zooming in and out. The intent of the example is to illustrate features of the language, not to demonstrate their best use.

5.3.2 The Prototype Language with Picture-Hierarchy

The language described in this section is a variant of the prototype language in which the structures allowed for pictures are broadened from ordered trees to general hierarchic structures (see Section 2.4). Instead of a structured picture data type, there is a global picture-hierarchy, into which simple (unstructured)

```
program circuit;
  const dt = .25, ds = 1.5;
  var running: boolean, windowed_circuit: picture,
    wndw_trans, posn_trans: grtrans;
  function transl(x1,x2: real): grtrans;
  begin
    transl ← grtrans(translate(x1,x2),universe)
  end;
  function seg(p1,p2: point): picture;
  begin
    seg ← lineto(moveto(nullpict,p1),p2)
  end;
  function arc(radius,theta1,theta2: real, center:point): picture;
    const dtheta = 10; var i,npoints: integer;
  begin
    npoints ← (theta2 – theta1) div dtheta;
    arc ← moveto(nullpict, center + polarpt(radius,theta1));
    for i ← 1 to npoints do begin
      angle ← theta1 + i*dtheta;
      arc ← lineto(arc, center + polarpt(radius,angle))
    end;
    arc ← lineto(arc, center + polarpt(radius,theta2))
  end;
  function andgate: picture;
  begin
    andgate ← arc(1,–90,90,origin);
    andgate ← lineto(lineto(lineto(andgate(0,1)),(–1,1)),(–1,–1))
  end;
  function orgate: picture;
  begin
    orgate ← arc(2,–90,–30,(–1,1) + arc(2,30,90,(–1,–1)
      + arc(4,–14.5,14.5,(–4.87,0))
  end;
  function circuit: picture;
  begin
    circuit ← nullpict;
    circuit ← insprogeny(circuit,andgate,transl(1,0),"");
    circuit ← insprogeny(circuit,andgate,transl(1,6),"");
    circuit ← insprogeny(circuit,orgate,transl(–8,6.5),"");
    circuit ← insprogeny(circuit,orgate,transl(–8,.5),"");
    circuit ← circuit + seg((–7.27,6.5), (0,6.5))
      + seg((–7.27,.5), (0,.5))
      + lineto(seg((–4,.5),(–4,5.5)), (0,5.5))
      + lineto(seg((–3.5,–4),(–3.5,–.5)), (0,–.5)
      + seg((2,0),(5,0)) + seg((2,6),(5,0))
  end;
```

Figure 5-2 Sample program in prototype language with tree-structured picture

```
function bndry: picture;
begin
  bndry ← moveto(nullpict,(−.9,−.8));
  bndry ← lineto(lineto(bndry,(.9,−.8)),.9,.9));
  bndry ← lineto(lineto(bndry,(−.9,.9)),(−.9,−.8))
end;
function menu: picture;
  var i: fixed, commands: array[1..7] of string;
  value commands ← ("left","right","up","down","in","out","exit");
begin
  menu ← nullpict;
  for i ← 1 to 7 do
    menu ← insprogeny(menu, text(nullpict,commands[i]),
      transl(.2*i−1,−.9), commands[i])
end;
procedure xformcircuit(gf: geomfcn);
begin
  posn_trans ← compose(grtrans(gf,universe), posn_trans);
  windowed_circuit ← instrans(windowed_circuit,"circuit",
    compose(wndw_trans,posn_trans))
end;
begin
  running ← true;
  wndw_trans ← grtrans(identity,rectangle(−.9,−.8,.9,.9));
  posn_trans ← identity;
  windowed_circuit ← insprogeny(nullpict,circuit,identity,"circuit");
  xformcircuit(scale(0.1));
  post(bndry,"boundary"); post(menu,"menu");
  while running do begin
    post(windowed_circuit,"circuit");
    case getpick of
      "":         ;
      "left":     xformcircuit(translate(−dt,0));
      "right":    xformcircuit(translate(dt,0));
      "up":       xformcircuit(translate(0,dt));
      "down":     xformcircuit(translate(0,−dt));
      "in":       xformcircuit(scale(ds));
      "out":      xformcircuit(scale(1/ds));
      "exit":     running ← false
    end
  end;
  post(text(nullpict,"program halt"),"")
end.
```

Figure 5-2   (continued)

pictures and graphical transformations are entered and linked together.

All of the non-Pascal data types included in this version of the language are listed below for reference, but descriptions are given only for those that have not already been discussed as part of the language with tree-structured pictures in the last section. The generation hierarchy is shown in Figure 5-3. Specifications are in Appendices B and D. Appendix D.1 contains an operation summary.

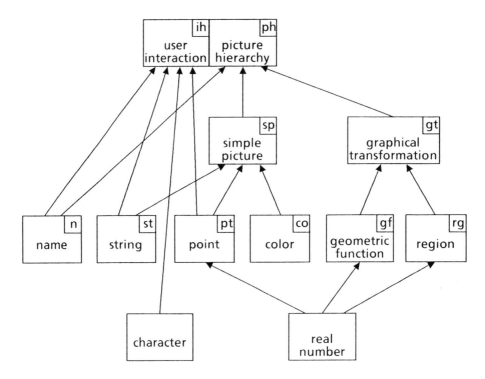

Figure 5-3 Generation hierarchy for prototype graphics language with picture-hierarchy

The Picture Hierarchy (ph)

All structuring of pictures is done within the global picture-hierarchy. Objects of type simple picture are entered into the structure as leaves, and graphical transformations as nodes. Nodes and leaves may be linked together to form an acyclic directed graph structure in which the leaves have no progeny. An attempt to build an invalid structure results in an error condition. The specification for the picture-hierarchy operations is in Section D.3.

procedure inspict(P: spicture, n: name)

Simple picture P is inserted into the picture-hierarchy as a leaf with name n. If there is already a node or leaf with name n, it is replaced, except that it is an error if n already has progeny assigned.

procedure insnode(T: grtrans, n: name)

Graphical transformation T is inserted into the picture-hierarchy as a node with name n, replacing any existing node or leaf by the same name.

procedure link(n_1,n_2: name)

Node or leaf n_2 is made a progeny of node n_1. An error condition is raised if n_1 does not exist in the picture-hierarchy, n_1 is a leaf, n_2 does not exist, n_2 is already a progeny of n_1, or the new link would create a cycle in the structure.

function getpict(n: name): spicture

Getpict returns the simple picture associated with n if n names a leaf in the picture-hierarchy; otherwise an error condition is returned.

function gettrans(n: name): grtrans

Gettrans returns the graphical transformation associated with name n if n names a node in the picture-hierarchy; otherwise an error condition is returned.

procedure comptrans(T: grtrans, n: name)

The graphical transformation associated with node n in the

picture-hierarchy is replaced by $T \circ T_n$, where T_n is the transformation previously associated with node n. An error condition is raised if there is no node n.

procedure unlink(n_1, n_2: name)
The link between node n_1 and node or leaf n_2, if any, is removed.

function progeny(n: name): set(name)
The progeny operation returns the set containing the names of all progeny of node n if such a node exists, the empty set otherwise.

Simple Picture (spicture, sp)

Simple picture is the data type for pictorial objects. Simple pictures and graphical transformations are the building blocks for structured pictures built up within the picture-hierarchy. Simple pictures contain lines and text of arbitrary colors and can be appended to one another to build larger pictures. The specification for type spicture is in Appendix B.3.

function nullpict(c: color): spicture
Empty spictures are created by the nullpict operation. The current color is c; the current position is the origin.

function setcolor(P: spicture, c: color): spicture
The resultant spicture is P with the current color set to c. Newly inserted lines and text will have the color c.

function moveto(P: spicture, p: point): spicture
The current position becomes p.

function lineto(P: spicture, p: point): spicture
Lineto inserts a line segment from the current position to point p. The current position becomes p.

function text(P: spicture, s: string): spicture
Text inserts the pictorial representation of string s starting at the current position, which remains unchanged.

function curpos(P: spicture): point
  Curpos returns the current position of P.

function curcolor(P: spicture): color
  Curcolor returns the current color of P.

function append(P_1,P_2: spicture): spicture
  Append forms a new **spicture** containing all the elements (lines and text) of P_1 followed by all those of P_2. The current color and current position are those of P_2. Append(P_1,P_2) can also be written $P_1 + P_2$.

The following data types are described in Section 5.3.1:

Graphical Transformation (grtrans, gt)

Geometric Transformation (geomfcn, gf)

Region (region, rg)

Point (point, pt)

String (string, st)

Color (color, co)

Name (name, n)

User Interaction (ih)

The interaction primitives are the same as those described in Section 5.3.1, except for **post** and **unpost**, which operate on names defined within the picture-hierarchy rather than pictorial objects. The operations for user interaction are specified in Appendix D.2.

procedure post(n: name)
  A call to **post** causes the picture represented by the structure with root n in the picture-hierarchy to be displayed. There is no effect if n was already being displayed. Any changes made within structure n while it is being displayed are immediately reflected on the screen.

```
program circuit;
   const dt = .25, ds = 1.5;
   var running: boolean,
      window_node, scaled_circuit, windowed_circuit: tree;
   function seg(p1,p2: point): picture;
   begin
      seg ← lineto(moveto(nullpict,p1),p2)
   end;
   function arc(radius,theta1,theta2: real, center:point): picture;
      const dtheta = 10; var i,npoints: integer;
   begin
      npoints ← (theta2 – theta1) div dtheta;
      arc ← moveto(nullpict, center + polarpt(radius,theta1));
      for i ← 1 to npoints do begin
         angle ← theta1 + i*dtheta;
         arc ← lineto(arc, center + polarpt(radius,angle))
      end;
      arc ← lineto(arc, center + polarpt(radius,theta2))
   end;
   procedure makeandgate;
      var ag: picture;
   begin
      ag ← arc(1,–90,90,origin);
      ag ← lineto(lineto(lineto(ag,(0,1)),(–1,1)),(–1,–1));
      inspict(ag,"andgate")
   end;
   procedure makeorgate;
      var og: picture;
   begin
      og ← arc(2,–90,–30,(–1,1)
         + arc(2,30,90,(–1,–1) + arc(4,–14.5,14.5,(–4.87,0));
      inspict(og,"orgate")
   end;
   procedure makecircuit;
      var wires: picture;
      procedure insgate(nodename,gatename: name, gf: geomfcn);
      begin
         insnode(grtrans(gf,universe), nodename);
         link(nodename,gatename); link("circuit",nodename)
      end;
   begin
      makeandgate; makeorgate;
      insgate("gate1","andgate",translate(1,0));
      insgate("gate2","andgate",translate(1,6));
      insgate("gate3","orgate",translate(–8,6.5));
      insgate("gate4","orgate",translate(–8,.5));
      wires ← seg((–7.27,6.5),(0,6.5)) + seg((–7.27,.5),(0,.5))
         + lineto(seg((–4,.5),(–4,5.5)),(0,5.5))
```

Figure 5-4 Sample program in prototype language with picture-hierarchy

```
      + lineto(seg((–3.5,–4),(–3.5,–.5)),(0,–.5)
        + seg((2,0),(5,0)) + seg((2,6),(5,0));
    insnode(grtrans(scale(0.1),universe), "circuit");
    inspict(wires,"wires"); link("circuit","wires");
    insnode(grtrans(identity,rectangle(–.9,–.8,.9,.9),"windowedcircuit");
    link("windowedcircuit","circuit")
  end;
  procedure makeoutline;
    var out: picture;
  begin
    out ← moveto(nullpict,(–.9,–.8));
    out ← lineto(lineto(out,(.9,–.8)),(.9,.9));
    out ← lineto(lineto(out,(–.9,.9)),(–.9,–.8));
    inspict(out,"outline")
  end;
  procedure makemenu;
    var i: fixed, commands: array[1..7] of string;
    value commands ← ("left","right","up","down","in","out","exit");
    procedure inslabel(str:string, gf: geomfcn): tree;
    begin
      inspict(text(nullpict,str),str ‖ "label");
      insnode(grtrans(gf,universe),str);
      link(str, str ‖ "label"); link("menu",str);
    end;
  begin
    insnode(grtrans(translate(–1,–.9),universe),"menu");
    for i ← 1 to 7 do inslabel(commands[i],translate(.2*i,0))
  end;
begin
  running ← true;
  makecircuit; makeoutline; makemenu;
  post("outline"); post("menu");
  while running do begin
    post("windowedcircuit");
    case getpick of
      "":          ;
      "left":    comptrans(grtrans(translate(–dt,0),universe),"circuit");
      "right":   comptrans(grtrans(translate(dt,0),universe),"circuit");
      "up":      comptrans(grtrans(translate(0,dt),universe),"circuit");
      "down":    comptrans(grtrans(translate(0,–dt),universe),"circuit");
      "in":      comptrans(grtrans(scale(ds),universe),"circuit");
      "out":     comptrans(grtrans(scale(1/ds),universe),"circuit");
      "exit":    running ← false
    end
  end;
  inspict(text(nullpict,"program halt"),"haltmsg");
  post("haltmsg")
end.
```

Figure 5-4   (continued)

procedure unpost(n: name)

    If a node or leaf named n in the picture-hierarchy was being displayed, its representative picture is removed from the screen.

User Actions

    User actions are the same as for the prototype language with tree-structured pictures (Section 5.3.1). The user operations are specified in Appendix D.2.

Sample Program

    The program shown in Figure 5-4 is a translation of the program in Figure 5-2 to use the version of the prototype language with a picture-hierarchy instead of type tree-structured picture.

5.4 Specification of Data Type Based Graphics Languages

    To give a complete specification of an interactive graphics language based on graphical data types, we must specify 1) the base language, 2) the graphical data types and 3) the interaction primitives. For the prototype language the base language is Pascal, and a semantic specification has already been written [HOAC73]. The specification of graphical data types was the subject of Chapter 3. Several of the data types in the prototype language were specified there and in Appendix B. In Chapter 4 we developed an equational specification technique for user interaction, and applied it to various primitives for doing user input/output. There is only one problem we have not yet addressed: the specification of pictorial program output.

    In Section 3.3.1 we defined the representative picture of a pictorial object as an idealization of what might actually be seen if the object were displayed. Display control primitives provide the means by which pictorial program objects can be displayed. An interactive program may display many different images during its lifetime, but each image represents one or more pictorial objects generated by the program.

We can model the images produced by programs in a manner analogous to images representing pictorial objects, but we must take into account that the image displayed by a program depends on the program's execution state. We define the *resultant picture* of a program in interactive state S as a unique object of type continuous picture, denoted image(S). The operation

> * image   state → picture,

is, in the notation of Section 4.2, an auxiliary function whose definition for an interactive interface describes the images produced by the display control primitives. (For systems supporting more than one view surface such as [GSPC79], there is more than one resultant picture at a given time, but this poses no difficulty, since the image function can be defined with an additional parameter.) The image function is exactly analogous to the generic operation display defined for pictorial objects in Section 3.3.1. In Chapter 6 we use both operations to write assertions about the pictorial output of programs.

It is because we treat the display control primitives as interaction primitives in our specifications that the resultant picture of a program can be expressed as a function of its interactive state. When user input and output are closely related as discussed in Section 5.1, the distinction between interaction primitives of the two kinds is less clear, but the resultant picture remains a function of the interactive state.

Other input-output relationships are handled similarly. For example, input from a pick device depends on the contents of the screen -- not just the image, but the meaning of the image, in terms of the picture structure it represents. Again, the interactive state contains the necessary information, because it records the complete history of updates to the display.

A note on modularity is in order here. We have claimed modularity as an advantage of the data type approach to graphics language design, yet we suggest that all interaction primitives should be specified together as a package. Modularity need not be lost entirely from the specification, however. By making use of the implicit axioms defined in Section 3.5, we can, for example, avoid mentioning input events in axioms for output operations and vice versa except where there is an actual relationship between the two. This is exactly what we want, because it draws attention to any relationships that exist between otherwise independent groups of operations.

Appendices C and D give specifications for the two versions of the prototype language discussed above. The data types common to both, namely point, region, geometric function, and graphical transformation, are specified in Appendix B. The special hidden data type continuous picture is also specified in Appendix B.

In the first version of the language, the picture structuring operations are all part of the data type tree-structured picture, and the axioms for the interaction primitives are grouped together. The second form of the language does not have a separate data type for structured pictures. Instead, there is a global data structure, the picture-hierarchy, within which all picture structuring is done. For specification purposes, we consider the picture-hierarchy to be a part of the interactive state. Thus the two groups of axioms labelled **user interaction** and **picture-hierarchy** in Appendix D are part of the same underlying shared data type. We have separated them for ease of understanding, and again, because of the implicit axioms, there are few references between the two.

Both versions of the language contain an example of a very complex input-output relationship: *hit processing*, that is, acquiring pointing input from a pick device. The result of the getpick operation depends on the structure of the pictorial objects being displayed at the time of the input. Coordinates received from the device are translated into the name of a picture subpart displayed at that position. For the language with tree structured pictures this involves searching through the tpicture objects currently posted for display. For the language with picture-hierarchy, the search is through substructures of the global hierarchy whose root nodes are currently posted. For both cases the required result is specified by the axioms.

5.5 Specification of Existing Systems

With the exception of the XPL/G input primitives, the graphics languages and data types that we have specified so far were created expressly to provide examples. In this section we examine how the same specification techniques can be applied to existing graphics languages. We specify a portion of the GSPC Core Graphics System to illustrate.

Method

As discussed in Section 5.2, most existing graphics languages consist of collections of subroutines (operations) that are called from a general purpose language to build, maintain, and display a global picture structure. The algebraic specification technique depends on operations being organized into data types, that is, independent modules, each accessing objects of a particular kind. Traditional graphics subroutine packages cannot be broken down in this way because the operations all must have access to the global picture structure. Equational axioms can be used to specify graphics subroutine packages, however, in the same way the picture-hierarchy of the prototype language was specified: by grouping all the operations that access the global picture structure together and treating them as a global data abstraction. In the prototype language only a few of the operations require access to the global picture structure because most picture-related concepts are embodied in separate types. In graphics languages whose design is not based on data types, however, nearly all of the operations generally make use of global data.

Specification of the Core Graphics System

As an example of a graphics language organized as a subroutine package, we give a specification for a portion of the

Core Graphics System in Appendix D. The Core Graphics System was developed by the Graphics Standards Planning Committee of ACM-SIGGRAPH. The first description of the system appeared in 1977 [GSPC77]. Our specification is based on the revised report issued in 1979 [GSPC79]. Although billed as a graphics standard, the document actually describes a comprehensive subroutine package for picture generation and user interaction. We chose to specify the Core Graphics System because it is a recent system that is widely known, completely documented, and of sufficient complexity to challenge formal specification methods.

Because of the size of the Core Graphics System, not all features described in the report are included in the specification in Appendix E. Our objective was to include as many of the interesting features of the system as possible, especially the user interaction, without an unreasonable amount of detail. Some features have been omitted outright; others have been treated at an abstract level by introducing extra data types to encompass them. The omitted features include multiple view surfaces, device initialization, various segment and primitive attributes, including those affecting the display of text strings, and some of the echo types for input devices.

The data types introduced for abstraction purposes have names that correspond to graphical data types presented in Chapter 3; however the types given earlier are not assumed to be the exact types referred to here. Type string allows character strings to be used without assuming a particular method of storage. Type point allows the concept of space to be treated abstractly without regard to coordinate systems or the number of dimensions. Where explicit reference to a coordinate system is necessary, such as for input device echoing, we use two dimensional Cartesian coordinates. Similarly, transformations are treated abstractly by use of the types geometric function (geomfcn) and graphical transformation (grtrans) to represent functions on points and functions on pictures respectively. The remaining added types -- class, device, name, echotype, and symbol -- are enumeration types introduced for increased clarity.

These could be implemented using type integer or a Pascal scalar type.

While an effort is been made to check for important errors, no distinction is made among errors of different kinds, and error recovery is not addressed.

The display control mechanism supported by the core graphics system corresponds to the segmented display discussed in Section 5.2. Pictorial objects are not a part of the core graphics system, but rather are associated with "modelling systems" built on top of the core. The input system is fairly complex. It includes routines for doing both "synchronous input", similar to that of XPL/G and the prototype language, and queued input, in which events are remembered by the system and reported to the program in FIFO order. Also, input devices can be associated with one another under program control so that several devices are sampled at the time of an input event.

We have mentioned that the input and output portions of an interactive graphics language cannot always be cleanly separated. The Core Graphics System exhibits three kinds of input-output relationships: 1) User input is influenced by the screen contents for pick (pointing) device input (axioms *ci23-24*, *ci82-89*). 2) The echoing of locator (positioning) device input with rubberband lines amounts to a screen overlay, that is, a special picture added to the representative picture otherwise generated by the program (axioms *cg94*, *ci131-134*). 3) A third kind of relationship is exemplified by most forms of valuator (scalar) device input echoing and the dragging of a picture with a locator device. Here the transformation applied to a picture segment is placed under control of an input device, so that the generated picture is changed directly by the device (axioms *ci64-65*).

Critique

In looking at the specification in Appendix E, it is both discouraging that it is so long and encouraging that it is even possible. The Core Graphics System is clearly very large and complex (requiring 105 dense pages of natural language description), much more so than most systems that have been described using formal methods to date. Our specification is kept manageable by virtue of the implicit axioms given in Sections 3.5 and 4.2. The total number of axioms that would be included in the specification if they were all written down is just under 2000; the number of axioms actually shown is only 228. Of course, a specification of the entire system would be considerably larger.

The size of the specification and the length of the published documentation both provide measures of the size and complexity of the Core Graphics System. A system of this size may well be necessary to provide a comprehensive set of tools for doing general purpose, device independent graphics. However, it does not follow that the system must be as complex as this one. A great deal of the complexity of the Core Graphics System arises because of its monolithic design: many operations have side effects on the behavior of other operations, so that the system can only be understood as a whole. In our view, the use of graphical data types, as illustrated by the prototype language, is an effective way to modularize large systems, reducing their overall complexity.

Because an algebraic specification can be organized in a way that guarantees the complete definition of the operations (see Section 3.7), any omissions in the description of a system become obvious during the process of specifying it. The Core Graphics description does extremely well in this regard. While a few small omissions were found in the 1977 version (such as the value returned by inquire_current_position after core initialization), no omissions were found in the 1979 version except for those features unavoidably system or device dependent. On the other hand, the information necessary to axiomatize a single operation was often found dispersed throughout the document, reflecting the monolithic design of the system.

Chapter 6

Graphics Program Verification

One of the benefits of writing a formal specification for a graphics programming language is that it becomes possible, in principle, to formally verify properties of programs written in the language. In practice, it may not be easy to construct the necessary proofs.

The major characteristics that distinguish interactive graphics programs from other programs are 1) they draw pictures, and 2) they interact with the user in real time. Both create special problems for graphics program verification. Correctness criteria for a graphics program can be expected to involve the pictorial output of the program, so it is necessary to express conditions on the pictures produced by a program (perhaps over time) as formal assertions. For interactive programs assertions are often needed to express correctness conditions involving the interaction itself, including assumptions about user actions. Finally, interactive programs contain special control structures (the interaction primitives) to control the user dialogue. The proof technique used for interactive programs must be able to handle these special control structures.

In this chapter we first show how auxiliary operations defined as part of the specifications for graphical data types (Chapter 3) and interaction primitives (Chapter 4) are used as the basis of an assertion language. Then we show how theorems necessary in the course of a program proof may themselves be proved from the axioms. Finally, we examine proof techniques suitable for graphics programs, both batch and interactive, and present some verification examples.

In related work, Lamport [LAML79] specifies by means of production rules an interactive program to format text and outlines a correctness proof. Picture generation is not considered, however, and it is not clear from the example how well the methods used generalize to other kinds of programs.

6.1 The Assertion Language

Whether the objective is a formal proof of correctness or just a better understanding of what a program does, it is useful to be able to state the desired properties of a program precisely. Statements about the behavior of a program are made in terms of *assertions*, that is predicates that are claimed to be true at particular points in the execution of a program. For ordinary sequential programs the assertions are usually expressed in terms of objects within the program, such as integers, arrays, and records.

For graphics programs, correctness criteria are often harder to express. An important class of objects in graphics programs are pictorial objects (Section 3.3.1), which represent pictures, and the representative pictures may be more important than the objects themselves. The most important determinant of correctness is often nothing more than a side effect, the displayed image, which can depend on both existent program objects and past execution history.

Consider the following program written in the prototype graphics language (Section 5.3.1):

```
program One;
   var P: tpicture, s: real;
begin
   P ← lineto(setcolor(nullpict,red),point(0,s));
   post(P,"up");
   P ← lineto(setcolor(nullpict,blue),point(s,0));
   post(P,"across")
end.
```

A number of objects exist at some time during execution of the program. The objects red (of type color), "up" (of type name), 0 (zero, of type real), and point(0,s) (of type point) are ordinary objects. The objects nullpict and setcolor(nullpict,red), of type tpicture, are pictorial objects. Variables P and s can store objects of type tpicture and real respectively. The two post statements (invocations of the operation post) control the image on the screen.

If s has value d, we expect program One to display the image depicted in Figure 6-1. In Section 5.4 we defined the resultant

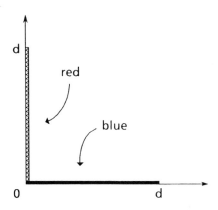

Figure 6-1 Resultant picture for program One

picture of a program to provide a formal model of displayed images. The resultant picture is an object of type continuous picture (Section 3.2), a special hidden data type used only for reasoning about programs. For now we denote the resultant picture for program One by P_{One}. The resultant picture we expect is

$$P_{One} = p.lineseg((0,0),(0,d),red) + p.lineseg((0,0),(d,0),blue),$$

where (a,b) is a synonym for point(a,b). Using notation similar to that of Hoare [HOAC69], we can express our expectation for program One by means of two assertions:

$\{s = d\}$
program One
$\{P_{One} = p.lineseg((0,0),(0,d),red) + p.lineseg((0,0),(d,0),blue)\},$

meaning that if s has value d initially, then P_{One} has the value we expect at termination of program One.

The resultant picture is the sum of the representative pictures of the pictorial objects displayed by the program in post statements. We can trace the steps leading to the final resultant picture by noting what these representative pictures are in assertions. Recall from Section 3.3.1 that the representative picture of a pictorial object is given by the hidden generic operation display. Showing just the executable statements from program One, we can write,

```
        {s = d}
P ← lineto(setcolor(nullpict,red),point(O,s));
        {display(P) = p.lineseg((0,0),(0,d),red)}
post(P,"up");
P ← lineto(setcolor(nullpict,blue),point(s,0));
        {display(P) = p.lineseg((0,0),(d,0),blue)}
post(P,"across")
        {P_One = p.lineseg((0,0),(0,d),red) +
            p.lineseg((0,0),(d,0),blue)}
```

What is still not clear is how the resultant picture P_{One} gets its final value. One of the pictorial objects displayed (the first assignment to P) isn't even around at program termination. Even though program One is not interactive, we can use the interactive interface concept (Sections 4.1 and 4.3) to describe the resultant picture presented to the outside world. We think of primitives like post as modifying the interactive state, denoted IS, and the resultant picture in turn is a function of the interactive state. We express the effect of post on IS as an assignment involving the event function post$return, in terms of which the semantics of post are specified in the appendix. Since the operation

$$*image \qquad\qquad state \rightarrow picture$$

is defined to map the interactive state of a program onto the corresponding resultant picture (Section 5.4), P_{One} can be expressed as image(IS), and the derivation of the resultant picture for program One can be shown explicitly.

```
          {s = d, IS = $init}
P ← lineto(setcolor(nullpict,red),point(0,s));
          {display(P) = p.lineseg((0,0),(0,d),red)}
IS ← post$return(IS,P,"up");
          {image(IS = p.lineseg((0,0),(0,d),red)}
P ← lineto(setcolor(nullpict,blue),point(s,0));
          {display(P) = p.lineseg((0,0),(d,0),blue),
           image(IS) = p.lineseg((0,0),(0,d),red)}
IS ← post$return(IS,P,"across")
          {image(IS) = p.lineseg((0,0),(0,d),red) + p.lineseg((0,0),(d,0),blue)}
```

Thus, the operations defined by the specification of graphical data types and interaction primitives have a dual role. They can be used in both the programming language and the assertion language. Hidden operations, on the other hand, can only appear in assertions. Some of the hidden operations specified in the appendices are included purely to enhance the assertion language. The most obvious example is the entire data type continuous picture, especially the picture predicates equal, contains, coincident, disjoint, visible, and bounded. This data type, together with the special generic operations display, for pictorial data types, and image, for interaction primitives, make it possible to write assertions about the pictures produced by graphics programs. The operations ispict, isnode, and isancestorof are useful for writing assertions about picture-hierarchies, and many similar examples can be found within the other graphical data types.

In Section 6.3 we show how the specification of the prototype graphics language can be used to prove program One correct with respect to the assertions above. Later on we look at verifying other kinds of program properties and properties of interactive programs. In each case, the assertions are built up from operations defined by the language specification.

Not explored in this work is the inclusion of assertions in a running program, to be checked automatically or to facilitate program optimization. Automatic assertion checking has been incorporated into general purpose languages already (for example Euclid [LAMB77]). As an example of assertion-directed optimization, assertions giving rectangular extents for pictorial objects allow the visibility test (see Section 2.4) to be applied with little computational overhead. The concept of "dimensioning in the master" is a realization of this idea that was successfully implemented in the graphics language Dial [NEWW70].

6.2 Theorems about Graphical Data Types

Formal specifications of graphical data types provide a basis not only for reasoning about graphics programs that use them, but also for deducing properties of the types themselves. The ability to prove theorems about data types has at least two uses:

First, as we will see in the following sections, the axioms sufficient to form a consistent and complete algebraic axiomatization generally do not state directly all of the facts necessary to complete a program proof. These needed facts can be filled in as theorems, which are in turn proved from the axioms. It is our experience that just a few theorems are needed fairly often, so that proving them separately eliminates needless repetition. For example, the specification of type continuous picture includes the axiom

$$p9 \quad \text{sum(P,nullpict)} = P$$

but not the fact

$$p4T \quad \text{sum(nullpict,P)} = P,$$

so the latter is presented as a theorem.

A second, and perhaps more important, purpose of proving theorems about data types can be to gain insight into the most difficult of the questions concerning the correctness of data type specifications: Does the specification capture the right abstraction? The notions of consistency and completeness are at least well defined, and in many practical cases they can be checked formally. The question of capturing what is intended, on the other hand, can never be fully answered by formal means, because it involves a concept that exists only in someone's mind.

The most obvious approach to this question, and the one most often used in practice, is to simply write programs that use the type and see if there are any surprises. This kind of test cannot be performed, however, until an implementation (possibly of the wrong abstraction) is available, and it involves the additional question of making sure the implementation meets the specification.

By using our intuitive understanding of a data type to write down theorems that we expect to be true, then showing that the theorems follow logically from the axioms, we can gain confidence that the abstraction captured by the axioms is the intended one.

As a simple example, consider the restriction transformation. The effect of the operation restriction(P,R) on continuous picture P should be to restrict the domain of P to the region lying inside R, that is, we would expect

$$p1T \; \text{domain(restriction(P,R)} = \text{domain(P)} \cap R,$$

but this is not stated directly in the axioms for type continuous picture.

To prove theorems like $p1T$, we can use a form of mathematical induction especially applicable to data types, called *generator induction* or *structural induction* [WEGB76]. The method takes advantage of the organization we have imposed on algebraic specifications (Section 3.5). Recall that all objects of a data type are generated by the basic generator operations for the type. For type continuous picture the basic generators are

- nullpict   → picture

and
- inspatch picture × region × color → picture.

A theorem TH about objects of type T can be expressed as a predicate

$$\text{TH} \qquad \text{T} \rightarrow \text{boolean},$$

which must be shown to be true for all objects of type T. Let t and t_i denote objects of type T (the type of interest), and o_i objects of outside type. We must show

$$\text{TH(t) for all t.}$$

All objects of type T are generated by expressions of the form

$$\text{B}(o_1,...,o_n) \qquad\qquad (n \geq 0)$$
$$\text{or} \quad \text{B}(t_1,...,t_k,o_{K+1},...,o_n), \quad (k \geq 1, n \geq k),$$

where B is a basic generator operation for T. (The order of parameters is arbitrary.) For type continuous picture the operation nullpict is of the first form, because it has no parameters of type continuous picture; the operation inspatch is of the second form.

The basis of induction is established by showing

$$\text{TH}(\text{B}(o_1,...,o_n))$$

for all $o_1,...,o_n$ and all basic generators B that do not operate on the type of interest. Then, in the induction step, we show

$$\text{TH}(\text{B}(t_1,...,t_k,o_{k+1},...,o_n))$$

for the remaining basic generators by assuming $\text{TH}(t_1)$, ..., $\text{TH}(t_k)$ each to be true.

For theorem *p1T* above, the proof proceeds as follows:

theorem
> *p1T* domain(restriction(P, R) = domain(P) ∩ R

basis of induction (Show *p1T*(nullpict).)
> domain(restriction(nullpict, R))
>> = domain(nullpict)   *p13*
>> = nullregion   *p1*

$$\text{domain(nullpicture)} \cap R$$
$$= \text{nullregion} \cap R$$
$$= \text{nullregion} \qquad \qquad \textit{p1}$$

induction step

(Assume $\textit{p1T}(P_0)$; show $\textit{p1T}(\text{inspatch}(P_0, R_0, c_0))$.)

$$\text{domain(restriction(inspatch}(P_0, R_0, c_0)), R)$$
$$= \text{domain(inspatch(restriction}(P_0,R), R_0 \cap R), c_0) \qquad \textit{p14}$$
$$= (R_0 \cap R) \cup \text{domain(restriction}(P_0,R)) \qquad \textit{p2}$$
$$= (R_0 \cap R) \cup (\text{domain}(P_0) \cap R) \qquad \text{hypothesis}$$
$$= R \cap (R_0 \cup \text{domain}(P_0))$$

$$\text{domain(inspatch}(P_0,R_0,c_0)) \cap R$$
$$= (R_0 \cup \text{domain}(P_0)) \cap R$$
$$= R \cap (R_0 \cup \text{domain}(P_0)), \qquad \textit{p2}$$

which completes the proof.

Lists of theorems appear after several of the specifications in the appendices. All of the theorems needed for proofs in this work are included, as well as some other interesting facts that follow from the axioms.

6.3 Verifying Non-Interactive Programs

Proof Technique

We now have the tools we need to prove facts about non-interactive graphics programs. First, the hypotheses to be verified are expressed as assertions. The assertions are then proven to agree with the program (if in fact they do) using the axioms for the language. The statement types in our prototype graphics language are taken from Pascal and have been axiomatized by Hoare and Wirth [HOAC73]. Axioms for operations used to build expressions are given in the type specifications in Appendices B, C, and D.

We will illustrate by showing that the assertions we gave for program One in Section 6.1 do indeed define its behavior. The first statement presents no difficulty.

$$\{s = d, IS = \$init\}$$
$$P \leftarrow lineto(setcolor(nullpict,red),(0,s));$$
$$\{display(P) = p.lineseg((0,0),(0,d),red)\}$$

The expression

$$display(lineto(setcolor(nullpict,red),(0,s)))$$

is reduced using axioms *tp27, tp3, tp2* (Appendix C.3) and theorem *p4T* (Appendix B.1). Verification of the second statement

$$\{display(P) = p.lineseg((0,0),(0,d),red)\}$$
$$IS \leftarrow post\$return(IS,P,"up");$$
$$\{image(IS) = p.lineseg((0,0),(0,d),red)\}$$

involves the auxiliary operation postpict (see Appendix C.2). Intuitively postpict(IS) is the tpicture object containing as progeny the tpictures currently posted for display. The resultant picture is just the representative picture of postpict(IS), as expressed by axiom *ip26*:

$$ip26 \quad image(S) = display(postpict(S)).$$

The value

$$insprogeny(nullpict,P,gt.identity,"up")$$

for postpict(IS) is determined by axioms *ip23, ip22*, and *tp15*, then the result

$$image(IS) = display(P)$$

follows from axioms *ip26, tp30, tp26* and theorems *p4T, gt2T*; display(P) is known to be unchanged because of the assignment axiom. The last two statements are verified in a similar manner.

A somewhat shorter derivation of the final resultant picture can be constructed by keeping track of postpict(IS) at each statement instead of image(IS). This version of the verification is shown below with axioms indicated at right. The axioms given in

[HOAC73] for the Pascal language statements (notably assignment) are assumed.

program One;
  var P: tpicture, s: real;
begin
        {postpict(IS) = tp.nullpict}
   P ← lineto(setcolor(nullpict,red),(0,s));
        {display(P) = p.lineseg(origin,(0,s),red),   *tp27,tp26,p4T,*
        postpict(IS) = tp.nullpict}   *tp3,tp2*
  IS ← post$return(IS,P,"up");
        {postpict(IS) = tp.insprogeny(tp.nullpict,P',gt.identity,"up"),
        where display(P') = p.lineseg(origin,(s,0),red)}   *ip23,tp15*
   P ← lineto(setcolor(nullpict,blue),(s,0));
        {display(P) = p.lineseg(origin,(s,0),blue),   *tp27,tp26,p4T,*
        postpict(IS) = tp.insprogeny(tp.nullpict,P',gt.identity,"up")} *tp3,tp2*
  IS ← post$return(IS,P,"across")
        {postpict(IS) = tp.insprogeny(tp.insprogeny(tp.nullpict,P',
        gt.identity,"up"),P",gt.identity,"across"),   *ip23,tp16,tp15*
          where display(P') = p.lineseg(origin,(0,s),red)
          and display(P") = p.lineseg(origin,(s,0),blue),
          image(IS) = p.lineseg(origin,(0,s),red)   *ip25,tp30,tp26,*
            + p.lineseg(origin,(s,0),blue)}   *p4T,gt2T*
end.

Thus, we have shown that

    {s = d}
program One
    {P$_{One}$ = p.lineseg(origin,(0,s),red)
      + p.lineseg(origin,(s,0),blue)},

and in so doing we have determined the manner in which the resultant picture was built. For non-interactive programs, such as this one, the final resultant picture is usually all that matters. For interactive programs, however, intermediate images are an integral part of the interaction, so it becomes important to be able to trace the progress of the resultant picture during program execution.

Now consider the two programs,

```
program Two;                        program Three;
    var P: tpicture, s: real            var P: tpicture, s: real;
begin                               begin
    P ← nullpict;                       P ← nullpict;
    P ← setcolor(P,red);                P ← setcolor(P,blue);
    P ← moveto(P,(0,s));                P ← moveto(P,(s,0));
    P ← lineto(P,origin);               P ← lineto(P,origin);
    P ← setcolor(P,blue);               P ← setcolor(P,red);
    P ← lineto(P,(s,0));                P ← lineto(P,(0,s));
    post(P,"Two")                       post(P,"Three")
end.                                end.
```

With s = d, we would expect them both to draw the picture shown in Figure 6-1. The only difference between them is that they draw the "L" shape from opposite ends. If the resultant pictures are the same, it should be provable from the axioms. We start by determining the picture drawn by each program.

Shown below is program Two with assertions written between statements. The axioms needed to prove the assertions are listed at the right.

```
program Two;
    var P: tpicture, s: real;
begin
```
{postpict(IS) = tp.nullpict}	ip22
P ← nullpict;	
{curpos(P) = origin, curcolor(P) = default,	tp3,tp1
display(P) = p.nullpict,	tp26
postpict(IS) = tp.nullpict}	
P ← setcolor(P,red);	
{curpos(P) = origin, curcolor(P) = red,	im2,tp2
display(P) = p.nullpict,	im2
postpict(IS) = tp.nullpict}	

```
P ← moveto(P,(0,s));
        {curpos(P) = (0,s), curcolor(P) = red,                    tp4,im2
        display(P) = p.nullpict,                                    im2
        postpict(IS) = tp.nullpict}
P ← lineto(P,origin);
        {curpos(P) = origin, curcolor(P) = red,                   tp5,im2
        display(P) = p.lineseg((0,s),origin,red),                tp27,p4T
        postpict(IS) = tp.nullpict}
P ← setcolor(P,blue);
        {curpos(P) = origin, curcolor(P) = blue,                  im2,tp2
        display(P) = p.lineseg((0,s),origin,red),                   im2
        postpict(IS) = tp.nullpict}
P ← lineto(P,(s,0));
        {curpos(P) = (s,0),curcolor(P) = blue,                    tp5,im2
        display(P) = p.lineseg((0,s),origin,red)
            + p.lineseg(origin,(s,0),blue),                         tp27
        postpict(IS) = tp.nullpict}
IS ← post$return(IS,P,"Two")
        {display(P) = p.lineseg((0,s),origin,red) + p.lineseg(origin,(s,0),blue),
        postpict(IS) = tp.insprogeny(tp.nullpict,P,
            gt.identity,"Two"),                                  ip23,tp15
        image(IS) = p.lineseg((0,s),origin,red)             ip26,tp30,tp26,
            + p.lineseg(origin,(s,0),blue)}                        p4T,gt2T
end.
```

Thus, the resultant picture for program Two is given by

P_{Two} = p.lineseg((0,s),origin,red) + p.lineseg(origin,(s,0),blue),

and in similar fashion we can show that

P_{Three} = p.lineseg((s,0),origin,blue) + p.lineseg(origin,(0,s),red).

If we assume the summing function for colors is commutative, we can use theorems *p5T* and *p10T* to obtain the result

$$P_{Two} = P_{Three}.$$

In fact, returning to our first example, and applying theorem $p10T$, we can show that

$$P_{One} = P_{Two} = P_{Three}.$$

But, suppose the summing operation for colors is not commutative. The expressions for P_{Two} and P_{Three} can then be compared more easily if we reduce them to basic generator operations (Section 3.5):

$P_{Two} =$
inspatch(inspatch(inspatch(nullpict,R_h,blue),R_v,red),R_o,red + blue)

$P_{Three} =$
inspatch(inspatch(inspatch(nullpict,R_v,red),R_h,blue),R_o,blue + red)

where
$\qquad R_h \approx \{(x_1,x_2) \mid x_1 = 0, 0 < x_2 \leq s\}$
$\qquad R_v \approx \{(x_1,x_2) \mid 0 < x_1 \leq s, x_2 = 0\}$
$\qquad R_o \approx \{(0,0)\}.$

(The axioms needed for the reduction are $p25$ and $p9$ through $p14$.) Now, using axiom $p23$, we can rewrite P_{Three} as

$P_{Three} =$
inspatch(inspatch(inspatch(nullpict,R_h,blue),R_v,red),R_o,blue + red)

Thus, as we would expect, P_{Three} is identical with P_{Two} except at the origin, where the color differs if blue + red $\neq$ red + blue. That is, if the color sum is not commutative,

$$P_{One} = P_{Two}, \quad \text{but} \quad P_{Two} \neq P_{Three}.$$

6.4 A Proof Technique for Interactive Programs

The methods used for verifying non-interactive graphics programs in Section 6.3 are not sufficient for handling programs with interaction. The principal new factor that comes into play is synchronization with a human user. As discussed in Section 4.3, the actions available to the user for interacting with a program can be modelled as a set of operations. These user actions and the interaction primitives called by the program both access the interactive interface. Interactive dialogues between a program and a user are modelled as a pair of programs; one of these, the user description, describes possible sequences of user actions.

For example, a program that reads in a location entered through a positioning device can by represented by the following program-user pair:

```
program Readloc;                    user Enterloc;
    var p: point;                       var q: point;
begin                               begin
    p ← getposn                         position(q)
end.                                end.
```

We might wish to verify that $p = q$ at completion. This requirement can be stated

$$\{IS = \$init\}$$
$$\textbf{program } Readloc \mathbin{/\!/} \textbf{user } Enterloc$$
$$\{p = q\},$$

with the meaning: if the interactive state is properly initialized, then after the concurrent execution of program Readloc and the actions given by user description Enterloc, p has value q.

A Program Transformation Using the Canonical Model

In an interactive context, treating calls to interaction primitives (and user actions) as assignments to a state variable is not adequate because more than one process can access the interactive state concurrently. The synchronization requirements specified for the interaction primitives can be conveniently represented using the canonical model for shared data type operations introduced in Section 4.2. The canonical model for an interaction primitive consists of both an assignment to the interactive state, and the necessary controls on synchronization.

The canonical model for the getposn statement of program Readloc is

with IS **when** true **do**
    IS ← getposn$call(IS);
with IS **when** ¬getposn:wait(IS) **do**
    begin
        p ← getposn:value(IS);
        IS ← getposn$return(IS)
end.

In our use of the canonical model for interaction, the resource variable referred to in critical section statements is always the interactive state, so the **with** clause can be omitted. Also, it was possible to write the specification of the prototype graphics language (Appendices C and D) so that call events are never referred to (this is not true of the Core Graphics system specified in Appendix E), so for the examples in this chapter, the first critical section statement of the canonical model can be omitted. With these simplifications program-user pair Readloc is transformed as follows:

program Readloc
    var p: point, IS: state;
begin
    when ¬getposn:wait(IS) **do**
    begin
        p ← getposn:value(IS);
        IS ← getposn$return(IS)
    end
end.

user Readloc;
    var q: point, IS: state;
    begin
when ¬position:wait(IS,q) **do**
    IS ← position$return(IS,q);
end.

This program transformation is useful because it localizes synchronization in the critical section statements and allows an existing proof technique for concurrent programs, developed by Owicki [OWIS75, OWIS76], to be applied. Before proceeding with a proof of the altered program, however, we must be sure such a proof is valid for the original program.

In a more general context, what we want to do is prove facts about programs that make use of certain abstractions. Here we use the term *abstraction* to refer to a logically related set of operations whose effects within programs are formally specified, but whose implementation is not (see also Section 3.1). Two kinds of abstractions appear in this work: sequential data types and shared data types. Other examples are control abstractions and procedure abstractons [LISB79]. In general, many different implementations of the same abstraction are possible. We assume an encapsulation mechanism surrounds the implementation of an abstraction, guaranteeing that only computations allowed for in the specification can occur.

We will say that a predicate is *true with respect to an abstraction* if and only if it is true for all correct implementations of the abstraction. In our view this is the appropriate sense in which to talk about program correctness, because a program should know nothing more about an abstraction it uses than its specification. However, the proof technique we have outlined above for shared data types requires that a program be modified by inserting a *particular* implementation for each abstraction and the proof based on the program that results. In general, such a proof is not valid for any implementation other than the one used in the proof.

Example 6.4-1

Consider a (data) abstraction for a set of items. Two useful operations on sets are

$$\begin{aligned} \text{insert} \quad & \text{set} \times \text{item} \rightarrow \text{set} \\ \text{and} \quad \text{select} \quad & \text{set} \rightarrow \text{item}. \end{aligned}$$

The insert operation adds a new item to a set. Select obtains an item from a set. The most reasonable specification for the select operation requires only that the item returned be a member of the set. This requirement can be stated

$$\neg empty(s) = >(select(s) \in s).$$

An implementation of select is thus free to choose any item whatsoever from the (non-empty) set. Let the variables s and x be declared by the statement

var s: set, x: item,

and let P denote the following sequence of statements:

s ← insert(s,itemA);
s ← insert(s,itemB);
x ← select(s).

For an implementation of select that always chooses the item that was first placed into the set, the assertion

$$\{s = \varnothing\} \quad P \quad \{x = itemA\}$$

is true. However, for an implementation of select that always chooses the last item placed in the set, the same assertion is false. Thus, an assertion provable for a particular implementation of a set is not true with respect to the set abstraction.

As the example illustrates, problems arise when, according to its specification, the use of an abstraction can have any of several correct results. An implementation is correct that always picks one of these correct results, but, as long as there is more than one choice, a predicate true of one implementation may not be true of another.

Inclusive Implementations (Models)

In what follows, we present criteria under which a proof based on one implementation of an abstraction is valid for all, and argue that the canonical model for shared data types meets these criteria. While we have tried to make the argument convincing, it is not intended as a formal proof.

We define a *program state* as the aggregate of all information necessary to fully describe the state of execution of a program at any time. The interactive state is part of the program state as are the values of all program variables and the location counter for each active process. For each possible use A of an abstraction we can define a mapping A_S that describes the change to the program state allowed by the specification and a mapping A_I determined by the implementation. Thus, for any beginning state S, $A_S(S)$ and $A_I(S)$ are sets of states describing the possible outcomes as specified and as implemented respectively. If $A_S(S)$ (or $A_I(S)$) has more then one element, the specification (or implementation) is *nondeterministic*. An implementation is *correct* if

$$\text{for all A and S,} \quad A_I(S) \subset A_S(S),$$

so that the implementation always picks a state allowed by the specification. An implementation is *inclusive* if

$$\text{for all A and S,} \quad A_I(S) \supset A_S(S).$$

An implementation that is both correct and inclusive, so that

$$\text{for all A and S,} \quad A_I(S) = A_S(S),$$

is a *model*. In its visible behavior it mirrors the specification exactly.

Any predicate that is true of a model of an abstraction is also true of the abstraction itself. We must show that the canonical model of a shared data type is indeed a model as we have defined it here.

For sequential data types the only influence an operation has on the calling program is through the parameters of the call and the value returned. We assume that calling parameters are always left unchanged. Then, if the specification determines a unique return value for each operation call, a correct implementation (provided it terminates) is always inclusive, since there is only one correct outcome of any operation.

Example 6.4-1 above illustrates a sequential data type operation whose return value is not completely determined by its specification. Because of this nondeterminism, there is a non-inclusive implementation, and, as we saw, an assertion true of this implementation does not apply to all other implementations. In order for an implementation of the set abstraction to be inclusive, the select operation would have to choose an element from the set nondeterministically.

<u>Example 6.4-2</u>

If the universe of possible set elements is finite, an inclusive implementation of the select operation can be written using guarded commands [DIJE75, HOAC78]. In the following implementation the possible set elements are the integers 1 through N:

```
function select(s: set): integer;
begin
    if (i: 1..N) i ∈ s ⇒ select ← i fi
end.
```

(The abbreviated form of the alternative command used above is equivalent to the expansion

```
if 1 ∈ s ⇒ select ← 1
□ 2 ∈ s ⇒ select ← 2
    . . .
□ N ∈ s ⇒ select ← N fi.)
```

For programs containing concurrent processes and shared data types, the situation is necessarily more complex. There is a new way in which an operation on a shared data type can affect the execution of a program: it can impose a delay before it returns. For sequential programs, delays are not important since they cannot alter the sequence of execution states that make up a computation. A delay in a parallel program, however, can affect the sequence of execution states by changing the synchronization between processes. In order for an implementation of a shared data type to be inclusive, it must allow not only all correct return values for the operations but all valid return times as well.

Analysis of the Canonical Model

To show that the canonical model of a shared data type is inclusive, we repeat below the body of the canonical model of an operation Op of a shared data type:

```
begin
    with S when true do
        S ← Op:call(S,a₁,...,aₙ);
    with S when ¬Op:wait(S,a₁,...,aₙ) do
        begin
            Op ← Op:value(S,a₁,...,aₙ);
            S ← Op:return(S,a₁,...,aₙ)
        end
end.
```

First let us look at the value returned by Op. The expression used to compute the return value is exactly the Op:value characteristic function from the specification, so none of the possible return values are excluded.

The range of possible return times for Op depends upon the semantics chosen for the **with/when** critical section statement. In the canonical implementation it is clear that the return event can only occur when Op:wait is false for the current object state S. It is tempting to also require that return occur at the earliest possible time, or, if several processes are waiting concurrently, that they be activated in first come first served order. To do so, however, is to impose constraints that are not part of the specification for Op, making the canonical implementation non-inclusive. Any return time that meets the criteria given by the Op:wait function must be allowed. Of course, the semantics of the **with/when** statement are ultimately determined by the proof rules we choose to use. Owicki [OWIS75] gives the following axiom for the **with/when** statement:

$$\frac{\{P \text{ \& } B \text{ \& } I(R)\} \ S \ \{Q \text{ \& } I(R)\}}{\{P\} \ \textbf{with } R \ \textbf{when } B \ \textbf{do } S \ \{Q\}}$$

According to this axiom, it is known only that condition B (and an invariant on resource R) is true when the critical section S is executed; nothing is assumed about the scheduling strategy. This is precisely the interpretation we need in order not to constrain the set of possible return times for Op beyond the requirements embodied in Op:wait. Thus, using the Hoare/Owicki proof rules, the canonical model of a shared data abstraction is inclusive, and proofs of interactive programs can be constructed by substituting the appropriate canonical model wherever an interaction primitive or user action is invoked.

6.5 Verification of Interactive Programs

An Illustrative Example

In the Section 6.4 we presented a very simple interaction example, the program-user pair Readloc-Enterloc:

```
program Readloc;              user Enterloc;
   var p: point;                 var q: point;
begin                         begin
   p ← getpos                    position(q)
end.                          end.
```

and showed how it can be transformed so that the synchronization between program and user is explicit. In this section we give a proof of

$$\{IS = \$init\}$$
$$\textbf{program } Readloc \ // \ \textbf{user } Enterloc$$
$$\{p = q\}$$

in some detail to illustrate the proof method we are using.

The purpose of transforming an interactive program as discussed in the last section is to allow the Owicki proof technique

[OWIS75] to be used. Owicki has extended the axioms of Hoare [HOAC69, HOAC73] for sequential programs to the realm of parallel programs by formulating axioms for two addition statements, a statement expressing concurrency and the with/when critical section statement. These axioms for Owicki's "restricted parallel language", as they apply to our notation, are as follows:

$$ow1 \quad \frac{\{P_i\} \; S_i \; \{Q_i\} \; \text{interference free, } 1 \le i \le n}{\{P_1 \; \&...\& \; P_n \; \& \; INV\} \; S_1 \; //...// \; S_n \; \{Q_1 \; \&...\& \; Q_n \; \& \; INV\}}$$

$$ow2 \quad \frac{\{P \; \& \; B \; \& \; INV\} \; S \; \{Q \; \& \; INV\}}{\{P\} \; \textbf{when } B \textbf{ do } S \; \{Q\}}$$

where INV is an invariant involving the interactive state.

Since we are not concerned with parallelism within programs, we use axiom *ow1* only at the outermost level to deal with concurrency between program and user. Potentially, there can be many processes involved in an interactive system, including multiple users, multiple programs, and clock processes, but, for simplicity, we confine this discussion to program-user pairs.

As we have noted, critical section statements(axiom *ow2*) are used only to guard a single resource, the interactive state. The program transformation that introduces the interactive state guarantees that it is not accessed outside a critical section. Similarly, assertions outside critical sections can involve only variables local to the process; inside critical sections they can also reference the interactive state IS.

A proof is usually carried out with the help of an *invariant* INV on the interactive state. The invariant is chosen according to what is needed to make the proof work, but it must be formulated in such a way that it is true initially and is preserved by each critical section statement.

The assertions for each program (process) are developed independently of the other program(s) running in parallel. When each program and its attached assertions conform to the restrictions above, the separate parallel proofs can be shown not to *interfere* with one another [OWIS75], as required by axiom *ow1*.

What we will prove of program **Readloc** then is the following:

$\{IS = \$init, INV\}$
program Readloc // **user** Enterloc
$\{p = q, INV\}.$

For the invariant we choose the expression

$INV \equiv \neg getposn:wait(IS) \Rightarrow (getposn:value(IS) = q),$

which states a property of the interactive dialogue important to the proof. INV is true initially because by axiom *ip6*,

$getposn:wait(\$init) = true.$

Showing that INV is preserved by each critical section will establish its validity at the end.

For program **Readloc** we can attach the following assertions:

program Readloc;
  var p: point;
begin
  when $\neg getposn:wait(IS)$ **do begin**
        $\{\neg getposn:wait(IS), INV, getposn:value(IS) = q\}$ (1)
    $p \leftarrow getposn:value(IS);$
    $IS \leftarrow getposn\$return(IS)$
        $\{p = q, INV\}$ (2)
  end
      $\{p = q\}$ (3)
end
    $\{p = q\}.$ (4)

There is no initial assertion because the only local variable is **p**, whose initial value is unknown. At the beginning of the critical section (1), we know that both the invariant, INV, and the condition of the **when** statement, $\neg getposn:wait(IS)$ must hold. It follows that $getposn:value(IS) = q$. The invariant now provides the key to the proof, for it allows us to conclude (with the help of the assignment axiom) that after the assignment to **p**, $p = q$

(assertion (2)). INV is preserved because, by axiom ip7, the assignment to IS makes getposn:wait(IS) true, which establishes the implication. By axiom *ow2*, we have p = q after the critical section statement (3) and hence at the end of program Readloc (4).

The verification of user Enterloc is similar:

user Enterloc;
   var q : point;
begin
   when true **do**
        {INV}   (5)
     IS ← position$return(IS,q)
         {getposn:value(IS) = q, INV}   (6)
end.

The **when** condition is identically true because, by implicit axiom *im6* (Section 4.2),

$$position:wait(S,q) = false.$$

Thus, at the beginning of the critical section, we know only that INV holds (5). To verify that it is preserved (6), we note that, by axiom *ip10*,

$$getposn:value(IS) = q$$

after the assignment to IS, and the implication is established. Since there are no local variables, there is nothing to assert at the end of user Enterloc.

Finally, using axiom *ow2*, we conclude that, after termination of the entire program-user pair Readloc-Enterloc, p = q as required.

The above proof was especially simple because of the small size of the program. The same methods apply to interactive programs of any size, except that it is often necessary to introduce *auxiliary variables* to keep track of execution states [OWIS75]. Auxiliary variables are added to a program in such a way that assertions not containing them are unaffected. The basic rule is that they may be assigned to but never used in computations. An example of a proof with auxiliary variables is given in Appendix F.

Pointing Device Input

Now that we have demonstrated the proof method with a simple example, we present some larger examples with details of proof omitted.

As we noted in Section 2.5, pointing (or pick) input involves both input and output in a close relationship. The value obtained from a pick device depends not just on user action, but on the image currently displayed on the screen, which depends, in turn, on the history of screen output operations. The resultant picture concept, discussed in Sections 5.4 and 6.1, allows us to express this relationship in the assertion language.

The examples in this section center around the following program-user pair:

```
program Boxes;
    var P1,P2,P3: tpicture;
begin
    P1 ← box(nullpict,(0,0),(1,1));
    P2 ← box(nullpict,(3,3),(5,5));
    P3 ← insprogeny(nullpict,P1,identity,"box1");
    P3 ← insprogeny(P3,P2,identity,"box2");
    post(P3,"boxes");
    prompt("delete box");
    P3 ← delprogeny(P3,getpick);
    post(P3,"boxes")
end
//
user Pickq;
    var q: point;
begin
    getprompt;
    pick(q)
end.
```

Program Boxes draws two filled square boxes, prompts the user to point at one of them, then deletes the selected box (if any). The user description Pickq models a user who waits for a prompt, then points at location q with the pick device.

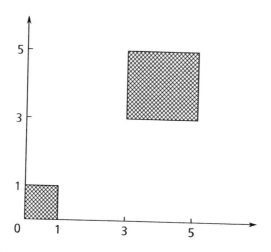

Figure 6-2 Resultant picture for program Boxes at time of prompt

The resultant picture at the time of the prompt is shown in Figure 6-2. We might wish to prove, for instance, that if the user points to the first box (labelled "box1" by the program), it does indeed disappear from the screen. Let R_1 denote the region occupied by box1. Then the statement, "the user points to the first box," can be expressed $q \in R_1$. The required screen image can be expressed in terms of the resultant picture using the domain operation:

$$\text{domain}(\text{image}(IS)) \cap R_1 = \text{nullregion}.$$

This outcome is illustrated in Figure 6-3a. A complete statement of the problem is

$\{q \in R_1\}$
program Boxes // **user** Pickq
$\{domain(image(IS)) \cap R_1 = nullregion\}$,

where $R_1 = rg.box((0,0),(1,1))$.

Using the methods discussed above, the following assertions can be shown to hold. Additional details of the proof are given in Appendix F.

$\{q \in rg.box((0,0),(1,1))\}$
program Boxes;
  var P1,P2,P3: tpicture;
begin
    $\{image(IS) = p.nullpict\}$
  P1 ← box(nullpict,(0,0),(1,1));
    $\{image(IS) = p.nullpict,$
    $tp.display(P1) = p.box((0,0),(1,1),fgnd)\}$
  P2 ← box(nullpict,(3,3),(5,5));
    $\{image(IS) = p.nullpict,$
    $tp.display(P1) = p.box((0,0),(1,1),fgnd),$
    $tp.display(P2) = p.box((3,3),(5,5),fgnd)\}$
  P3 ← insprogeny(nullpict,P1,identity,"box1");
    $\{image(IS) = p.nullpict,$
    $tp.display(P2) = p.box((3,3),(5,5),fgnd),$
    $tp.display(P3) = p.box((0,0),(1,1),fgnd)\}$
  P3 ← insprogeny(P3,P2,identity,"box2");
    $\{image(IS) = p.nullpict,$
    $tp.display(P3) = p.box((0,0),(1,1),fgnd) + p.box((3,3),(5,5),fgnd)\}$
  post(P3,"boxes");
    $\{image(IS) = p.box((0,0),(1,1),fgnd) + p.box((3,3),(5,5),fgnd)\}$
  prompt("delete box");
    $\{image(IS) = p.box((0,0),(1,1),fgnd) + p.box((3,3),(5,5),fgnd)\}$

```
    P3 ← delprogeny(P3,getpick);
        {image(IS) = p.box((0,0),(1,1),fgnd) + p.box((3,3),(5,5),fgnd),
        getpick:value(IS) = "box1",
        tp.display(P3) = p.box((3,3),(5,5),fgnd)}
    post(P3,"boxes");
        {image(IS) = p.box((3,3),(5,5),fgnd)}
end.

//

user Pickq;
    var q: point;
begin
        {q ∈ rg.box((0,0),(1,1))}
    getprompt;
        {image(IS) = p.box((0,0),(1,1),fgnd) + p.box((3,3),(5,5),fgnd),
        pickname(IS,q) = "box1"}
    pick(q);
        {getpick:value(IS) = "box1"}
end.
        {image(IS) = p.box((3,3),(5,5),fgnd)}
```

The final assertion

$$\text{domain(image(IS))} \cap R_1 = \text{nullregion}$$

is established by using axioms *p1* and *p2* to compute the domain of the resultant picture.

The following are additional criteria that might be required of program Boxes, stated both informally and as assertions on the program-user pair; each is illustrated in Figure 6-3.

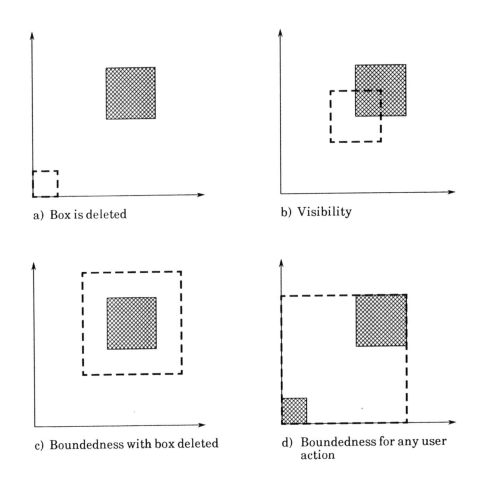

a) Box is deleted

b) Visibility

c) Boundedness with box deleted

d) Boundedness for any user
action

Figure 6-3 Theorems about program Boxes

1) If the user points within box 1, the resultant picture is visible within the region box((2,2),(4,4)) (Figure 6-3b),

$$\{q \in R_1\}$$
$$\textbf{program } \text{Boxes } \textit{//} \textbf{ user } \text{Pickq}$$
$$\{\text{visible(image(IS),rg.box((2,2),(4,4)))}\}$$

2) If the user points within box 1, the resultant picture is bounded by the region box((2,2),(6,6)) (Figure 6-3c),

$$\{q \in R_1\}$$

program Boxes // **user** Pickq

$$\{bounded(image(IS), rg.box((2,2),(6,6)))\}.$$

3) Regardless of user action, the resultant picture is bounded by the region box((0,0),(5,5)) (Figure 6-3d),

$$\{true\}$$

program Boxes // **user** Pickq

$$\{bounded(image(IS), rg.box((0,0),(5,5)))\}.$$

Since criteria 1) and 2) assume the same user behavior (pointing to box 1) that we have already analyzed, they can be verified from the resultant picture derived above, using axioms *p33* and *p34* respectively.

Criterion 3) requires that the final image lie within given bounds no matter where the user points. Since the user action is now unconstrained, the assertions given above are no longer valid. Tracking the progress of the resultant picture after each statement, as we have done up to now, would require splitting the proof into several cases, because the resultant picture depends on where the user points. What we can do instead is keep track of an extent (see Section 2.1) of the resultant picture in our assertions, rather than the resultant picture itself. It can be shown that after each statement of program Boxes, the region rg.box((0,0),(5,5)) bounds (is an extent of) the resultant picture, regardless of the value of q.

An "Equivalent" Program

To avoid confusion, the examples given so far have all been written in the first version of the prototype graphics language. An interesting comparison can be made by rewriting program Boxes in the second version of the prototype language, which uses a global picture-hierarchy instead of tree-structured picture objects.

```
program Boxes2;
    var P1: spicture;
begin
    insnode(identity,"root");  post("root");
    P1 ← box(nullpict(green),origin,(1,1));
    inspict(P1,"box1");  link("root","box1");
    P1 ← box(nullpict(yellow),(3,3),(5,5));
    inspict(P1,"box2");  link("root","box2");
    prompt("delete box");
    unlink("root",getpick);
end.
```

To compare the behavior of program **Boxes2** with that of program Boxes above, we pair it with the same user description Pickq. Assuming $q \in R_1$ (the user points to box 1), the following assertions result:

```
    {q ∈ rg.box((0,0),(1,1))}
program Boxes2;
    var P1: spicture;
begin
    insnode(identity,"root"); post("root");
        {image(IS) = p.nullpict}
    P1 ← box(nullpict(green),origin,(1,1));
        {image(IS) = p.nullpict,
        sp.display(P1) = p.box((0,0),(1,1),fgnd)}
    inspict(P1,"box1"); link("root","box1");
        {image(IS) = p.box((0,0),(1,1),fgnd)}
    P1 ← box(nullpict(yellow),(3,3),(5,5));
        {image(IS) = p.box((0,0),(1,1),fgnd),
        sp.display(P1) = p.box((3,3),(5,5),fgnd)}
    inspict(P1,"box2"); link("root","box2");
        {image(IS = p.box((0,0),(1,1),fgnd) + p.box((3,3),5,5),fgnd)}
    prompt("delete box");
        {image(IS) = p.box((0,0),(1,1),fgnd) + p.box((3,3),(5,5),fgnd)}
```

```
    unlink("root",getpick);
        {getpick:value = "box1",
        image(IS) = p.box((3,3),(5,5),fgnd)}
end

//

user Pickq;
    var q: point;
begin
        {q ∈ rg.box((0,0),(1,1))}
    getprompt;
        {image(IS) = p.box((0,0),(1,1),fgnd) + p.box((3,3),(5,5),fgnd),
        pickname(IS,q) = "box1"}
    pick(q);
        {getpick:value(IS) = "box1"}
end.
        {image(IS) = p.box((3,3),(5,5),fgnd)}
```

Several observations can be made in comparing program Boxes2 above with program Boxes:

1) The data structures used by the two programs are totally different.

2) The evolution of the resultant picture, as shown in the assertions, differs between the two programs. Program Boxes produces the first image "all at once", whereas program Boxes2 builds it piecewise.

3) With $q \in R_1$, the final resultant picture is the same for both programs.

4) The same assertions hold within the user description in both cases.

5) At the point in the user description where the behavior of the two programs does differ, (before the getprompt statement), it is not possible to determine the resultant picture for either companion program.

Thus, even though the two programs are outwardly very different, when paired with user description Pickq, they produce the same resultant picture at termination, and, in fact, the same assertions can be shown to hold throughout the user description in the two cases. We interpret this to mean that, from the viewpoint of a user who behaves according to Pickq, the two programs are functionally equivalent. Without developing a formal definition of equivalence for interactive programs, we can at least conclude that the analysis of user descriptions in program-user pairs, by suppressing transient effects not relevant to the interactive dialogue, provides a practical measure of whether two or more interactive programs are equivalent from the user view.

Chapter 7

Conclusions

In this chapter we evaluate several issues fundamental to the research we have described and indicate some areas where future work is needed.

Specification of Graphics Languages

We have demonstrated the feasibility of writing complete formal specifications for graphics programming languages. A language design framework based on the data type construct makes specification especially straightforward and at the same time contributes a desirable uniformity and modularity to the language design. It is apparent, however, that a formal specification is not by itself an adequate description for all purposes. An informal description (based on the formal one) is still needed for user documentation and to make the formal specification easier to grasp.

The value of the design framework and specification methods we have proposed can be proven only through experience with their use in a variety of graphics programming environments. A major area not included in our examples is three-dimensional graphics.

Graphical Data Types

As the examples show, a wide variety of graphics concepts can be expressed in convenient form as data types. While strict adherence to the data type model imposes restrictions on the form of the operations, most of these can be overcome easily using devices suggested in [GUTJ77] and [GUTJ80]. Additional graphical data type examples need to be defined and evaluated, such as other graphical transformations, other picture structures (possibly non-hierarchic), and types that support realistic renderings of solid objects. Extensible graphics languages could easily be developed by providing facilities for user definition of graphical data types.

Alternative ways of describing images that represent pictorial objects should be investigated. For example, instead of using a hidden data type like our continuous picture, Guttag and Horning [GUTJ80] rely entirely on generic operations to describe screen images.

It remains to be seen whether graphical data types can contribute to some of the current problems in raster graphics. Much of the active research in the area concerns the rendering of realistic scenes with raster output devices. Our work characterizes the graphical output of programs in terms of mathematical functions on a continuous space, but does not address the translation of these conceptual pictures into pixel arrays.

The Algebraic Specification Technique

We have chosen to use algebraic specifications primarily because they combine formality with flexibility. The examples in Chapter 6 show them to be well suited for reasoning about programs also. Unfortunately, we have found one data type (region) for which an algebraic specification clearly is not the best choice, and while, with experience, algebraic specification are easy enough to use, they can seem unnatural to the uninitiated.

Algebraic specifications have one potential advantage we have not explored. Since the axioms are essentially rewrite rules, it is possible to interpret them directly (even if slowly) without benefit of a separate implementation. A number of systems capable of such *direct execution* have already been developed [GOGJ79, BURR80, MUSD80, NOLG80]. Using such a system and an existing base language, it would be possible in principle to test alternative designs for a graphics language before an implementation is done. Even event algebra specifications could be handled by interfacing a suitable scheduler to the system that interprets the axioms.

Specification of User Interaction

By treating interaction as a problem in parallel computation, our specification method is able to handle virtually any form of interaction that can be envisioned. Perhaps it is more powerful than it needs to be, and a simpler model (such as coroutines) would suffice in enough cases to be worth considering.

The generality of the event algebra specification method makes it worth studying in the broader context of resource sharing. It brings together the specification of synchronization and data flow in a common language while maintaining a logical separation between the two.

An area we have not touched upon is the specification of graphics software at the user dialogue level. Such a specification represents the highest level of abstraction, in that only the behavior of the interface as it is seen by the user is determined.

Logic of Graphics Programs

We have shown that formal specifications aid in reasoning about graphics programs, both formally and informally, but the work is incomplete. For example, we have dealt only with partial correctness. Work by Owicki [OWIS76b] and Dahl [DAHO80] would suggest that our methods should extend without difficulty to liveness properties (e.g. termination and deadlock), at least some of which are pertinent to problems in interaction.

More importantly, only a few examples are considered in Chapter 6. Further examination is needed of the kinds of properties it is useful to require of graphics programs and how these criteria can be stated in ways that are amenable to proof.

Appendix A

Proof That T^g and T^r
Distribute over Picture Sum

For a hierarchic composition algorithm to be valid, the graphical transformations used in hierarchic picture structures must distribute over the picture sum operation (see Section 2.4). Below we outline proofs of this distributive law for geometric transformations and restriction transformations.

A.1 Geometric Transformations

We must show that

$$T^g\langle G\rangle(P_1) + T^g\langle G\rangle(P_2) = T^g\langle G\rangle(P_1 + P_2),$$

where pictures P_1 and P_2 have domains D_1 and D_2 respectively. Making use of the definitions for picture sum and graphical transformation (see Section 2.2) and the fact,

$$\text{domain}(T^g\langle G\rangle(P)) = G(\text{domain}(P)),$$

the two sides evaluate as follows:

$$T^g\langle G\rangle(P_1) + T^g\langle G\rangle(P_2) = \{(x,P'(x)) \mid x \in G(D_1) \cup G(D_2)\},$$

$$\text{where } P'(x) = \begin{cases} P_1 \circ G^{-1}(x) & \text{for all } x \in G(D_1) - G(D_2) \\ P_2 \circ G^{-1}(x) & \text{for all } x \in G(D_2) - G(D_1) \\ P_1 \circ G^{-1}(x) + P_2 \circ G^{-1}(x) & \text{for all } x \in G(D_1) \cap G(D_2) \end{cases}$$

$$T^g\langle G\rangle(P_1 + P_2) = \{(x,P''(x)) \mid x \in G(D_1 \cup D_2)\},$$

$$\text{where } P''(x) = \begin{cases} P_1 \circ G^{-1}(x) & \text{for all } x \in G(D_1 - D_2) \\ P_2 \circ G^{-1}(x) & \text{for all } x \in G(D_2 - D_1) \\ P^* \circ G^{-1}(x) & \text{for all } x \in G(D_1 \cap D_2) \end{cases}$$

and $P^*(x) = P_1(x) + P_2(x)$.

The fact that

$$P_1 \circ G^{-1}(x) + P_2 \circ G^{-1}(x) = P^* \circ G^{-1}(x)$$

follows from the definition of function composition; the corresponding regions are the same (e.g. $G(D_1) - G(D_2) = G(D_1 - D_2)$) because G is one-to-one.

A.2 Restriction Transformations

To show that

$$T^r\langle R\rangle(P_1) + T^r\langle R\rangle(P_2) = T^r\langle R\rangle(P_1 + P_2),$$

we use the definitions for picture sum and restriction transformation:

$$T^r\langle R\rangle(P_1) + T^r\langle R\rangle(P_2) = \{(x, P'(x)) \mid x \in (R \cap D_1) \cup (R \cap D_2)$$

$$\text{where } P'(x) = \begin{cases} P_1(x) \text{ for all } x \in (R \cap D_1) - (R \cap D_2) \\ P_2(x) \text{ for all } x \in (R \cap D_2) - (R \cap D_1) \\ P_1(x) + P_2(x) \text{ for all } x \in (R \cap D_2) \cap (R \cap D_1). \end{cases}$$

$$T^r\langle R\rangle(P_1 + P_2) = \{(x, P''(x)) \mid x \in R \cap (D_1 \cup D_2)\}$$

$$\text{where } p''(x) = \begin{cases} P_1(x) \text{ for all } x \in R \cap (D_1 - D_2) \\ P_2(x) \text{ for all } x \in R \cap (D_2 - D_1) \\ P_1(x) + P_2(x) \text{ for all } x \in R \cap (D_1 \cap D_2). \end{cases}$$

The equivalence of corresponding regions in the two expressions is established using the properties of sets.

Appendix B

Specifications for
Some Graphical Data Types

Special Symbols Used in Specifications

- * indicates a hidden operation (Section 3.3.1)
- • indicates a basic generator operation (Section 3.5.2)
- : (within an identifier) denotes a characteristic function for a shared data type operation (Section 4.2.2)
- $ (within an identifier) denotes an event function for a shared data type operation (Section 4.2.2)

Implicit Axioms

exception conditions (Section 3.5.5):

  im0   The result of applying any operation to the value undefined (in any argument) is the value undefined.

inquiry operations (Section 3.5.6):

  im1 $I(B(o_1,...,o_{n(B)}),a_1,...,a_{n(I)}) = $ undefined

  im2 $I(B(t,b_1,...,b_{n(B)}),a_1,...,a_{n(I)}) = I(t,a_1,...,a_{n(I)})$

generator operations (Section 3.5.6):

  im3 $G(B(o_1,...,o_{n(B)}),a_1,...,a_{n(G)}) = B(o_1,...,o_{n(B)})$

  im4 $G(B(t,b_1,...,b_{n(B)}),a_1,...,a_{n(G)}) =$
     $B(G(t,b_1,...,b_{n(G)}),b_1,...,b_{n(B)}),$

where I is an inquiry operation, G is a generator operation, and B is a basic generator operation.

characteristic functions for shared data types (Section 4.2.3):

  im5 $Op:value(S,a_1,..,a_n) = $ undefined

  im6 $Op:wait(S,a_1,..,a_n) = $ false

event functions that are not basic state generators:

  im7 $Op\$call(S,a_1,...,a_n) = S$

  im8 $Op\$return(S,a_1,...,a_n) = S$

B.1 Data Type Continuous Picture (picture, p)

operations

*• nullpict		$\rightarrow$ picture
*• inspatch	picture $\times$ region $\times$ color	$\rightarrow$ picture
* domain	picture	$\rightarrow$ region
* colors	picture $\times$ region	$\rightarrow$ set(color)
* getpatch	picture $\times$ color	$\rightarrow$ region
* getcolor	picture $\times$ point	$\rightarrow$ color
* sum	picture $\times$ picture	$\rightarrow$ picture
* addpatch	picture $\times$ region $\times$ color	$\rightarrow$ picture
* restriction	picture $\times$ region	$\rightarrow$ picture
* geomtrans	picture $\times$ geomfcn	$\rightarrow$ picture
* colortrans	picture $\times$ colorfcn	$\rightarrow$ picture
* fill	picture $\times$ color	$\rightarrow$ picture

synonyms

$sum(P_1, P_2) \equiv P_1 + P_2$

axioms

p1   domain(nullpict) = nullregion

p2   domain(inspatch(P,R,c)) = R $\cup$ domain(P)

p3   colors(nullpict) = $\varnothing$

p4   colors(inspatch(P,R_1,c), R_2) =
        if rg.empty($R_1 \cap R_2$) **then** colors(P,R_2)
        else {c} $\cup$ colors(restriction(P,$\sim R_1$), R_2)

p5   getpatch(nullpict,c) = nullregion

p6   getpatch(inspatch(P,R,c_1),c_2) =
        if c_1 = c_2 **then** R $\cup$ getpatch(P,c_1)
        else getpatch(restriction(P,$\sim R$),c_2)

p7   getcolor(nullpict,p) = undefined

p8   getcolor(inspatch(P,R,c),p) =
        if p ϵ R **then** c **else** getcolor(P,c)

p9   sum(P,nullpict) = P

p10   sum(P_1,inspatch(P_2,R,c)) =
        sum(addpatch(P_1,R,c),restriction(P_2,$\sim R$))

$p11$ addpatch(nullpict,R,c) = inspatch(nullpict,R,c)

$p12$ addpatch(inspatch(P,R_1,c_1),R_2,c_2) =
     inspatch(inspatch(addpatch(P,R_2-R_1,c_2),R_1-R_2,c_1),
     $R_1 \cap R_2$, $c_1 + c_2$)

$p13$ restriction(nullpict,R) = nullpict

$p14$ restriction(inspatch(P,R_1,c),R_2) =
     inspatch(restriction(P,R_2), $R_1 \cap R_2$, c)

$p15$ geomtrans(nullpict,G) = nullpict

$p16$ geomtrans(inspatch(P,R,c),G) =
     inspatch(geomtrans(P,G), rg.transform(G,R), c)

$p17$ colortrans(nullpict,C) = nullpict

$p18$ colortrans(inspatch(P,R,c),C) =
     inspatch(colortrans(P,C), R, c.transform(C,c))

$p19$ fill(nullpict,c) = inspatch(nullpict,universe,c)

$p20$ fill(inspatch(P,R,c_1),c_2) = inspatch(fill(P,c_2), R, c_1)

$p21$ inspatch(P,nullregion,c) = P

$p22$ inspatch(inspatch(P,R_1,c),R_2,c) = inspatch(P,$R_1 \cup R_2$,c)

$p23$ inspatch(inspatch(P,R_1,c_1),R_2,c_2) =
     inspatch(inspatch(P,R_2,c_2),R_1-R_2,c_1)

Picture Primitives
(extension of type continuous picture)

operations

dot	point × color → picture
lineseg	point × point × color → picture
box	point × point × color → picture
text	string × point × color → picture

axioms

$p24$ $dot(p,c) = inspatch(nullpict, rg.point(p), c)$

$p25$ $lineseg(p_1, p_2, c) = inspatch(nullpict, rg.lineseg(p_1, p_2), c)$

$p26$ $box(p_1, p_2, c) = inspatch(nullpict, rg.box(p_1, p_2), c)$

$p27$ $text(s, p, c) = inspatch(nullpict, rg.text(s, p), c)$

Picture Predicates
(extension of type continuous picture)

operations

equal	picture × picture → boolean
contains	picture × picture → boolean
coincident	picture × picture → boolean
disjoint	picture × picture → boolean
visible	picture × region → boolean
bounded	picture × region → boolean

synonyms

equal(P_1,P_2) ≡ P_1 = P_2

contains(P_1,P_2) ≡ P_2 C P_1

axioms

p28   equal(nullpict,P) = empty(domain(P))

p29   equal(inspatch(P_1,R,c),P_2) =
        rg.contains(domain(P_2),R) &
        s.equal(colors(P_2,R), {c}) &
        equal(restriction(P_1,~R), restriction(P_2,~R))

p30   contains(P_1,P_2) =
        rg.contains(domain(P_1),domain(P_2)) &
        equal(restriction(P_1,domain(P_2)), P_2)

p31   coincident(P_1,P_2) = rg.equal(domain(P_1), domain(P_2))

p32   disjoint(P_1,P_2) = rg.empty(domain(P_1) ∩ domain(P_2))

p33   visible(P,R) = ~rg.empty(domain(P) ∩ R)

p34   bounded(P,R) = rg.contains(R,domain(P))

Theorems for Type Continuous Picture

p1T   domain(restriction(P,R)) = domain(P) $\cap$ R

p2T[†]   N(addpatch(P,R,c)) $\leq$ 2*N(P) + 1

p3T[†]   N(sum(P_1,P_2)) $\leq$ N(P_1)*N(P_2) + N(P_1) + N(P_2)

p4T   sum(nullpict,P) = P

p5T   operation " + " for colors commutative $\Rightarrow$
       sum(P_1,P_2) = sum(P_2,P_1)

p6T   operation " + " for colors associative $\Rightarrow$
       sum(sum(P_1,P_2),P_3) = sum(P_1,sum(P_2,P_3))

p7T   restriction(P,universe) = P

p8T   restriction(P,nullregion) = nullpict

p9T   fill(P,c) = inspatch(P,$\sim$domain(P),c)

p10T   lineseg(x_1,x_2,c) = lineseg(x_2,x_1,c)

p11T $P_1 = P_2$ $\Leftrightarrow$ equal(P_1,P_2)

p12T   visible(gt.transform(T,P), R) =
       visible(P, rg.transform(gpartof(T)$^{-1}$,R) $\cap$ rpartof(T))

[†]   where N(P) is the number of colors in P, that is, s.size(colors(P,universe))

B.2 Data Type Picture-Tree (tree, tr)

operations

• leaf	spicture × name → tree
• node	grtrans × name → tree
• insprogeny	tree × tree → tree
instrans	tree × grtrans → tree
delprogeny	tree × name → tree
getname	tree → name
getpict	tree → spicture
gettrans	tree → grtrans
getprogeny	tree × name → tree
isleaf	tree → boolean
* display	tree → picture

axioms

tr1   instrans(leaf(p,n),T) = error

tr2   instrans(node(T_1,n),T_2) = node(T_2,n)

tr3   instrans(insprogeny(t_1,t_2),T) = instrans(t_1,T)

tr4   delprogeny(leaf(p,n_1),n_2) = error

tr5   delprogeny(node(T,n_1),n_2) = node(T,n_1)

tr6   delprogeny(insprogeny(t_1,t_2),n) =
         if getname(t_2) = n **then** delprogeny(t_1,n)
         else insprogeny(delprogeny(t_1,n),t_2)

tr7   getname(leaf(p,n)) = n

tr8   getname(node(T,n)) = n

tr9   getname(insprogeny(t_1,t_2)) = getname(t_1)

tr10   getpict(leaf(p,n)) = p

tr11   getpict(node(T,n)) = error

tr12   getpict(insprogeny(t_1,t_2)) = error

tr13   gettrans(leaf(p,n)) = error

tr14   gettrans(node(T,n)) = T

tr15   gettrans(insprogeny(t_1,t_2)) = gettrans(t_1)

tr16   getprogeny(leaf(p,n_1),n_2) = error

tr17   getprogeny(node(T,n_1),n_2) = error

tr18   getprogeny(insprogeny(t_1,t_2),n) =
         if getname(t_2) = n **then** t_2 **else** getprogeny(t_1,n)

tr19   isleaf(leaf(p,n)) = true

tr20   isleaf(node(T,n)) = false

tr21   isleaf(insprogeny(t_1,t_2)) = false

tr22   display(leaf(p,n)) = sp.display(p)

tr23   display(node(T,n)) = p.nullpict

tr24   display(insprogeny(t_1,t_2)) =
         p.sum(display(t_1), gt.transform(gettrans(t_1),display(t_2)))

tr25   insprogeny(leaf(n),P) = error

B.3 Data Type Simple Picture (spicture, sp)

operations
- nullpict $\qquad$ color $\rightarrow$ spicture
- setcolor $\qquad$ spicture x color $\rightarrow$ spicture
- moveto $\qquad$ spicture x point $\rightarrow$ spicture
- lineto $\qquad$ spicture x point $\rightarrow$ spicture
- box $\qquad$ spicture x point x point $\rightarrow$ spicture
- text $\qquad$ spicture x string $\rightarrow$ spicture
  - curpos $\qquad$ spicture $\rightarrow$ point
  - curcolor $\qquad$ spicture $\rightarrow$ color
  - append $\qquad$ spicture x spicture $\rightarrow$ spicture
- * display $\qquad$ spicture $\rightarrow$ picture

synonyms

append(P_1,P_2) $\equiv$ $P_1 + P_2$

axioms

$sp1$	curpos(nullpict(c)) = origin
$sp2$	curpos(setcolor(P,c)) = curpos(P)
$sp3$	curpos(moveto(P,x)) = x
$sp4$	curpos(lineto(P,x)) = x
$sp5$	curpos(box(P,x_1,x_2)) = curpos(P)
$sp6$	curpos(text(P,s)) = curpos(P)

$sp7$	curcolor(nullpict(c)) = c
$sp8$	curcolor(setcolor(P,c)) = c
$sp9$	curcolor(moveto(P,x)) = curcolor(P)
$sp10$	curcolor(lineto(P,x)) = curcolor(P)
$sp11$	curcolor(box(P,x_1,x_2)) = curcolor(P)
$sp12$	curcolor(text(P,s)) = curcolor(P)

$sp13$	append(P,nullpict(c)) = moveto(setcolor(P,c),origin)
$sp14$	append(P_1,setcolor(P_2,c)) = setcolor(append(P_1,P_2),c)
$sp15$	append(P_1,moveto(P_2,x)) = moveto(append(P_1,P_2),x)
$sp16$	append(P_1,lineto(P_2,x)) = lineto(append(P_1,P_2),x)
$sp17$	append(P_1,box(P_2,x_1,x_2)) = box(append(P_1,P_2),x_1,x_2)
$sp18$	append(P_1,text(P_2,s)) = text(append(P_1,P_2),s)

sp19   display(nullpict(c)) = p.nullpict
sp20   display(setcolor(P,c)) = display(P)
sp21   display(moveto(P,x)) = display(P)
sp22   display(lineto(P,x)) =
        p.sum(display(P), p.lineseg(curpos(P),x,curcolor(P)))
sp23   display(box(P,x_1,x_2)) =
        p.sum(display(P), p.box(x_1,x_2,curcolor(P)))
sp24   display(text(P,s)) =
        p.sum(display(P), p.text(curpos(P),s,curcolor(P)))

theorems
sp1T   display(nullpict(c) + P) = display(P)
sp2T   display(P + nullpict(c)) = display(P)

B.4 Data Type Graphical Transformation (grtrans, gt)

operations

- grtrans   geomfcn x region $\rightarrow$ grtrans
  identity $\rightarrow$ grtrans
  gpartof   grtrans $\rightarrow$ geomfcn
  rpartof   grtrans $\rightarrow$ region
  compose   grtrans x grtrans $\rightarrow$ grtrans
- * transform   grtrans x picture $\rightarrow$ picture

synonyms

grtrans(G,R) $\equiv$ $T^{gr}\langle G,R\rangle$
compose(T_1,T_2) $\equiv$ $T_1 \circ T_2$
transform(T,P) $\equiv$ T(P)

axioms

gt1   identity = grtrans(gf.identity,rg.universe)

gt2   gpartof(grtrans(G,R)) = G

gt3   rpartof(grtrans(G,R)) = R

gt4   compose(grtrans(G_1,R_1),grtrans(G_2,R_2)) =
        grtrans(gf.compose(G_1,G_2), rg.transform(G_2^{-1},R_1)$\cap R_2$)

gt5   transform(grtrans(G,R),P) = geomtrans(restriction(P,R),G)

theorems

gt1T   grtrans(gpartof(T),rpartof(T)) = T

gt2T   transform(identity,P) = P

gt3T   compose(T,identity) = compose(identity,T) = T

gt4T   p.domain(transform(T,P)) =
        rg.transform(gpartof(T), p.domain(P) $\cap$ rpartof(T))

B.5 Data Type Geometric Function (geomfcn, gf)

operations
- scale   real → geomfcn
- translate   real x real → geomfcn
- compose   geomfcn x geomfcn → geomfcn
  identity   → geomfcn
* invertible   geomfcn → boolean
  inverse   geomfcn → geomfcn
  transform   geomfcn x point → point

synonyms

$compose(G_1, G_2) = G_1 \circ G_2$

$inverse(G) = G^{-1}$

axioms

gf1 $identity = scale(1) = translate(0,0)$

gf2 $invertible(scale(x)) = (x \neq 0)$

gf3 $invertible(translate(x_1, x_2)) = true$

gf4 $invertible(compose(G_1, G_2)) = invertible(G_1)\,\&\,invertible(G_2)$

gf5 $inverse(scale(x)) = $ **if** $x = 0$ **then** error **else** $scale(1/x)$

gf6 $inverse(translate(x_1, x_2)) = translate(-x_1, -x_2)$

gf7 $inverse(compose(G_1, G_2)) =$
          $compose(inverse(G_2), inverse(G_1))$

gf8 $transform(scale(x_1), point(x_2, x_3)) = point(x_1 * x_2, x_1 * x_3)$

gf9 $transform(translate(x_1, x_2), point(x_3, x_4)) =$
          $point(x_1 + x_3, x_2 + x_4)$

gf10 $transform(compose(G_1, G_2), p) =$
          $transform(G_1, transform(G_2, p))$

gf11 compose(compose(G_1,G_2),G_3) =
        compose(G_1,compose(G_2,G_3))

gf12 compose(scale(x_1),scale(x_2)) = scale(x_1*x_2)

gf13 compose(translate(x_1,x_2),translate(x_3,x_4)) =
        translate($x_1 + x_3$, $x_2 + x_4$)

gf14 compose(scale(x_1),translate(x_2,x_3)) =
        compose(translate(x_1*x_2,x_1*x_3), scale(x_1))

theorems

gf1T compose(G,identity) = compose(identity,G) = G

gf2T inverse(identity) = identity

gf3T inverse(inverse(G)) = G

gf4T compose(G,inverse(G)) = compose(inverse(G),G) = identity

gf5T transform(identity,p) = p

B.6 Data Type Region (region,rg)

Type region is a data type for which an algebraic specification is cumbersome, and an operational specification is more convenient. Because a region is most naturally thought of as a set of points (see Section 2.1), each operation on regions is easily specified in terms of the equivalent operation on sets. The finite set data type specified in Appendix B.9, however, is not adequate for this purpose. We need instead the mathematical notion of set, possibly containing an uncountably infinite number of elements.

The specification below determines the defining algebra (Section 3.4.1) for type region by defining a one-to-one mapping into the algebra of sets of points. The space of region objects is defined by the transitive closure of the generator operations (Section 3.5). For each object of type region, the specification gives a corresponding object in the algebra of sets. Just as for algebraic specifications, all variables are universally quantified over the object spaces for their types. The notation "$r \approx s$" means "region object r corresponds to set s", and " r' " means "the set corresponding to region r".

Based on the mapping defined here, set objects and operations are freely substituted for their corresponding region objects and operations in derivations elsewhere in this work. For ease of expression, set operation symbols are ambiguously defined as synonyms for the corresponding region operations. The well known properties of sets are taken as given without further specification.

The hidden operation pickregion is included to represent a "window of sensitivity" around a pick device (see Section 2.5). The actual definition of pickregion depends on the hardware or software imposed characteristics of the pick device(s). For simplicity in this work, we define the window to always contain just a single point.

operations

null	region $\rightarrow$	region
universe	$\rightarrow$	region
lineseg	point $\times$ point $\rightarrow$	region
box	point $\times$ point $\rightarrow$	region
complement	region $\rightarrow$	region
intersect	region $\times$ region $\rightarrow$	region
union	region $\times$ region $\rightarrow$	region
difference	region $\times$ region $\rightarrow$	region
transform	geomfcn $\times$ region $\rightarrow$	region
empty	region $\rightarrow$	boolean
contains	region $\times$ region $\rightarrow$	boolean
contains	ptregion $\times$ point $\rightarrow$	boolean
equal	region $\times$ region $\rightarrow$	boolean
* pickregion	point $\rightarrow$	region

synonyms

nullregion $\equiv \varnothing$

universe $\equiv U$

complement(R) $\equiv \sim$R

intersect(R_1,R_2) $\equiv R_1 \cap R_2$

union(R_1,R_2) $\equiv R_1 \cup R_2$

difference(R_1,R_2) $\equiv R_1 - R_2$

transform(G,R) $\equiv$ G(R)

contains(R_1,R_2) $\equiv R_2 \subseteq R_1$

containspt(R,p) $\equiv p \in R$

object mapping

rg1   nullregion $\approx$ { }

rg2   universe $\approx$ {q | q is in the universe}

rg3   lineseg(q_1, q_2) $\approx$ {(x,y) | $x_1 \leq x \leq x_2$, $y_1 \leq y \leq y_2$, $(y_2 - y_1) * x - (x_2 - x_1) * y = x_1 * y_2 - x_2 * y_1$}†

rg4   box(q_1, q_2) $\approx$ {(x,y) | $x_1 \leq x \leq x_2$, $y_1 \leq y \leq y_2$}†

rg5   complement(R) $\approx$ $\sim$(R')

rg6   intersect(R_1, R_2) $\approx$ $R_1' \cap R_2'$

rg7   union(R_1, R_2) $\approx$ $R_1' \cup R_2'$

rg8   difference(R_1, R_2) $\approx$ $R_1' - R_2'$

rg9   transform(G,R) $\approx$ {G(q) : q $\in$ R'}

rg10 empty(R) = (R' = { })

rg11 contains(R_1, R_2) = $R_2' \subseteq R_1'$

rg12 containspt(R,q) = q $\in$ R'

rg13 equal(R_1, R_2) = ($R_1' = R_2'$)

rg14 pickregion(q) $\approx$ {q}

† where x_1 = abscissa(q_1), y_1 = ordinate(q_1), x_2 = abscissa(q_2), and y_2 = ordinate(q_2).

B.7 Data Type Point (point, pt)

operations

• point	real x real →	point
polarpt	real x real →	point
origin	→	point
abscissa	point →	real
ordinate	point →	real
radius	point →	real
angle	point →	real
sum	point x point →	point
difference	point x point →	point

synonyms

$point(x_1,x_2) \equiv (x_1,x_2)$

$sum(p_1,p_2) \equiv p_1 + p_2$

$difference(p_1,p_2) \equiv p_1 - p_2$

axioms

pt1 $polarpt(x_1,x_2) = point(x_1*cos(x_2), x_1*sin(x_2))$

pt2 $origin = point(0,0)$

pt3 $abscissa(point(x_1,x_2)) = x_1$

pt4 $ordinate(point(x_1,x_2)) = x_2$

pt5 $radius(point(x_1,x_2) = (x_1^2 + x_2^2)^{1/2}$

pt6 $angle(p) = $ **if** $radius(p) = 0$ **then** 0

        else if $ordinate(p) \geq 0$

        then $arccos(abscissa(p)/radius(p))$

        else $360 - arccos(abscissa(p)/radius(p))$

pt7 $sum(point(x_1,x_2),point(x_3,x_4)) = point(x_1 + x_3, x_2 + x_4)$

pt8 $difference(point(x_1,x_2),point(x_3,x_4)) = point(x_1 - x_3, x_2 - x_4)$

B.8 Data Types Color (color, co) and Name (name, n)

Types color and name, for our purposes, are very simple. Each consists of a finite set of arbitrary constants (denoted here with subscripts) and an equality operation for telling the objects apart. Type name contains the hidden operation lessthan, which must define a total ordering but is otherwise unconstrained.

Data Type Color (color, co)

$color_1$	$\rightarrow$ color
...	
$color_n$	$\rightarrow$ color
equals	color $\times$ color $\rightarrow$ boolean

Data Type Name (name, n)

$name_1$	$\rightarrow$ name
...	
$name_m$	$\rightarrow$ name
equals	name $\times$ name $\rightarrow$ boolean
* lessthan	name $\times$ name $\rightarrow$ boolean

B.9 Data Type Ordered Set of Items (set(item), s)

operations

• nullset	$\to$ set
• insert	set $\times$ item $\to$ set
empty	set $\to$ boolean
contains	set $\times$ item $\to$ boolean
size	set $\to$ integer
remove	set $\times$ item $\to$ set
first	set $\to$ item
rest	set $\to$ set
select	set $\to$ item
union	set $\times$ set $\to$ set
intersect	set $\times$ set $\to$ set
difference	set $\times$ set $\to$ set
equal	set $\times$ set $\to$ boolean

synonyms

nullset $\equiv \emptyset$

insert(...(insert(nullset,x_1),...),x_n) $\equiv \{x_1,...,x_n\}$

contains(s,x) $\equiv x \in s$

union(s_1,s_2) $\equiv s_1 \cup s_2$

intersect(s_1,s_2) $\equiv s_1 \cap s_2$

difference(s_1,s_2) $\equiv s_1 - s_2$

axioms

s1   empty(nullset) = true

s2   empty(insert(s,x)) = false

s3   contains(nullset,x) = false

s4   contains(insert(s,x_1),x_2) = **if** $x_1 = x_2$ **then** true
            else contains(s,x_2)

s5   size(nullset) = 0

s6   size(insert(s,x)) = **if** contains(s,x) **then** size(s) **else** 1 + size(s)

s7   remove(nullset,x) = nullset

s6   remove(insert(s,x_1),x_2) = **if** $x_1 = x_2$ **then** remove(s,x_2)
            else insert(remove(s,x_2),x_1)

s9 first(nullset) = undefined

s10 first(insert(s,x)) =
      if empty(s) **then** x
      else if $x <$ first(s) **then** x **else** first(s)

s11 rest(s) = **if** empty(s) **then** s **else** remove(s,first(s))

s12 select(nullset) = undefined

s13 contains(insert(s,x), select(insert(s,x))) = true

s14 union(nullset,s) = s

s15 union(insert(s_1,x),s_2) = insert(union(s_1,s_2),x)

s16 intersect(nullset,s) = nullset

s17 intersect(insert(s_1,x),s_2) =
      if contains(s_2,x) **then** insert(intersect(s_1,s_2),x)
      else intersect(s_1,s_2)

s18 difference(nullset,s) = nullset

s19 difference(insert(s_1,x),s_2) =
      if contains(s_2,x) **then** difference(s_1,s_2)
      else insert(difference(s_1,s_2),x)

s20 equal(nullset,s) = empty(s)

s21 equal(insert(s_1,x),s_2) =
      contains(s_2,x) & equal(remove(s_1,x), remove(s_2,x))

s22 insert(insert(s,x_1),x_2) = insert(insert(s,x_2),x_1)

s23 insert(insert(s,x),x) = insert(s,x)

theorems

s1T union(s,nullset) = s

s2T intersect(s,nullset) = nullset

s3T difference(s,nullset) = s

B.10 Data Type String (string, st)

operations
- nullstr $\quad\qquad\qquad\qquad\qquad\qquad\qquad \rightarrow$ string
- inschar $\qquad\qquad\qquad$ string $\times$ char $\rightarrow$ string
- concat $\qquad\qquad\qquad$ string $\times$ string $\rightarrow$ string

synonyms

nullstr $\equiv$ " "

inschar(...(inschar(nullstr,a_1),...),a_n) $\equiv$ "$a_1...a_n$"

concat(s_1,s_2) $\equiv$ $s_1 \| s_2$

axioms

st1 $\quad$ concat(s,nullstr) = s

st2 $\quad$ concat(s_1,inschar(s_2,a)) = inschar(concat(s_1,s_2),a)

theorems

st1T $\quad$ concat(nullstr,s) = s

Appendix C

Prototype Graphics Language
with Tree-Structured Pictures

C.1 Summary of Operations

User Interaction (ip)   Appendix C.2

prompt	string $\rightarrow$	
getkey		$\rightarrow$ char
getposn		$\rightarrow$ point
getpick		$\rightarrow$ name
post	tpicture x name $\rightarrow$	
unpost	name $\rightarrow$	

Tree-Structured Picture (tpicture,tp)   Appendix C.3

nullpict		$\rightarrow$ tpicture
setcolor	tpicture x color	$\rightarrow$ tpicture
moveto	tpicture x point	$\rightarrow$ tpicture
lineto	tpicture x point	$\rightarrow$ tpicture
box	tpicture x point x point	$\rightarrow$ tpicture
text	tpicture x string	$\rightarrow$ tpicture
insprogeny	tpicture x tpicture x grtrans x name	$\rightarrow$ tpicture
curcolor	tpicture	$\rightarrow$ color
curpost	picture	$\rightarrow$ point
getprogeny	tpicture x name	$\rightarrow$ tpicture
gettrans	tpicture x name	$\rightarrow$ grtrans
delprogeny	tpicture x name	$\rightarrow$ tpicture
instrans	tpicture x name x grtrans	$\rightarrow$ tpicture
append	tpicture x tpicture	$\rightarrow$ tpicture

synonyms

append(P_1,P_2) $\equiv$ $P_1 + P_2$

Graphical Transformation (grtrans,gt)   Appendix B.4

grtrans	geomfcn x region → grtrans
identity	→ geomfcn
gpartof	grtrans → geomfcn
rpartof	grtrans → region
compose	grtrans x grtrans → grtrans

synonyms

grtrans(G,R) ≡ $T^{gr}\langle G,R\rangle$

compose(T_1,T_2) ≡ $T_1 \circ T_2$

Geometric Function (geomfcn,gf)   Appendix B.5

scale	real → geomfcn
translate	real x real → geomfcn
compose	geomfcn x geomfcn → geomfcn
identity	→ geomfcn
inverse	geomfcn → geomfcn
transform	geomfcn x point → point

synonyms

compose(G_1,G_2) ≡ $G_1 \circ G_2$

inverse(G) ≡ G_{-1}

Region (rg)   Appendix B.6

nullregion	→ region
universe	→ region
lineseg	point x point → region
box	point x point → region
intersect	region x region → region
union	region x region → region
difference	region x region → region
empty	region → boolean

synonyms
   nullregion $\equiv$ $\emptyset$
   universe $\equiv$ U
   intersect(R_1,R_2) $\equiv$ $R_1 \cap R_2$
   union(R_1,R_2) $\equiv$ $R_1 \cup R_2$
   difference(R_1,R_2) $\equiv$ $R_1 - R_2$

Point (point,pt)   Appendix B.7

point	real × real →	point
polarpt	real × real →	point
origin	→	point
absissa	point →	real
ordinate	point →	real
radius	point →	real
angle	point →	real
sum	point × point →	point
difference	point × point →	point

synonyms
   sum(p_1,p_2) $\equiv$ $p_1 + p_2$
   difference(p_1,p_2) $\equiv$ $p_1 - p_2$

String (string,st)   Appendix B.10

nullstr	→	string
inschar	string × char →	string
concat	string × string →	string

synonyms
   nullstr $\equiv$ " "
   inschar(...(inschar(nullstr,a_1),...),a_n) $\equiv$ "$a_1...a_n$"
   concat(s_1,s_2) $\equiv$ $s_1 \| s_2$

C.2 User Interaction (ip)

program operations

promptstring	→	
getkey	→	char
getposn	→	point
getpick	→	name
post	tpicture x name →	
unpost	name →	

user actions

getprompt	→	string
keystroke	char →	
position	point →	
pick	point →	boolean

basic state generators

(The event functions are the basic state generators.)

auxiliary functions

* postpict	state →	tpicture
* pickname	state x point →	name
* image	state →	picture

axioms

getkey

    ip1   :wait($init) = true

    ip2   :wait(getkey$return(S)) = true

    ip3   :wait(keystroke$return(S,c)) = false

    ip4   :value($init) = undefined

    ip5   :value(keystroke$return(S,c)) = c

getposn

    ip6   :wait($init) = true

    ip7   :wait(getposn$return(S)) = true

    ip8   :wait(position$return(S,p)) = false

ip9　:value($init) = undefined
ip10　:value(position$return(S,p)) = p

getpick
　　ip11　:wait($init) = true
　　ip12　:wait(getpick$return(S)) = true
　　ip13　:wait(pick$return(S,p)) =
　　　　　　　¬p.visible(image(S),rg.pickregion(p))
　　ip14　:value($init) = undefined
　　ip15　:value(pick$return(S,p)) = pickname(S,p)

getprompt
　　ip16　:wait($init) = true
　　ip17　:wait(prompt$return(S,s)) = false
　　ip18　:wait(getprompt$return(S)) = true
　　ip19　:value($init) = nullstring
　　ip20　:value(prompt$return(S,s)) = s

pick
　　ip21　:value(S,p) = ¬p.visible(image(S),rg.pickregion(p))

ip22　postpict($init) = tp.nullpict
ip23　postpict(post$return(S,P,n)) =
　　　　　tp.insprogeny(tp.delprogeny(postpict(S),n),P,gt.identity,n)
ip24　postpict(unpost$return(S,n)) =
　　　　　tp.delprogeny(postpict(S),n)

ip25　pickname(S,p) =
　　　　　if s.empty(tp.picknames(postpict(S),rg.pickregion(p))
　　　　　then n.null
　　　　　else s.first(tp.picknames(postpict(S),rg.pickregion(p)))

ip26　image(S) = tp.display(postpict(S))

C.3 Tree-Structured Picture (tpicture,tp)

operations

• nullpict	→	tpicture
• setcolor	tpicture x color →	tpicture
• moveto	tpicture x point →	tpicture
• lineto	tpicture x point →	tpicture
• box	tpicture x point x point →	tpicture
• text	tpicture x string →	tpicture
• insprogeny	tpicture x tpicture x grtrans x name →	tpicture
curcolor	tpicture →	color
curpos	tpicture →	point
getprogeny	tpicture x name →	tpicture
gettrans	tpicture x name →	grtrans
delprogeny	tpicture x name →	tpicture
instrans	tpicture x name x grtrans →	tpicture
append	tpicture x tpicture →	tpicture
* display	tpicture →	picture
* nodedisplay	tpicture →	picture
* picknames	tpicture x region →	set(name)

synonyms

append(P_1,P_2) = P_1 + P_2

axioms

tp1 curcolor(nullpict) = fgnd

tp2 curcolor(setcolor(P,c)) = c

tp3 curpos(nullpict) = origin

tp4 curpos(moveto(P,x)) = x

tp5 curpos(lineto(P,x)) = x

tp6 getprogeny(nullpict,n) = undefined

tp7 getprogeny(setcolor(P,c),n) = getprogeny(P,n)

tp8 getprogeny(moveto(P,x),n) = getprogeny(P,n)

tp9 getprogeny(lineto(P,x),n) = getprogeny(P,n)

tp10 getprogeny(box(P,x_1,x_2),n) = getprogeny(P,n)
tp11 getprogeny(text(P,s),n) = getprogeny(P,n)
tp12 getprogeny(insprogeny(P_1,P_2,T,n_1),n_2) =
　　　　if n_1 = n_2 **then** P_2 **else** getprogeny(P_1,n_2)

tp13 gettrans(nullpict,n) = undefined
tp14 gettrans(insprogeny(P_1,P_2,T,n_1),n_2) =
　　　　if n_1 = n_2 **then** T **else** gettrans(P_1,n_2)

tp15 delprogeny(nullpict,n) = nullpict
tp16 delprogeny(insprogeny(P_1,P_2,T,n_1),n_2) =
　　　　if n_1 = n_2 **then** delprogeny(P_1,n_2)
　　　　else insprogeny(delprogeny(P_1,n_2),P_2,T,n_1)

tp17 instrans(nullpict,n,T) = nullpict
tp18 instrans(insprogeny(P_1,P_2,T_1,n_1),n_2,T_2) =
　　　　if n_1 = n_2 **then** insprogeny(instrans(P_1,n_2,T_2),P_2,T_2,n_1)
　　　　else insprogeny(instrans(P_1,n_2,T_2),P_2,T_1,n_1)

tp19 append(P,nullpict) = moveto(setcolor(P,default),origin)
tp20 append(P_1,setcolor(P_2,c)) = setcolor(append(P_1,P_2),c)
tp21 append(P_1,moveto(P_2,x)) = moveto(append(P_1,P_2),x)
tp22 append(P_1,lineto(P_2,x)) = lineto(append(P_1,P_2),x)
tp23 append(P_1,box(P_2,x_1,x_2)) = box(append(P_1,P_2),x_1,x_2)
tp24 append(P_1,text(P_2,s)) = text(append(P_1,P_2),s)
tp25 append(P_1,insprogeny(P_2,P_3,T,n)) =
　　　　insprogeny(append(P_1,P_2),P_3,T,n)

tp26 display(nullpict) = p.nullpict
tp27 display(lineto(P,x)) =
　　　　p.sum(display(P), p.lineseg(curpos(P),x,curcolor(P)))
tp28 display(box(P,x_1,x_2)) =
　　　　p.sum(display(P), p.box(x_1,x_2,curcolor(P)))
tp29 display(text(P,s)) =
　　　　p.sum(display(P), p.text(curpos(P),s,curcolor(P)))
tp30 display(insprogeny(P_1,P_2,T,n)) =
　　　　p.sum(display(P_1), gt.transform(T,display(P_2)))

tp31 picknames(nullpict,R) = nullset

tp32 picknames(insprogeny(P_1,P_2,T,n),R) =
      if visible(gt.transform(T,nodedisplay(P_2)))
      then {n} ∪ picknames(P_1,R) ∪
        picknames(P_2, rg.transform(gpartof(T)$^{-1}$,R) ∩ rpartof(T))
      else picknames(P_1,R) ∪
        picknames(P_2, rg.transform(gpartof(T)$^{-1}$,R) ∩ rpartof(T))

tp33 nodedisplay(nullpict) = p.nullpict

tp34 nodedisplay(lineto(P,x)) =
      p.sum(nodedisplay(P), p.lineseg(curpos(P),x,curcolor(P)))

tp35 nodedisplay(box(P,x_1,x_2)) =
      p.sum(nodedisplay(P), p.box(x_1,x_2,curcolor(P)))

tp36 nodedisplay(text(P,s)) =
      p.sum(nodedisplay(P), p.text(curpos(P),s,curcolor(P)))

tp37 nodedisplay(insprogeny(P_1,P_2,T,n)) = nodedisplay(P_1)

theorems

tp1T (P_1 + P_2) + P_3 = P_1 + (P_2 + P_3)

tp2T display(P_1 + P_2) = display(P_1) + display(P_2)

tp3T display(P_1 + P_2) = display(P_2 + P_1)

Prototype Graphics Language
with Picture-Hierarchy

D.1 Summary of Operations

User Interaction(ih)   Appendix D.2

prompt	string →	
getkey		→ char
getposn		→ point
getpick		→ name
post	name →	
unpost	name →	

Picture-Hierarchy (ph)   Appendix D.3

inspict	spicture × name →	
insnode	grtrans × name →	
link	name × name →	
getpict	name →	spicture
gettrans	name →	grtrans
comptrans	grtrans × name →	
unlink	name × name →	
progeny	name →	set(name)

Simple Picture (spicture,sp)   Appendix B.3

nullpict	color →	spicture
setcolor	spicture × color →	spicture
moveto	spicture × point →	spicture
lineto	spicture × point →	spicture
box	spicture × point × point →	spicture
text	spicture × string →	spicture
curpos	spicture →	point
curcolor	spicture →	color
append	spicture × spicture →	spicture

synonyms

$append(P_1, P_2) \equiv P_1 + P_2$

Graphical Transformation (grtrans,gt)   Appendix B.4

grtrans	geomfcn × region → grtrans
identity	→ geomfcn
gpartof	grtrans → geomfcn
rpartof	grtrans → region
compose	grtrans × grtrans → grtrans

synonyms

grtrans(G,R) ≡ T^{gr}⟨G,R⟩
compose(T$_1$,T$_2$) ≡ T$_1$ ∘ T$_2$

Geometric Function (geomfcn,gf)   Appendix B.5

scale	real → geomfcn
translate	real × real → geomfcn
compose	geomfcn × geomfcn → geomfcn
identity	→ geomfcn
inverse	geomfcn → geomfcn
transform	geomfcn × point → point

synonyms

compose(G$_1$,G$_2$) ≡ G$_1$ ∘ G$_2$
inverse(G) ≡ G^{-1}

Region (rg)   Appendix B.6

nullregion	→ region
universe	→ region
lineseg	point × point → region
box	point × point → region
intersect	region × region → region
union	region × region → region
difference	region × region → region
empty	region → boolean

synonyms
    nullregion $\equiv \emptyset$
    universe $\equiv$ U
    intersect$(R_1,R_2) \equiv R_1 \cap R_2$
    union$(R_1,R_2) \equiv R_1 \cup R_2$
    difference$(R_1,R_2) \equiv R_1 - R_2$

Point (point,pt)   Appendix B.7

point	real × real → point
polarpt	real × real → point
origin	→ point
absissa	point → real
ordinate	point → real
radius	point → real
angle	point → real
sum	point × point → point
difference	point × point → point

synonyms
    sum$(p_1,p_2) \equiv p_1 + p_2$
    difference$(p_1,p_2) \equiv p_1 - p_2$

String (string,st)   Appendix B.10

nullstr	→ string
inschar	string × char → string
concat	string × string → string

synonyms
    nullstr $\equiv$ " "
    inschar$(...(inschar(nullstr,a_1),...),a_n) \equiv$ "$a_1...a_n$"
    concat$(s_1,s_2) \equiv s_1 \parallel s_2$

D.2 User Interaction (ih)

program operations
prompt	string →
getkey	→ char
getposn	→ point
getpick	→ name
post	name →
unpost	name →

user actions
getprompt	→ string
keystroke	char →
position	point →
pick	point → boolean

basic state generators
*• $init	→ state
*• $prompt	state × string → state
*• $getkey	state → state
*• $getposn	state → state
*• $getpick	state → state
*• $post	state × name → state
*• $getprompt	state → state
*• $keystroke	state × char → state
*• $position	state × point → state
*• $pick	state × point → state

auxiliary functions
* postset	state → set(name)
* image	state → picture

axioms

prompt
   ih1 $return(S,s) = $prompt(S,s)

getkey
   ih2   :wait($init) = true
   ih3   :wait($getkey(S)) = true
   ih4   :wait($keystroke(S,c)) = false
   ih6   :value($init) = undefined
   ih7   :value($keystroke(S,c)) = c
   ih8 $return(S) = $getkey(S)

getposn
   ih9   :wait($init) = true
   ih10 :wait($getposn(S)) = true
   ih11 :wait($position(S,p)) = false
   ih13 :value($init) = undefined
   ih14 :value($position(S,p)) = p
   ih12 $return(S) = $getposn(S)

getpick
   ih16 :wait($init) = true
   ih17 :wait($getpick(S)) = true
   ih18 :wait($pick(S,p)) = ¬visible(image(S),pickregion(p))
   ih20 :value($init) = undefined
   ih21 :value($pick(S,p)) =
               if (s.empty(ph.picksetnames(S,postset(S),pickregion(p)))
               then n.null
               else s.first(ph.picksetnames(S,postset(S),pickregion(p)))
   ih19 $return(S) = $getpick(S)

post
   ih23 $return(S,n) = $post(S,n)

unpost
   ih24 $return($init,n) = $init
   ih25 $return($post(S,n_1),n_2) = **if** $n_1 = n_2$ **then** $return(S,$n_2$)
               else $post($return(S,n_2),n_1)

getprompt
    ih26   :wait($init) = true
    ih27   :wait($prompt(S,s)) = false
    ih28   :wait($getprompt(S)) = true
    ih30   :value($init) = nullstring
    ih31   :value($prompt(S,s)) = s
    ih29 $return(S) = $getprompt(S)

keystroke
    ih33 $return(S,c) = $keystroke(S,c)

position
    ih34 $return(S,p) = $position(S,p)

pick
    ih35   :value(S,p) = ¬visible(image(S),pickregion(p))
    ih36 $return(S,p) = $pick(S,p)

ih37   postset($init) = nullset
ih38   postset($post(S,n)) = insert(postset(S),n)

ih39   image(S) = ph.displayset(S,postset(S))

D.3 The Picture-Hierarchy (ph)

program operations
inspict	spicture × name →
insnode	grtrans × name →
link	name × name →
getpict	name → spicture
gettrans	name → grtrans
comptrans	grtrans × name →
unlink	name × name →
progeny	name → set(name)

basic state generators
- $init   → state
- $inspict   state × spicture × name → state
- $insnode   state × grtrans × name → state
- $link   state × name × name → state

auxiliary operations
- ⋆ ispict   state × name → boolean
- ⋆ isnode   state × name → boolean
- ⋆ isancestorof   state × name × name → boolean
- ⋆ display   state × name → picture
- ⋆ displayset   state × set(name) → picture
- ⋆ picknames   state × name × region → set(name)
- ⋆ picksetnames   state × set(name) × region → set(name)

axioms

inspict

ph1 $return(S,P,n) = **if** $\neg$empty(progeny:value(S,n))
           then error **else** $inspict(S,P,n)

insnode

ph2 $return(S,T,n) = $insnode(S,T,n)

link

ph3 $return(S,$n_1$,$n_2$) =
        if $\neg$isnode(S,n_1)|($\neg$isnode(S,n_2) & $\neg$ispict(S,n_2))
          |isancestorof(S,n_2,n_1)
          |s.contains(progeny:value(S,n_1), n_2)
        then error
        else $link(S,$n_1$,$n_2$)

getpict

ph4   :value($init,n) = error
ph5   :value($inspict(S,P,$n_1$),$n_2$) =
        if $n_1 = n_2$ **then** P **else** :value(S,n_2)
ph6   :value($insnode(S,T,$n_1$),$n_2$) =
        if $n_1 = n_2$ **then** error **else** :value(S,n_2)
ph7   :value($link(S,$n_1$,$n_2$),$n_3$) = :value(S,$n_3$)
ph8 $return(S,n) = S

gettrans

ph9: value($init,n) = error
ph10 :value($inspict(S,P,$n_1$),$n_2$) =
        if $n_1 = n_2$ **then** error **else** :value(S,n_2)
ph11 :value($insnode(S,T,$n_1$),$n_2$) =
        if $n_1 = n_2$ **then** T **else** :value(S,n_2)
ph12 :value($link(S,$n_1$,$n_2$),$n_3$) = :value(S,$n_3$)
ph13 $return(S,n) = S

comptrans

ph14 $return(S,T,n) =
      $insnode(S, gt.compose(T,gettrans:value(S,n)), n)

unlink
    ph15 return($\$init,n_1,n_2$) = $\$init$
    ph16 $\$return(\$link(S,n_1,n_2),n_3,n_4)$ = **if** $n_1 = n_3$ & $n_2 = n_4$ **then** S
            else $\$link(\$return(S,n_3,n_4),n_1,n_2)$

progeny
    ph17 :value($\$init,n$) = nullset
    ph18 :value($\$link(S,n_1,n_2),n_3$) =
            if $n_1 = n_3$ **then** $\{n_2\}$ ∪ :value(S,n_3)
            else :value(S,n_3)
    ph19 $\$return(S,n)$ = S

ph20 ispict($\$init,n$) = false
ph21 ispict($\$inspict(S,P,n_1),n_2$) =
           if $n_1 = n_2$ **then** true **else** ispict(S,n_2)
ph22 ispict($\$insnode(S,T,n_1),n_2$) =
           if $n_1 = n_2$ **then** false **else** ispict(S,n_2)
ph23 ispict($\$link(S,n_1,n_2),n_3$) = ispict($S,n_3$)

ph24 isnode($\$init,n$) = false
ph25 isnode($\$inspict(S,P,n_1),n_2$) =
           if $n_1 = n_2$ **then** false **else** isnode(S,n_2)
ph26 isnode($\$insnode(S,T,n_1),n_2$) =
           if $n_1 = n_2$ **then** true **else** isnode(S,n_2)
ph27 isnode($\$link(S,n_1,n_2),n_3$) = isnode($S,n_3$)

ph28 isancestorof($\$init,n_1,n_2$) = $(n_1 = n_2)$
ph29 isancestorof($\$link(S,n_1,n_2),n_3,n_4$) =
           isancestorof(S,n_3,n_4)
           |(isancestorof(S,n_3,n_1) & isancestorof(S,n_2,n_4))

ph30 display(S,n) = **if** ¬ispict(S,n) & ¬isnode(S,n) **then** p.nullpict
           else if ispict(S,n) **then** sp.display(getpict:value(S,n))
           else gt.transform(displayset(S,progeny:value(S,n)),
             gettrans:value(S,n))

ph31 displayset(S,N) =
        if s.empty(N) **then** p.nullpict
        else p.sum(display(S,s.first(N)), displayset(S,s.rest(N)))

ph32 picknames(S,n,R) =
      if ¬p.visible(display(S,n),R) **then** ∅
      else if isleaf(S,n) **then** {n}
      else picksetnames(S,progeny:value(S,n),
          rg.transform(inverse(gpartof(gettrans:value(S,n))), R)
         ∩ rpartof(gettrans:value(S,n)))

ph33 picksetnames(S,N,R) =
      if s.empty(N) **then** ∅
      else picknames(S,s.first(N),R)
         ∪ picksetnames(S,s.rest(N),R)

theorems

ph1T isancestorof(S,n,n) = true
ph2T ispict(S,n_1) & $n_1 \neq n_2$ ⇒ isancestorof(S,n_1,n_2) = false
ph3T ¬isancestorof(S,n_2,n_1) ⇒
      display($inspict(S,P,$n_1$),$n_2$) = display(S,$n_2$)
ph4T ¬isancestorof(S,n_2,n_1) ⇒
      display($insnode(S,T,$n_1$),$n_2$) = display(S,$n_2$)
ph5T ¬isancestorof(S,n_3,n_1) ⇒
      display($link(S,$n_1$,$n_2$),$n_3$) = display(S,$n_3$)

Appendix E

A Specification for
the Core Graphics System

The following specification describes a portion of the Core Graphics system, which is defined in the revised report of the ACM SIGGRAPH Graphics Standards Planning Committee [GSPC79]. A discussion and evaluation are given in Section 5.5. The specification is presented as an event algebra (Section 4.2) in two parts with a common state object. The first part contains the operations for generating pictures and has abbreviation cg; the second part contains the interactive input primitives and has abbreviation ci. The operations are grouped according to the categories used in the report. Operation names are the same as in the report, except that some of the longer names are shortened. As discussed in Section 5.5, several data types have been introduced to mask out details, and operation functionalities are altered accordingly.

Some of the notation used here does not appear elsewhere in the dissertation:

1) For each operation Op that returns more than one result, such as await_event in Section E.2, value functions are defined with names Op:value1, Op:value2, etc. as needed.

2) In conditional tests, the notation

$$(x_1,...,z_n) = (y_1,...,y_n)$$

is an abbreviation for

$$(x_1 = y_1) \& ...\& (x_n = y_n).$$

3) The value default refers to a system defined default (as specified by the standard), and default(x) indicates a default that varies with x.

A number of auxiliary functions (including basic state generators) are defined; some are necessary to make an algebraic specification possible (see Section 3.5.3) and others are introduced for increased clarity. The name of each auxiliary function is chosen to suggest its meaning. The axiomatizations for the operations $picked_primitive and $current_event_report make use of implicit axiom $im4$ rather than axiom $im2$ as would be expected from the discussion in Section 3.5.6. The other operations conform to convention.

To illustrate how the axioms should be interpreted, consider axioms $ci6$ through $ci10$ for the operation await_event in Section E.2. The effect on the interactive state when await_event is called (axiom $ci6$) is to set the elapsed time to zero (using the $time\_zero function, a basic state generator). Await_event cannot return ($ci7$) until either the elapsed time (time function, $ci67$-$ci69$) exceeds the time-out period given by parameter t, or the event queue is empty (queue_empty function, $ci103$-$ci107$). Two values are then returned (see the functionality specification for await_event). The first value ($ci8$) is the device class (current_class function, $ci116$) of the current event report, after the previous event report has been dequeued ($dequeue_event function, $ci96$-$ci100$). The second value ($ci9$) is the device name(current_device function, $ci117$) from the same event report. The effect on the interactive state at return ($ci10$) is to dequeue the previous event report ($dequeue_event function, $ci96$-$ci100$), unless the queue is already empty (queue_empty function, $ci103$-$ci107$).

E.1 Picture Generation (cg)

output primitives

move_abs	point →
move_rel	point →
line_abs	point →
line_rel	point →
marker_abs	point →
marker_rel	point →
text	string →
current_position	→ point

segmentation

create_ret_segment	name →
close_ret_segment	→
delete_ret_segment	name →
delete_all_ret_segments	→
rename_ret_segment	name x name →
open_ret_segment	→ name
create_temp_segment	name →
close_temp_segment	→
open_temp_segment→	boolean

segment attributes

set_visibility	name x boolean →
set_detectability	name x integer →
set_image_trans	name x geomfcn →
segment_visibility	name → boolean
segment_detectability	name → integer
image_trans	name → geomfcn

primitive attributes

set_color	color →
set_marker_symbol	symbol →
set_pickid	name →
color	→ color
marker_symbol	→ symbol
pickid	→ name

viewing operations

set_viewing_parameters	grtrans →
viewing_parameters	→ grtrans
set_world_coord_trans	geomfcn →
world_coord_trans	→ geomfcn
ndc_to_world	point → point
world_to_ndc	point → point

control

initialize_core	→
new_frame	→

basic state generators

*• $init	→ state
*• $move	state × point → state
*• $line	state × point → state
*• $marker	state × point → state
*• $text	state × string → state
*• $ret_segment	state × name × boolean × integer × geomfcn → state
*• $temp_segment	state → state
*• $close_segment	state → state
*• $color	state × color → state
*• $marker_symbo	lstate × symbol → state
*• $pickid	state × name → state
*• $viewing_trans	state × grtrans → state
*• $world_coord_trans	state × geomfcn → state

auxiliary functions

* $delete_ret_segment   state x name → state
* $set_visibility   state x name x boolean → state
* $set_image_trans state x name x geomfcn → state
* $new_frame   state → state
* segment_exists   state x name → boolean
* segment_open   state → boolean
* current_segment_visible   state → boolean
* any_ret_segment_visible   state → boolean
* current_segment_detectability   state → integer
* world_to_ndc_trans   state → geomfcn
* world_to_view_surface_trans   state → grtrans
* program_image   state → picture
* image   state → picture

axioms

move_abs

  cg1 $return(S,x) = **if** segment_open(S)
     then $move(S,x) **else** error

move_rel

  cg2 $return(S,x) = **if** segment_open(S)
     then $move(s, x + current_position:value(S)) **else** error

line_abs

  cg3 $return(S,x) = **if** segment_open(S)
     then $line(S,x) **else** error

line_rel

  cg4 $return(S,x) = **if** segment_open(S)
     then $line(S,x + current_position:value(S)) **else** error

marker_abs

  cg5 $return(S,x) = **if** segment_open(S)
     then $marker(S,x) **else** error

marker_rel

  cg6 $return(S,x) = **if** segment_open(S)
     then $marker(S, x + current_position:value(S)) **else** error

text

  cg7 $return(S,s) = **if** segment_open(S)
     then $text(S,s) **else** error

current_position
- *cg8*   :value($init) = origin
- *cg9*   :value($move(S,x)) = x
- *cg10* :value($line(S,x)) = x
- *cg11* :value($marker(S,x)) = x

create_ret_segment
- *cg12* $return(S,a) = **if** segment_open(S) | segment_exists(S,a)
      then error
      else $move($ret_segment(S,a,true,0,gf.identity),
       current_position(S))

close_ret_segment
- *cg13* $return(S) = $close_segment(S)

delete_ret_segment
- *cg14* $return(S,a) = **if** segment_visibility:value(S,a)
      then $new_frame($delete_ret_segment(S,a))
      else $delete_ret_segment(S,a)

delete_all_ret_segments
- *cg15* $return(S) = **if** any_ret_segment_visible(S)
      then $new_frame($delete_ret_segment(S,null))
      else $delete_ret_segment(S,null)

rename_ret_segment
- *cg16* $return($init,a_1,a_2) = error
- *cg17* $return($ret_segment(S,a_1,v,d,G),a_2,a_3) =
      if a_1 = a_2 **then** $ret_segment(S,$a_3$,v,d,G)
      else $ret_segment($return(S,a_2,a_3),a_1,v,d,G)

open_ret_segment
- *cg18* :value($init) = null
- *cg19* :value($ret_segment(S,a,v,d,G)) = a
- *cg20* :value($close_segment(S)) = null

create_temp_segment
- *cg21* $return(S,a) = **if** segment_open(S) | segment_exists(S,a)
      then error
      else $move($temp_segment(S),current_position(S))

close_temp_segment
    cg22 $return(S) = $close_segment(S)

open_temp_segment
    cg23 :value($init) = false
    cg24 :value($temp_segment(S)) = true
    cg25 :value($close_segment(S)) = false

set_visibility
    cg26 $return(S,a,v) = **if** ¬segment_exists(S,a) **then** error
            else if ¬v & segment_visibility:value(S,a)
            then $new_frame($set_visibility(S,a,v))
            else $set_visibility(S,a,v)

set_detectability
    cg27 $return($init,a,d) = error
    cg28 $return($ret_segment(S,a_1,v,d_1,G),a_2,d_2) =
                if a_1 = a_2 **then** $ret_segment(S,$a_1$,v,$d_2$,G)
                else $ret_segment($return(s,a_2,d_2),a_1,v,d_1,G)

set_image_trans
    cg29 $return(S,a,G) = **if** ¬segment_exists(S,a) **then** error
                else $new_frame($set_image_trans(S,a,G))

segment_visibility
    cg30 :value($init,a) = error
    cg31 :value($ret_segment(S,$a_1$,v,d,G),$a_2$) =
                if a_1 = a_2 **then** v **else** :value(S,a_2)

segment_detectability
    cg32 :value($init,a) = error
    cg33 :value($ret_segment(S,$a_1$,v,d,G),$a_2$) =
                if a_1 = a_2 **then** d **else** :value(S,a_2)

image_trans
    cg34 :value($init,a) = error
    cg35 :value($ret_segment(S,$a_1$,v,d,G),$a_2$) =
                if a_1 = a_2 **then** G **else**   :value(S,a_2)

set_color
    cg36 $return(S,c) = $color(S,c)

set_marker_symbol
   cg37 $return(S,m) = $marker_symbol(S,m)

set_pickid
   cg38 $return(S,n) = $pickid(S,n)

color
   cg39   :value($init) = default
   cg40   :value($color(S,c)) = c

marker_symbol
   cg41   :value($init) = default
   cg42   :value($marker_symbol(S,m)) = m

pickid
   cg43   :value($init) = default
   cg44   :value($pickid(S,n)) = n

set_viewing_parameters
   cg45 $return(S,T) = $viewing_trans(S,T)

viewing_parameters
   cg46   :value($init) = gt.identity
   cg47   :value($viewing_trans(S,T) = T

set_world_coord_trans
   cg48 $return(S,G) = $world_coord_trans(S,G)

world_coord_trans
   cg49   :value($init) = gf.identity
   cg50   :value($world_coord_trans(S,G)) = G

ndc_to_world
   cg51   :value(S,p) =
              if gf.transform(world_coord_trans:value(S),p)
                 ε rpartof(viewing_parameters:value(S))
              then error
              else gf.transform(world_to_ndc_trans:value(S),p)

world_to ndc

 cg52   :value(S,p) =

    if ¬invertible(world_to_ndc_trans:value(S))

    then error

    else if gf.transform(gpartof(

     viewing_parameters:value(S))$^{-1}$,p)

       ∉ rpartof(viewing_parameters:value(S))

    then error

    else gf.transform(world_to_ndc_trans:value(S)$^{-1}$,p)

initialize_core

 cg53   \$return(S) = \$init

new_frame

 cg54   \$return(S) = \$new_frame(S)

cg55   \$delete_ret_segment(\$init,a) =

    if a = null **then** \$init **else** error

cg56   \$delete_ret_segment(\$move(S,x),a) =

    if a = null | open_ret_segment:value(S) = a

    then \$delete_ret_segment(S,a)

    else \$move(\$delete_ret_segment(S,a),x)

cg57   \$delete_ret_segment(\$line(S,x),a) =

    if a = null | open_ret_segment:value(S) = a

    then \$delete_ret_segment(S,a)

    else \$line(\$delete_ret_segment(S,a),x)

cg58   \$delete_ret_segment(\$marker(S,m),a) =

    if a = null | open_ret_segment:value(S) = a

    then \$delete_ret_segment(S,a)

    else \$marker(\$delete_ret_segment(S,a),m)

cg59   \$delete_ret_segment(\$text(S,s),a) =

    if a = null | open_ret_segment:value(S) = a

    then \$delete_ret_segment(S,a)

    else \$text(\$delete_ret_segment(S,s),c)

cg60   \$delete_ret_segment(\$ret_segment(S,a_1,v,d,G),a_2) =

    if a_2 = null | a_1 = a_2 **then** S

    else \$ret_segment(\$delete_ret_segment(S,a_2),a_1,v,d,G)

cg61 $delete_ret_segment($close_segment(S),a) =
  if a = null | open_ret_segment:value(S) = a
  then $delete_ret_segment(S,a)
  else $close_segment($delete_ret_segment(S,a))

cg62 $delete_ret_segment(ci.$set_echo_segment(S,c,d,a_1),a_2) =
  if a_2 = null | a_1 = a_2 **then** $delete_ret_segment(S,$a_2$)
  else ci.$set_echo_segment(
    $delete_ret_segment(S,$a_2$,),c,d,$a_1$)

cg63 $set_visibility($init,a,v) = error

cg64 $set_visibility($ret_segment(S,a_1,v_1,d,G),a_2,v_2) =
  if a_1 = a_2 **then** $ret_segment(S,$a_1$,$v_2$,d,G)
  else $ret_segment($set_visibility(s,a_2,v_2),a_1,v_1,d,G)

cg65 $set_image_trans($init,a,G) = error

cg66 $set_image_trans($ret_segment(S,a_1,v,d,G_1),a_2,G_2) =
  if a_1 = a_2 **then** $ret_segment(S,$a_1$,v,d,$G_2$)
  else $ret_segment($set_image_trans(s,a_2,G_2),a_1,v,G_1)

cg67 $new_frame($init,a) = $init

cg68 $new_frame($move(S,x),a) =
  if open_temp_segment:value(S) **then** $new_frame(S)
  else $move($new_frame(S,a),x)

cg69 $new_frame($line(S,x),a) =
  if open_temp_segment:value(S) **then** $new_frame(S)
  else $line($new_frame(S,a),x)

cg70 $new_frame($marker(S,m),a) =
  if open_temp_segment:value(S) **then** $new_frame(S)
  else $marker($new_frame(S,a),m)

cg71 $new_frame($text(S,s),a) =
  if open_temp_segment:value(S) **then** $new_frame(S)
  else $text($new_frame(S,s),c)

cg72 $new_frame($temp_segment(S)) = $new_frame(S)

cg73 $new_frame($close_segment(S),a) =
  if open_temp_segment:value(S) **then** $new_frame(S)
  else $close_segment($new_frame(S,a))

cg74 segment_exists($init,a) = false

cg75 segment_exists($ret_segment(S,$a_1$,v,d,G),$a_2$) =
      if a_1 = a_2 **then** true **else** segment_exists(S,a_2)

cg76 segment_open($init) = false

cg77 segment_open($ret_segment(S,a,v,d,G)) = true

cg78 segment_open($temp_segment(S)) = true

cg79 segment_open($close_segment(S)) = false

cg80 current_segment_visible($init) = false

cg81 current_segment_visible($ret_segment(S,a,v,d,G)) = v

cg82 current_segment_visible($temp_segment(S)) = true

cg83 any_ret_segment_visible($init) = false

cg84 any_ret_segment_visible($ret_segment(S,a,v,d,G)) =
      if v **then** true **else** any_ret_segment_visible(S)

cg85 current_segment_detectability($init) = 0

cg86 current_segment_detectability($ret_segment(S,a,v,d,G)) = d

cg87 current_segment_detectability($temp_segment(S)) = 0

cg88 world_to_ndc_trans(S) =
      gpartof(viewing_parameters:value(S)) ∘
       world_coord_trans:value(S)

cg89 world_to_view_surface_trans(S) =
      if open_temp_segment:value(S)
      then viewing_parameters:value(S) ∘
       grtrans(world_coord_trans:value(S),universe)
      else grtrans(image_trans:value(
       S,open_ret_segment:value(S)), universe) ∘
       viewing_parameters:value(S) ∘
       grtrans(world_coord_trans:value(S),universe)

cg90 program_image($init) = p.nullpict

cg91 program_image($line(S,x)) =
   if current_segment_visible(S)
   then program_image(S) +
      gt.transform(world_to_view_surface_trans(S),
      p.lineseg(current_position:value(S),x,color:value(S))
   else program_image(S)

cg92 program_image($text(S,s)) =
   if current_segment_visible(S)
   then program_image(S) +
      gt.transform(world_to_view_surface_trans(S),
      p.text(s,current_position:value(S),color:value(S))
   else program_image(S)

cg93 program_image($marker(S,m)) =
   if current_segment_visible(S)
   then program_image(S) +
      gt.transform(world_to_view_surface_trans(S),
      p.symbol(m,current_position:value(S),color:value(S))
   else program_image(S)

cg94 image(S) = program_image(S) + ci.echo_image(S)

E.2 User Interaction (ci)

input level 3

enable_device	class × device →
disable_device	class × device →
disable_all	→
read_locator	device → point
read_valuator	device → integer
await_event	integer → class × device
flush_device_events	class × device →
flush_all_events	→
associate	class × device × class × device →
disassociate	class × device × class × device →
disassociate_device	class × device →
disassociate_all	→
get_pick_data	→ name × name
get_keyboard_data	→ string
get_locator_data	device → point
get_valuator_data	device → real

input level 2

await_any_button   integer → device
await_pick   integer →
                                    device × name × name
await_keyboard   integer → device × string
await_any_button_get_locator
                   integer × device → device × point
await_any_button_get_valuator
                   integer × device → device × real

device control

set_echo   class × device × echotype →
set_echo_segment   class × device × name →
set_echo_position   class × device × point →
set_pick   device × region →

user actions

pick_event	device × point →
keyboard_event	device × char →
button_event	device →
new_locator_data	device × point →
new_valuator_data	device × real →

clock operation

next_second	→

basic state generators

*• $init	→ state
*• $enable_device	state × class × device → state
*• $disable_device	state × class × device → state
*• $enable_all	state → state
*• $disable_all	state → state
*• $time_zero	state → state
*• $queue_head	state → state
*• $associate	
	state × class × device × class × device → state
*• $disassociate	
	state × class × device × class × device → state
*• $disassociate_device	state × class × device → state
*• $disassociate_allstate	→ state
*• $set_echo	state × class × device × echotype → state
*• $set_echo_segment	
	state × class × device × name → state
*• $set_echo_position	
	state × class × device × point → state
*• $set_pick	state × device × region → state
*• $pick_event	state × device × point → state
*• $keyboard_event	state × device × char → state
*• $button_event	state × device → state
*• $new_locator_data	state × device × point → state
*• $new_valuator_data	state × device × real → state
*• $next_second	state → state

auxiliary functions

*	time	state → integer
*	enabled	state × class × device → boolean
*	associated	
		state × class × device × class × device → boolean
*	pick_region	state × device → region
*	picked_detectability	state × region → integer
*	$picked_primitive	state × region → state
*	keyboard_data	state × device → string
*	locator_data	state × device → point
*	valuator_dat	state × device → real
*	$dequeue_event	state → state
*	$current_event_report	state → state
*	queue_empty	state → boolean
*	event_class	state → class
*	event_device	state → device
*	current_class	state → class
*	current_device	state → device
*	sampled	class → boolean
*	echo_type	state × class × device → echotype
*	echo_segment	state × class × device → name
*	echo_position	state × class × device → point
*	pick_aperture	state × device → region
*	keyboard_image	state × device → picture
*	locator_image	state × device → picture
*	echo_image	state × state → picture

axioms

enable_device

    ci1 $return(S,c,d) = **if** enabled(S,c,d)

             then error **else** $enable_device(S,c,d)

disable_device

    ci2 $return(S,c,d) = **if** ¬enabled(S,c,d)

             then error **else** $disable_device(S,c,d)

disable_all

  ci3 $return(S) = $disable_all(S)

read_locator

  ci4   :value(S,d) = **if** ¬enabled(S,locator,d) **then** error
            else locator_data(S,d)

read_valuator

  ci5   :value(S,d) = **if** ¬enabled(S,valuator,d) **then** error
            else valuator_data(S,d)

await_event

  ci6 $call(S,t) = $time_zero(S)
  ci7   :wait(S,t) = time(S) < t & queue_empty(S)
  ci8   :value1(S,t) = current_class($dequeue_event(S))
  ci9   :value2(S,t) = current_device($dequeue_event(S))
  ci10 $return(S,t) =
            if queue_empty(S) **then** S **else** $dequeue_event(S)

flush_device_events

  ci11 $return($init,c,d) = $init
  ci12 $return($pick_event(S,d_1,x),c,d_2) =
            if c = pick & d_1 = d_2 **then** $return(S,c,$d_2$)
            else $pick_event($return(S,c,d_2),d_1,x)
  ci13 $return($keyboard_event(S,d_1,s),c,d_2) =
            if c = keyboard & d_1 = d_2 **then** $return(S,c,$d_2$)
            else $keyboard_event($return(S,c,d_2),d_1,s)
  ci14 $return($button_event(S,d_1),c,d_2) =
            if c = button & d_1 = d_2 **then** $return(S,c,$d_2$)
            else $button_event($return(S,c,d_2),d_1)

flush_all_events

  ci15 $return($init) = $init
  ci16 $return($pick_event(S,d,x)) = $return(S)
  ci17 $return($keyboard_event(S,d,s)) = $return(S)
  ci18 $return($button_event(S,d)) = $return(S)

associate
 ci19 $\$return(S,c_1,d_1,c_2,d_2) = $ **if** $\neg sampled(c_1)$ & $sampled(c_2)$ &
     $\neg\,associated(S,c_1,d_1,c_2,d_2)$
   then $\$associate(S,c_1,d_1,c_2,d_2)$ **else** error

disassociate
 ci20 $\$return(S,c_1,d_1,c_2,d_2) = $ **if** $\neg sampled(c_1)$ & $sampled(c_2)$ &
     $associated(S,c_1,d_1,c_2,d_2)$
   then $\$disassociate(S,c_1,d_1,c_2,d_2)$ **else** error

disassociate_device
 ci21 $\$return(S,c,d) = \$disassociate\_device(S,c,d)$

disassociate_all
 ci22 $\$return(S) = \$disassociate\_all(S)$

get_pick_data
 ci23 :value1(S) = **if** current_class(S) $\neq$ pick **then** error
   else cg.open_ret_segment:value(
    $picked_primitive(current_event_report(S),
    pick_region($current_event_report(S),
    current_device(S))))
 ci24 :value2(S) = **if** current_class(S) $\neq$ pick **then** error
   else cg.pickid:value(
    $picked_primitive(current_event_report(S),
    pick_data($current_event_report(S),
    current_device(S))))

get_keyboard_data
 ci25 :value(S) = **if** current_class(S) $\neq$ keyboard **then** error
   else keyboard_data($current_event_report(S),
    current_device(S))

get_locator_data
 ci26 :value(S,d) =
   if associated(S,current_class(S),current_device(S),
    locator,d)
    & enabled($current_event_report(S),locator,d)
   then locator_data($current_event_report(S),d)
   else error

get-valuator_data
   ci27   :value(S,d) =
               if associated(S,current_class(S),current_device(S),
                   valuator,d)
                   & enabled($current_event_report(S),valuator,d)
               then valuator_data($current_event_report(S),d)
               else error

await_any_button
   ci28 $call(S,t) =
               $time_zero($enable_all(flush_all_events$return(S)))
   ci29   :wait(S,t) = time(S) < t & event_class(S) ≠ button
   ci30   :value(S,t) = **if** event_class(S) = button
               then event_device(S) **else** null
   ci31 $return($init,t) = $init
   ci32 $return($enable_all(S),t) = $return(S,t)
   ci33 $return($pick_event(S,d,x),t) = $return(S,t)
   ci34 $return($keyboard_event(S,d,s),t) = $return(S,t)
   ci35 $return($button_event(S,d),t) = $return(S,t)

await_pick
   ci36 $call(S,t) = await_any_button$call(S,t)
   ci37   :wait(S,t) = time(S) < t & event_class(S) ≠ pick
   ci38   :value1(S,t) = **if** event_class(S) ≠ pick **then** null
               else event_device(S)
   ci39   :value2(S,t) = **if** event_class(S) ≠ pick **then** null
               else cg.open_ret_segment:value($picked_primitive(S,
                   pick_region(S,event_device(S))))
   ci40   :value3(S,t) = **if** event_class(S) ≠ pick **then** null
               else cg.pickid:value($picked_primitive(S,
                   pick_region(S,event_device(S))))
   ci41 $return(S,t) = await_any_button$return(S,t)

await_keyboard

ci42　$call(S,t) = await_any_button$call(S,t)

ci43　:wait(S,t) = time(S) < t & event_class(S) ≠ keyboard

ci44　:value1(S,t) = **if** event_class(S) ≠ keyboard **then** null
　　　　　　else event_device(S)

ci45　:value2(S,t) = **if** event_class(S) ≠ keyboard **then** null
　　　　　　else keyboard_data(S,event_device(S))

ci46　$return(S,t) = await_any_button$return(S,t)

await_any_button_get_locator

ci47　$call(S,t,d) = await_any_button$call(S,t)

ci48　:wait(S,t,d) = time(S) < t & event_class(S) ≠ button

ci49　:value1(S,t,d) = **if** event_class(S) ≠ button **then** null
　　　　　　else event_device(S)

ci50　:value2(S,t,d) = **if** event_class(S) ≠ button **then** null
　　　　　　else locator_data(S,d)

ci51　$return(S,t,d) = await_any_button$return(S,t)

await_any_button_get_valuator

ci52　$call(S,t,d) = await_any_button$call(S,t)

ci53　:wait(S,t,d) = time(S) < t & event_class(S) ≠ button

ci54　:value1(S,t,d) = **if** event_class(S) ≠ button **then** null
　　　　　　else event_device(S)

ci55　:value2(S,t,d) = **if** event_class(S) ≠ button **then** null
　　　　　　else valuator_data(S,d)

ci56　$return(S,t,d) = await_any_button$return(S,t)

set_echo

ci57　$return(S,c,d,e) = $set_echo(S,c,d,e)

set_echo_segment

ci58　$return(S,c,d,a) = **if** ¬segment_exists(S,a) **then** error
　　　　　　else $set_echo_segment(S,c,d,a)

set_echo_position

ci59　$return(S,c,d,x) = $set_echo_position(S,c,d,x)

set_pick

ci60　$return(S,d,R) = $set_pick(S,d,R)

pick_event

  ci61 $return(S,d,x) = **if** enabled(S,pick,d) &
            picked_detectability(S,pick_region(
            $pick_event(S,d,x))) ≠ 0
         then $pick_event(S,d,x) **else** S

keyboard_event

  ci62 $return(S,d,s) = **if** enabled(S,keyboard,d)
         then $keyboard_event(S,d,s) **else** S

button_event

  ci63 $return(S,d) = **if** enabled(S,button,d)
         then $button_event(S,d) **else** S

new_locator_data

  ci64 $return(S,d,x) = **if** ¬enabled(S,locator,d) |
         echo_segment(S,locator,d) = null **then** S
         else if echo_type(S,locator,d) = 7
         then cg.set_image_trans$return(
            $new_locator_data(S,d,x),
            echo_segment(S,locator,d),
            gf.translate(abscissa(x - echo_position(S,locator,d)),
            ordinate(x - echo_position(S,locator,d)))))
         else $new_locator_data(S,d,x)

new_valuator_data

  ci65 $return(S,d,r) =
            if ¬enabled(S,valuator,d) |
              echo_segment(S,valuator,d) = null
            then S
            else if echo_type(S,valuator,d) = 2
            then cg.set_image_trans$return(
              $new_valuator_data(S,d,r),
              echo_segment(S,valuator,d),gf.translate(r,0))
            else if echo_type(S,valuator,d) = 3
            then cg.set_image_trans$return(
              $new_valuator_data(S,d,r),
              echo_segment(S,valuator,d),gf.translate(0,r))
            else $new_valuator_data(S,d,r)

next_second
   ci66 $\$return(S) = \$next\_second(S)$

ci67 $time(\$init) = 0$
ci68 $time(\$time\_zero(S)) = 0$
ci69 $time(\$next\_second(S)) = 1 + time(S)$

ci70 $enabled(\$init,c,d) = false$
ci71 $enabled(\$enable\_device(S,c_1,d_1),c_2,d_2) =$
     if $(c_1,d_1) = (c_2,d_2)$ **then** true **else** $enabled(S,c_2,d_2)$
ci72 $enabled(\$disable\_device(S,c_1,d_1),c_2,d_2) =$
     if $(c_1,d_1) = (c_2,d_2)$ **then** false **else** $enabled(S,c_2,d_2)$
ci73 $enabled(\$disable\_all(S),c,d) = false$
ci74 $enabled(\$synchronous\_wait(S),c,d) = true$

ci75 $associated(\$init,c_1,d_1,c_2,d_2) = false$
ci76 $associated(\$associate(S,c_1,d_1,c_2,d_2),c_3,d_3,c_4,d_4) =$
     if $(c_1,d_1,c_2,d_2) = (c_3,d_3,c_4,d_4)$ **then** true
     else $associated(S,c_3,d_3,c_4,d_4)$

ci77 $associated(\$disassociate(S,c_1,d_1,c_2,d_2),c_3,d_3,c_4,d_4) =$
     if $(c_1,d_1,c_2,d_2) = (c_3,d_3,c_4,d_4)$ **then** false
     else $associated(S,c_3,d_3,c_4,d_4)$
ci78 $associated(\$disassociate\_device(S,c_1,d_1),c_2,d_2,c_3,d_3) =$
     if $(c_1,d_1) = (c_2,d_2) \,|\, (c_1,d_1) = (c_3,d_3)$ **then** false
     else $associated(S,c_2,d_2,c_3,d_3)$
ci79 $associated(\$disassociate\_all(S),c_1,d_1,c_2,d_2) = false$

ci80 $pick\_region(\$init,d) = undefined$
ci81 $pick\_region(\$pick\_event(S,d_1,x),d_2) =$
     if $d_1 \neq d_2$ **then** $pick\_region(S,d_2)$
     else $rg.transform(gf.translate(absissa(x),ordinate(x)),$
       $pick\_aperture(S,d_2))$

ci82   picked_detectability($init,R) = 0

ci83   picked_detectability(cg.$line(S,x),R) =
   if cg.current_segment_visible(S) &
    ¬cg.open_temp_segment(S) &
    p.visible(gt.transform(cg.world_to_view_surface_trans(S),
     p.lineseg(cg.current_position:value(S),x,cg.color:value(S)),R)
    & cg.current_segment_detectability(S)
      > picked_detectability(S,R)
   then cg.current_segment_detectability(S)
   else picked_detectability(S,R)

ci84   picked_detectability(cg.$text(S,s),R) =
   if cg.current_segment_visible(S) & ¬cg.open_temp_segment(S)
    & p.visible(gt.transform(cg.world_to_view_surface_trans(S),
    p.text(s,cg.current_position:value(S),cg.color:value(S)),R)
    & cg.current_segment_detectability(S)
      > picked_detectability(S,R)
   then cg.current_segment_detectability(S)
   else picked_detectability(S,R)

ci85   picked_detectability(cg.$marker(S,m),R) =
   if cg.current_segment_visible(S) & ¬cg.open_temp_segment(S)
    & p.visible(gt.transform(cg.world_to_view_surface_trans(S),
    p.marker(m,cg.current_position:value(S),cg.color:value(S)),R)
    & cg.current_segment_detectability(S)
     > picked_detectability(S,R)
   then cg.current_segment_detectability(S)
   else picked_detectability(S,R)

ci86 $picked_primitive($init,R) = $init

ci87 $picked_primitive(cg.$line(S,x),R) =
      if picked_detectability(cg.$line(S,x),R)
       > picked_detectability(S,R)
     then cg.$line(S,x) **else** $picked_primitive(S,R)

ci88 $picked_primitive(cg.$text(S,s),R) =
     if picked_detectability(cg.$text(S,s),R)
       > picked_detectability(S,R)
     then cg.$text(S,s) **else** $picked_primitive(S,R)

ci89 $picked_primitive(cg.$marker(S,m),R) =
     if picked_detectability(cg.$marker(S,m),R)
       > picked_detectability(S,R)
     then cg.$marker(S,m) **else** $picked_primitive(S,R)

ci90 keyboard_data($init,d) = undefined
ci91 keyboard_data($keyboard_event(S,$d_1$,s),$d_2$) =
     if d_1 = d_2 **then** s **else** keyboard_data(S,d_2)

ci92 locator_data($init,d) = undefined
ci93 locator_data($new_locator_data(S,$d_1$,x),$d_2$) =
     if d_1 = d_2 **then** x **else** locator_data(S,d_2)

ci94 valuator_data($init,d) = undefined
ci95 valuator_data($new_valuator_data(S,$d_1$,r),$d_2$) =
     if d_1 = d_2 **then** r **else** valuator_data(S,d_2)

ci96 $dequeue_event($init) = $init
ci97 $dequeue_event($queue_head(S)) =
     flush_all_events$return(S)
ci98 $dequeue_event($pick_event(S,d,x)) =
   if ¬queue_empty(S) **then** $pick_event($dequeue_event(S),d,x)
   else $queue_head($pick_event($dequeue_event(S),d,x))
ci99 $dequeue_event($keyboard_event(S,d,s)) =
   if ¬queue_empty(S)
   then $keyboard_event($dequeue_event(S),d,s)
   else $queue_head($keyboard_event($dequeue_event(S),d,s))
ci100 $dequeue_event($button_event(S,d)) =
   if ¬queue_empty(S) **then** $button_event($dequeue_event(S),d)
   else $queue_head($button_event($dequeue_event(S),d))

ci101 $current_event_report($init) = error
ci102 $current_event_report($queue_head(S)) = S

ci103 queue_empty($init) = true
ci104 queue_empty($queue_head(S)) = true
ci105 queue_empty($pick_event(S,d,x)) = false
ci106 queue_empty($keyboard_event(S,d,s)) = false
ci107 queue_empty($button_event(S,d)) = false

ci108 event_class($init) = undefined
ci109 event_class($pick_event(S,d,x)) = pick
ci110 event_class($keyboard_event(S,d,s)) = keyboard
ci111 event_class($button_event(S,d)) = button

ci112 event_device($init) = undefined
ci113 event_device($pick_event(S,d,x)) = d
ci114 event_device($keyboard_event(S,d,s)) = d
ci115 event_device($button_event(S,d)) = d

ci116 current_class(S) = **if** queue_empty(S) **then** null
       else event_class($current_event_report(S))

ci117 current_device(S) = **if** queue_empty(S) **then** null
       else event_device($current_event_report(S))

ci118 sampled(pick) = false
ci119 sampled(keyboard) = false
ci120 sampled(button) = false
ci121 sampled(locator) = true
ci122 sampled(valuator) = true

ci123 echo_type($init,c,d) = 1
ci124 echo_type($set_echo(S,$c_1$,$d_1$,e),$c_2$,$d_2$) =
    if (c_1,d_1) = (c_2,d_2) **then** e **else** echo_type(S,c_2,d_2)

ci125 echo_segment($init,c,d) = null

ci126 echo_segment($set_echo_segment(S,$c_1$,$d_1$,n),$c_2$,$d_2$) =
if (c_1,d_1) = (c_2,d_2) **then** n **else** echo_segment(S,c_2,d_2)

ci127 echo_position($init,c,d) = default(c,d)

ci128 echo_position($set_echo_position(S,$c_1$,$d_1$,x),$c_2$,$d_2$) =
if (c_1,d_1) = (c_2,d_2) **then** x **else** echo_position(S,c_2,d_2)

ci129 pick_aperture($init,d) = default(d)

ci130 pick_aperture($set_pick(S,$d_1$,R),$d_2$) =
if d_1 = d_2 **then** R **else** pick_aperture(S,d_2)

ci131 keyboard_image(S,d) =
if echo_type(S,keyboard,d) = 1
then p.text(keyboard_data(S,d),
echo_position(S,keyboard,d), cg.color:value(S))
else p.nullpict

ci132 locator_image(S,d) =
if echo_type(S,locator,d) = 1
then p.symbol(dot,locator_data(S,d),cg.color:value(S))
else if echo_type(S,locator,d) = 2
then p.lineseg(echo_position(S,c,d),locator_data(S,d),
cg.color:value(S))
else p.nullpict

ci133 echo_image($init,S) = p.nullpict

ci134 echo_image($enable_device($S_1$,c,d),$S_2$) =
if ¬enabled(S_2,c,d) **then** echo_image(S_1,S_2)
else if c = keyboard
then keyboard_image(S_2,d) +
echo_image(S_1,$disable_device($S_2$,c,d))
else if c = locator
then locator_image(S_2,d) +
echo_image(S_1,$disable_device($S_2$,c,d))
else echo_image(S_1,S_2)

Appendix F

Proof of an Interactive Program

In Section 6.5 the interactive program-user pair Boxes-Pickq was presented, and assertions were attached without proof. In what follows, we give details of the proof of

$$\{q \in rg.box((0,0),(1,1))\}$$
program Boxes // **user** Pickq
$$\{image(IS) = p.box((3,3),(5,5))\},$$

particularly those aspects concerning synchronization between program and user. We start by substituting the canonical implementation for each of the operations that access the interactive state (see Section 6.5), and introducing two auxiliary variables a1 and a2. Variable a1 is true between the time the program issues the prompt and receives a response from the user; a2 is true from the time the user notices the prompt until he points to something on the screen.

```
program Boxes;
  var P1,P2,P3: tpicture, a1: boolean;
begin
  P1 ← box(nullpict,(0,0),(1,1));
  P2 ← box(nullpict,(3,3),(5,5));
  P3 ← insprogeny(nullpict,P1,identity,"box1");
  P3 ← insprogeny(nullpict,P1,identity,"box1");
  when true do begin
    IS ← post$return(IS,P3,"boxes");
  end;
  when true do begin
    IS ← prompt$return(IS,"delete box");
    a1 ← true
  end;
```

```
        when ¬getpick:wait(IS) do begin
            P3 ← delprogeny(P3,getpick:value(IS));
            IS ← getpick$return(IS);
            a1 ← false
        end;
        when true do begin
            IS ← post$return(IS,P3,"boxes")
        end;
    end.

    //

    user Pickq;
        var q: point, a2: boolean;
    begin
        when ¬getprompt:wait(IS) do begin
            IS ← getprompt$return(IS);
            a2 ← true
        end;
        when true do begin
            IS ← pick$return(IS,q);
            a2 ← false
        end;
    end.
```

It is easy to see from the form of the interactive dialogue that a2 ⇒ a1. This and other facts that are always true between accesses to the interactive state and are useful in the proof of the program are combined to form the invariant,

INV ≡

$$
\begin{array}{llr}
a2 \Rightarrow & a1\ \& & (1)\\
& \text{pickname(IS,q)} = \text{"box1"}\ \& & (2)\\
& \text{getprompt:wait(IS)}\ \& & (3)\\
& \text{getpick:wait(IS),} & (4)\\
\neg\text{getprompt:wait(IS)} \Rightarrow & a1\ \& & (5)\\
& \text{pickname(IS,q)} = \text{"box1",} & (6)\\
\neg\text{getpick:wait(IS)} \Rightarrow & a1\ \& & (7)\\
& \text{getpick:value(IS)} = \text{"box1"}\ \& & (8)\\
& \text{getprompt:wait(IS).} & (9)
\end{array}
$$

Assertions sufficient to establish both the invariance of INV and the result {image(IS) = p box((3,3),(5,5))} are now imbedded in the altered program:

```
            {q ∊ rg.box((0,0),(1,1)),IS = $init,¬a1,¬a2,INV}
program Boxes;
   var P1,P2,P3: tpicture;
begin
   P1 ← box(nullpict,(0,0),(1,1));
            {tp.display(P1) = p.box((0,0),(1,1),fgnd)}
   P2 ← box(nullpict,(3,3),(5,5));
            {tp.display(P1) = p.box((0,0),(1,1),fgnd),
             tp.display(P2) = p.box((3,3),(5,5),fgnd)}
   P3 ← insprogeny(nullpict,P1,identity,"box1");
            {tp.display(P2) = p.box((3,3),(5,5),fgnd),
             tp.display(P3) = p.box((0,0),(1,1),fgnd)}
   P3 ← insprogeny(nullpict,P1,identity,"box1");
            {tp.display(P3) = p.box((0,0),(1,1),fgnd)
             + p.box((3,3),(5,5),fgnd)}
```

when true **do begin**
  {¬a1,INV,¬a2,getpick:wait(IS),getprompt:wait(IS)}
  IS ← post$return(IS,P3,"boxes");
  {¬a2,getpick:wait(IS),getprompt:wait(IS),INV}
end;
  {image(IS) = p.box((0,0),(1,1),fgnd)
  + p.box((3,3),(5,5),fgnd)}
when true **do begin**
  {¬a1,INV,getpick:wait(IS),¬a2}
  IS ← prompt$return(IS,"delete box");
  a1 ← true
  {pickname(IS,q) = "box1",a1,getpick:wait(IS),¬a2,INV}
end;
  {image(IS) = p.box((0,0),(1,1),fgnd) + p.box((3,3),(5,5),fgnd)}
when ¬getpick:wait(IS) **do begin**
  {¬getpick:wait(IS),INV,
  getpick:value(IS) = "box1",getprompt:wait(IS),¬a2}
  P3 ← delprogeny(P3,getpick:value(IS));
  IS ← getpick$return(IS);
  a1 ← false
  {getpick:wait(IS),getprompt:wait(IS),¬a2,INV}
end;
  {image(IS) = p.box((0,0),(1,1),fgnd) + p.box((3,3),(5,5),fgnd),
  p3 = insprogeny(nullpict,p2,identity,"box2"),
  tp.display(p3) = p.box((3,3),(5,5),fgnd)}
when true **do begin**
  {¬a1,INV,getprompt:wait(IS),getpick:wait(IS),¬a2}
  IS ← post$return(IS,P3,"boxes")
  {pickname(IS,q) ≠ "box1",getprompt:wait(IS),
  getpick:wait(IS),¬a2,INV}
end;
  {image(IS) = p.box((3,3),(5,5),fgnd)}
end.

//

```
user Pickq;
   var q: point;
begin
   when ¬getprompt:wait(IS) do begin
                {¬getprompt:wait(IS),INV,
                 pickname(IS,q) = "box1",getpick:wait(IS),a1}
      IS ← getprompt$return(IS);
      a2 ← true
                {getpick:wait(IS),pickname(IS,q) = "box1",
                 getprompt:wait(IS),a1,INV}
      end;
                {a2}
   when true do begin
                {a2,INV,pickname(IS,q) = "box1",getprompt:wait(IS),a1}
      IS ← pick$return(IS,q);
      a2 ← false

{¬a2,getprompt:wait(IS),getpick:value(IS) = "box1",a1,INV}
      end;
end.
                {image(IS) = p.box((3,3),(5,5),fgnd)}
```

Invariant INV is easily shown to be true initially: ¬a2 establishes clauses (1) through (4), IS = $init and axiom *ip16* establish (5) and (6), and IS = $init and axiom *ip11* establish (7) through (9).

As an example, we will show that the first critical section in program Boxes maintains INV. The other critical sections are verified in a similar manner.

At the beginning of the critical section, we know that a1 is false and INV is true. From this we can establish ¬a2 (by INV(1)), getpick:wait(IS) (by INV(7)), and getprompt:wait(IS) (by INV(5)). Because a2 is accessed only inside critical sections, ¬a2 still holds at the end of the critical section. By implicit axiom *im2*, getpick:wait(IS) and getprompt:wait(IS) also still hold. Now, at the end of the critical section, ¬a2 establishes clauses (1) through (4) of INV, getpick:wait(IS) establishes (7) through (9), and getprompt:wait(IS) establishes (5) and (6).

References

[BERJ79]   Bergstra, J.A. On the adequacy of finite equational methods for data type specification, *ACM SIGPLAN Notices 14*, 11 (1979), 13-18.

[BERV79]   Berzins, V.A. Abstract model specifications for data abstractions, Technical Report 221, Laboratory for Computer Science, Massachusetts Institute of Technology, July 1979.

[BOSJ80]   van den Bos, J. High level graphics input tools and their semantics, in Guedj, R.A. et al (eds.) *Methodology of Interaction*, North-Holland, New York, 1980, 159-169.

[BOUP72]   Boullier, P, Gros, J., Jancene, P. Lemaire, A., Prusker, F., and Saltel, E. Metavisu - a general purpose graphic system, in Nake, F. and Rosenfeld, A. (eds.) *Graphic Languages*, North-Holland, New York, 1972.

[BURR80]   Burstall, R.M. and Goguen,J.A. The semantics of CLEAR, a specification language, Proc. Copenhagen Winter School on Abstract Software Specifications, D. Bjorner (ed.), in *Lecture Notes in Computer Science 86*, 1980, 292-332.

[CAMR74]   Campbell, R.H. and Habermann, A.N. The specification of process synchronization by path expressions, *Lecture Notes in Computer Science 16*, Springer Verlag, New York, 1974, 89-102.

[CARL77]   Caruthers, L.C., van den Bos, J., and van Dam, A. GPGS - a device-independent general purpose graphics system for stand-alone and satellite graphics, Proceedings Fourth Annual Conference on Computer Graphics and Interactive Techniques, *Computer Graphics 11*, 2 (Summer 1977), 112-119.

[DAHO80]   Dahl, 0.-J. Time sequences as a tool for describing program behavior, Proc. Copenhagen Winter School on Abstract Software Specifications, D. Bjorner (ed.), in *Lecture Notes in Computer Science 86*, 1980, 273-291.

[DEMA78]   Demers, A., Donahue, J., and Skinner, G. Data types as values: polymorphism, type-checking, encapsulation, Proc. Fifth Symposium on Principles of Programming Languages, 1978, 23-30.

[DIJE75]   Dijkstra, E.W. Guarded commands, nondeterminacy, and the formal derivation of programs, *Comm. ACM 18*, 8 (August 1975), 453-457.

[ECKR77]   Eckert, R. Functional aspects and specification of graphics systems, part II, Technical Report GDV77-3, Fachbereich Informatik, Technische Hochschule Darmstadt, 1977.

[FOLJ74]   Foley, J.D. and Wallace, V.L. The art of natural graphic man-machine conversation, *Proceedings IEEE 62*, 4 (April 1974), 462-471.

[GOGJ77]   Goguen, J.A. Abstract errors for abstract data types, in Hewhold, E.J. (ed.) *Formal Description of Programming Concepts*, North Holland, 1978, 491-522.

[GOGJ78]   Goguen, J.A., Thatcher, J.W., and Wagner, E.G. An initial algebra approach to the specification, correctness and implementation of abstract data types, in Yeh, R.T. (ed.) *Current Trends in Programming Methodology, vol. IV, Data Structuring*, Prentice Hall, Englewood Cliffs, New Jersey, 1978.

[GOGJ79]   Goguen, J.A. and Tardo, J.J. An introduction to OBJ: a language for writing and testing formal algebraic program specifications, Proc. IEEE Conference on Reliable Software, 1979, 170-189.

[GREI77]   Greif, I. A language for formal problem specification, *Comm. ACM 20*, 12 (December 1977), 931-935.

[GSPC77]   Status report of the ACM SIGGRAPH graphics standards planning committee, *ACM Computer Graphics Quarterly 11*, 3 (Fall 1977).

[GSPC79]   Status report of the ACM SIGGRAPH graphics standards planning committee, *ACM Computer Graphics Quarterly 13*, 3 (August 1979).

[GUER79]   Guedj, R.A. and Tucker, H.A. *Methodology in Computer Graphics*, North-Holland, New York, 1979.

[GUER80]   Guedj, R.A., ten Hagen, P.J.W., Hopgood, F.R.A., Tucker, H.A., and Duce, D.A. (eds.) *Methodology of Interaction*, North-Holland, New York, 1980.

[GUTJ75]   Guttag, J.V. The specification and application to programming of abstract data types, Tech. Report CSRG-59, University of Toronto, Toronto, Canada, September 1975.

[GUTJ77]   Guttag, J.V., Horowitz, E., and Musser, D.R. Some extensions to algebraic specifications, Proc. ACM Conference on Language Design for Reliable Software, *ACM SIGPLAN Notices 12*, 3 (March 1977), 63-67.

[GUTJ78a]   Guttag, J.V. and Horning J.J. The algebraic specification of abstract data types, *Acta Informatica 10* (1978), 27-52.

[GUTJ78b] Guttag, J.V., Horowitz, E., and Musser, D.R. The design of data type specifications, in Yeh, R.T. (ed.) *Current Trends in Programming Methodology, Vol. IV, Data Structuring*, Prentice Hall, Englewood Cliffs, New Jersey, 1978, 60-79.

[GUTJ78c] Guttag, J.V., Horowitz, E., and Musser, D.R. Abstract data types and software validation, *Comm. ACM 21*, 12 (December 1978), 1048-1063.

[GUTJ80] Guttag, J. and Horning J.J. Formal specification as a design tool, Proc. Seventh Symposium on Principles of Programming Languages, January 1980, 251-261.

[HOAC69] Hoare, C.A.R. An axiomatic approach to computer programming, *Comm. ACM 12*, 10 (October 1969), 576-580.

[HOAC72a] Hoare, C.A.R. Proof of correctness of data representations, *Acta Informatica 1* (1972), 271-281.

[HOAC72b] Hoare, C.A.R. Towards a theory of parallel programming, in Hoare, C.A.R. and Perrott, R.H. (eds.) *Operating Systems Techniques*, Academic Press, New York, 1972, 61-71.

[HOAC73] Hoare, C.A.R. and Wirth, N. An axiomatic definition of the programming language Pascal, *Acta Informatica 2* (1973), 335-355.

[HOAC78] Hoare, C.A.R. Communicating sequential processes, *Comm. ACM 21*, 8 (August 1978), 666-677.

[JENK76] Jensen, K. and Wirth, N. *Pascal User Manual and Report*, Springer-Verlag, New York, 1976.

[KAMS79] Kamin, S. Some definitions for algebraic data type specifications, *ACM SIGPLAN Notices 14*, 3 (1979), 28-37.

[KELJ55] Kelley, J.L. *General Topology*, Van Nostrand, New York, 1955.

[KJET72] Kjeldaas, T.S. Class draughting, Publication S.39, Norwegian Computing Center, Oslo, Norway, June 1972.

[KNUD73] Knuth, D.E. *The Art of Computer Programming*, Vol. 1, second ed., Addison-Wesley, Reading, Mass., 1973.

[LAMB77] Lampson, B.W., Horning J.J., London R.L., Mitchell, J.G., Popek, G.L. Report on the programming language Euclid, *ACM SIGPLAN Notices 12*, 2 (February 1977).

[LAML79] Lamport L. The specification and proof of correctness of interactive programs, *Lecture Notes in Computer Science 75*, Springer Verlag, New York, 1979, 474-537.

[LAVM79]   Laventhal, M.S. Synchronization specifications for data abstractions, *Proc. IEEE Conf. on Specifications of Reliable Software*, 1979, 119-125.

[LEVM80]   Levy, M.R. Specifying data types with variables and referencing, Department of Computer Science, University of Victoria, Victoria, B.C., Canada, December 1980.

[LISB74]   Liskov, B. and Zilles, S. Programming with abstract data types, *ACM SIGPLAN Notices 9*, 4 (April 1974), 50-59.

[LISB77]   Liskov, B. and Zilles, S. An introduction to formal specifications of data abstractions, in Yeh, R.T. (ed.) *Current Trends in Programming Methodology, Vol. 1*, Prentice-Hall, 1977, 1-32.

[LISB79]   Liskov, B. and Berzins, V.A. An appraisal of program specifications, in Wegner P. (ed.) *Research Directions in Software Technology*, M.I.T. Press, 1979.

[LONR78]   London, R.L., Guttag, J.V., Horning, J.J., Lampson, Michell, and Popek. Proof rules for the programming language Euclid, *Acta Informatica 10* (1978), 1-26.

[MAJM79]   Majster, M.E. Treatment of partial operations in the algebraic specification technique, *Proc. IEEE Conf. on Specifications of Reliable Software*, 1979, 190-197.

[MALW76]   Mallgren, W.R. and Turrill, C.N. XPL/G -- a programming system for easy computer graphics, Technical Note 60, Computer Science Teaching Laboratory, University of Washington, Seattle, Washington, 1976.

[MALW78]   Mallgren, W.R. and Shaw, A.C. Graphical transformations and hierarchic picture structures, *Computer Graphics and Image Processing 8* (1978), 237-258.

[MALW80]   Mallgren, W.R. Formal specification of graphic data types, *ACM Transactions on Programming Languages and Systems 4*, 4 (October 1982), 687-710.

[MARM76]   Marcotty, M., Ledgard, H.F., and Bochman, G.V. A sampler of formal definitions, *Computing Surveys 8*, 2 (June 1976), 191-276.

[MUSD80]   Musser, D.R. Abstract data type specification in the Affirm system, *IEEE Trans. on Software Engineering SE-6*, 1 (January 1980), 24-31.

[NEWW70]   Newman, W.M. An experimental display programming language for the PDP-10 computer, Technical Report UTEC-CSc-70-104, University of Utah, Salt Lake City, Utah, July 1970.

[NEWW72]   Newman, W.M. Display procedures, *Comm ACM 14*, 10 (October 1972), 651-660.

[NEWW78]   Newman, W.M. and van Dam, A. Recent efforts toward graphics standardization, *Computing Surveys 10*, 4 (December 1978), 356-380.

[NEWW79]   Newman, W.M. and Sproull, R.F. *Principles of Interactive Computer Graphics*, second ed., McGraw-Hill, New York, 1979.

[NOLG80]   Nolan, G.J. DASIM1: a practical exercise in data abstraction, Proc. Symposium on Language and Programming Methodology, Sydney, Australia, in *Lecture Notes in Computer Science 79*, 1980, 225-254.

[ORGE72]   Organick, E.I. *The Multics System: An Examination of Its Structure*, The MIT Press, Cambridge, Massachusetts, 1972.

[OWIS75]   Owicki, S.S. Axiomatic proof techniques for parallel programs, Technical Report 75-251, Department of Computer Science, Cornell University, Ithaca, New York, July 1975.

[OWIS76a]   Owicki, S.S. and Gries, D. Verifying properties of parallel programs: an axiomatic approach, *Comm. ACM 19*, 5 (May 1976), 279-285.

[OWIS76b]   Owicki, S.S. An axiomatic proof technique for parallel programs II: shared data abstractions, Stanford University, 1976.

[PARD72]   Parnas, D.L. A technique for the specification of software modules with examples, *Comm. ACM 15*, 5 (May 1972), 330-336.

[PARD74]   Parnas, D.L. On a "buzzword": hierarchical structure, *IFIP 74 Proceedings*, 1974, 336-339.

[PARD76]   Parnas, D.L. Some hypotheses about the "uses" hierarchy for operating systems, Forschungsbericht BS I 76/1, Fachbereich Informatik, Technische Hochschule Darmstadt, 1976.

[RIEJ75]   Rieber, J. and Shaw A.C. Interactive picture generation and manipulation through formal descriptions, *Computers and Graphics 1* (1975), 95-107.

[ROSA69]   Rosenfeld, A. *Picture Processing by Computer*, Academic Press, New York, 1969.

[SCHG76]   Schrack, G. Specifications, representations and manipulation of the data type GRAPHICAL, Departments of Electrical Engineering and Computer Science, University of British Columbia, Vancouver, Canada, February 1976.

[SCHG80] Schrack, G. The data type GRAPHICAL for high level graphical programming languages, Proc. Computer Graphics 80 International Conference, Brighton, U.K., August 1980.

[SHAA78] Shaw, A.C. Software descriptions with flow expressions, *IEEE Transactions on Software Engineering SE-4*, 3 (May 1978), 242-254.

[SHAA79] Shaw, A.C. Software specification languages based on regular expressions, Technical Report 31, Institut fuer Informatik, ETH, Zurich, Switzerland, June 1979, also in Riddle, W.E. and Fairley, R.E. (eds.) *Software Development Tools*, Springer-Verlag, New York, 1980, 148-175.

[SHAA80a] Shaw, A.C. On the specification of graphics command languages and their processors, in Guedj, R.A. et al (eds.) *Methodology of Interaction*, North-Holland, New York, 1980, 377-392.

[SHAA80b] Shaw, A.C. A model for document preparation systems, Technical Report 80-04-02, Department of Computer Science, University of Washington, Seattle, Washington, April 1980.

[SHOR79] Shoup, R.G. Color table animation, Proc. Sixth Annual Conference on Computer Graphics and Interactive Techniques, in *ACM Computer Graphics Quarterly 13*, 2 (August 1979), 8-13.

[SIGP81] Proc. of the Workshop on Data Abstraction, Databases, and Conceptual Modelling, in *ACM SIGPLAN Notices 16*, 1 (January 1981).

[SPIJ75] Spitzen, J. and Wegbreit, B. The verification and synthesis of data structures, *Acta Informatica 4* (1975), 127-144.

[STAT78] Standish, T.A. Data structures -- an axiomatic approach, in Yeh, R.T. (ed.) *Current Trends in Programming Methodology, Vol. IV, Data Structuring*, Prentice Hall, 1978, 30-59.

[SUBP79] Subrahmanyam, P.A. Nondeterminism in abstract data types, Department of Computer Science, University of Utah, Salt Lake City, Utah, December 1979.

[TANS80] Tanimoto, S.L. Image data structures, in Tanimoto, S.L. and Klinger A. (eds.) *Structured Computer Vision*, Academic Press, New York, 1980.

[THAD79] Thalmann, D. and Thalmann N. Design and implementation of abstract graphical data types, Publication 332, Departement d'informatique et de recherche operationnelle, Universite de Montreal, August 1979, also in Proc Third IEEE Computer Software and Applications Conf., November 1979.

[THAJ78]   Thatcher, J.W., Wagner, E.G., and Wright, J.B. Data type specification: parameterization and the power of specification techniques, Proc. Tenth ACM SIGACT Symposium on Theory of Computing, May 1978.

[TRAU75]   Trambacz, U. Towards device independent graphics systems, *Computer Graphics 9*, 1 (Spring 1975), 49-51.

[TURC75]   Turrill, C.N. and Mallgren W.R. XPL/G -- experiences in implementing an experimental interactive graphics programming system, *Computers and Graphics 1* (1975), 55-63.

[WALV76]   Wallace, V.L. The semantics of graphic input devices, Proceedings ACM Siggraph Symposiom of Graphic Languages, *Computer Graphics 10*, 1 (Spring 1976), 61-63.

[WEGB76]   Wegbreit, B. and Spitzen, J.M. Proving properties of complex data structures, *Journal ACM 13*, 2 (April 1976), 389-396.

[WOOP71]   Woodsford, P.A. The design and implementation of the GINO-F graphics software package, *Software Practice and Experience 1* (October 1971).

[WULW76]   Wulf, W.A., London, R.L., Shaw M. An introduction to the construction and verification of Alphard programs, *IEEE Transactions on Software Engineering SE-2*, 4 (December 1976), 253-264.

[ZILS74]   Zilles, S.N. Algebraic specification of data types, *Project MAC Progress Report 11* (1974), Massachusetts Institute of Technology, Cambridge, Mass., 52-58.

[ZILS80]   Zilles, S.N. An introduction to data algebras, Proc. Copenhagen Winter School on Abstract Software Specifications, D. Bjorner (ed.), in *Lecture Notes in Computer Science 86*, 1980, 248-272.

Index